Hong Kong's Hou

MW01711502

Hong Kong University Press thanks Xu Bing for writing the Press's name in his Square Word Calligraphy for the covers of its books. For further information, see p. iv.

Hong Kong's Housing Policy
A Case Study in Social Justice

Betty Yung

香港大學出版社
Hong Kong University Press

Hong Kong University Press
14/F Hing Wai Centre
7 Tin Wan Praya Road
Aberdeen
Hong Kong

Hardback ISBN 978-962-209-904-3
Paperback ISBN 978-962-209-905-0

British Library Cataloguing-in-Publication Data
A catalogue record for this book is available from the British Library.

Secure On-line Ordering
http://www.hkupress.org

Printed and bound by Liang Yu Printing Factory Ltd., Hong Kong, China.

Hong Kong University Press is honoured that Xu Bing, whose art explores the complex themes of language across cultures, has written the Press's name in his Square Word Calligraphy. This signals our commitment to cross-cultural thinking and the distinctive nature of our English-language books published in China.

"At first glance, Square Word Calligraphy appears to be nothing more unusual than Chinese characters, but in fact it is a new way of rendering English words in the format of a square so they resemble Chinese characters. Chinese viewers expect to be able to read Square Word Calligraphy but cannot. Western viewers, however are surprised to find they can read it. Delight erupts when meaning is unexpectedly revealed."

— Britta Erickson, *The Art of Xu Bing*

Contents

Preface

Philosophy is often thought of as detached from real life, and as a discipline without any practical application. I think that philosophizing should not be merely an intellectual pursuit; on the contrary, some philosophical insights and conclusions, when thoughtfully applied, can enrich our lives in practice as well as in theory. Social and political philosophy focuses on concepts such as rights, justice, equality, and liberty. These concepts should not be ignored in public policy-making. Public policies affect everyone in society: when public policies are sensible, each citizen benefits. Thus, applying social philosophy to public policy is worthwhile, although some philosophers might disdain the "pedestrian" application (in their eyes) of their abstract theories. As a person trained in both philosophy and public policy studies, I believe I may make some contributions, both in the academic and policy-making spheres, by applying philosophy to examine policies.

As a person who grew up in Hong Kong, I would like to research into Hong Kong policy issues which I am more familiar with and would like to contribute to. As about half of Hong Kong people live in public housing, rental or self-owned, unparalleled in other countries, second only to Singapore, Hong Kong's housing policy will be a prominent and special case study. Though there have been many researches done on Hong Kong's housing policy, there were few related to social justice in Hong Kong's housing policy. Thus, I would like to research into this topic, combining social philosophy and housing policy studies, hoping to bring fresh insights to the discussions on housing issues.

This book largely rests on my PhD research done at the University of Bristol's School for Policy Studies. I would like to thank my supervisors, Professor Ray Forrest and Professor Gary Bridge, for their guidance and support. I would also like to thank the Centre of Asian Studies, University of Hong Kong, for providing research facilities to me when I conducted fieldwork in Hong Kong. Both my journal article (entitled "An Interplay Between Western and Confucian Concepts of

Justice: Development of Hong Kong Housing Policy," published in *Housing, Theory and Society* in June 2007) and Chapters 2 and 5 of this book rest mainly on the same research. Thus, there may be some overlap of content between the two, with the latter being an elaborated and much extended version of the former. I would like to acknowledge both the journal and Hong Kong University Press for permitting me to do so.

May 2008
Hong Kong

1

Philosophy, Justice and Hong Kong Housing Policy

We often talk about the question of justice in its different aspects, yet we use the term with only a vague concept of its meaning. When asked to define "justice", we may struggle to do so. Of course, "what is justice" is a complex philosophical question, one without a clear answer: for centuries philosophers have debated it without reaching a consensus. Insoluble for philosophers, such a question is difficult for common people to answer, too. Yet we all have enough of a general idea of what justice is to be able to discuss the term in our daily lives. An examination and analysis of the concept seem constructive and important, enabling us to lead a more enlightened life.

Whenever confronted with injustices, we may think that something is wrong, feel angry and frustrated, and believe that the situation should be rectified. The question of social justice occurs whenever there is a clash over limited resources. Exactly how to distribute limited resources is an issue we all face in our everyday lives: whether as a mother distributing one cake among several children, or a boss awarding bonuses to his/her staff. Just as individuals confront the problem of justice every day, a government, through its policy-making, must distribute resources among different groups in society. For example, it must resolve whether free education should be available to all or only limited to the needy, and it must determine whether housing subsidies should be made accessible to potential home-owners. Thus, the discussion of social justice is highly relevant to public policy studies. Public policy injustices are of critical importance; sometimes they can result in life-and-death situations, for example, when insufficient public resources are allocated to take care of those with long-term illness. Such injustices can also create serious and widespread misery, as in the cross-generational poverty that results from the lack of social security for the worse-off. Thus, justice in public policy remains an issue of enormous importance, not just to all policy-makers and academics, but also to all citizens, as it directly affects their interests.

Housing policy involves the distribution of housing resources among different groups of stakeholders, from waitlist households to public tenants and home-owners. Because the lack of housing resources creates other problems (diseases, limited access to job opportunities, and crime), a just distribution of housing resources should be of prime concern to policy-makers and citizens alike.

Justice plays, or should play, an important role in formulating housing policy, or indeed, all public policy. Any policy that does not take justice into consideration may be criticized as a bad policy. This book will investigate justice in public and housing policy in general, and justice in Hong Kong housing policy in particular. During my research, I found that although public and housing policy issues were well researched by many academics, justice in public and housing policy was a greatly neglected topic. This is quite surprising, given that the issue affects every member of society to a significant extent. This omission may reflect the rigid compartmentalization of knowledge into different disciplines, which are taught and researched by academics from different faculties. Philosophy is essentially an arts subject, whereas policy and housing studies are classed with the social sciences. Since cross-faculty research collaboration is rare (though such studies have increased in recent years), the question of justice in public and housing policy is quite neglected as a research topic, despite its importance to all aspects of society. This book is an attempt to bridge this gap. It is largely an application of social philosophy to policy and housing studies, employing the art of philosophizing to social science empirical research. I hope this book may throw light on the much neglected philosophical debates on housing issues, contributing both to the philosophical discussion on justice and the empirical study of housing policy.

In recent years, there has been a global trend toward privatizing public services. Governments have also promoted home ownership as an explicit housing strategy. These trends have significant impacts on the distribution of resources within a society, making the question of justice highly relevant. The time is ripe to ask whether these trends result in a just distribution in society and if not, how can we improve public policy?

Housing policy is an important public policy in Hong Kong: the government intervenes on a scale unparalleled in any other country, except Singapore. About half of Hong Kong's population lives in public housing, either rented or self-owned. Thus, Hong Kong's housing policy will definitely serve as an interesting case for the investigation of justice in housing policy, since the question of housing subsidy distribution looms large in view of the fact that a considerable proportion of people in Hong Kong receive housing support from the government. While many studies of Hong Kong's public housing sector exists, very little has been written about how the question of justice influences housing policy. This book will endeavour to fill this gap. The problem is made more complex because Hong Kong was essentially a Chinese society ruled by the British before the transfer of sovereignty to China in 1997. It was, and is, fundamentally a place where East meets West. It therefore serves as a favourable testing ground for a hybrid of Eastern and Western concepts of justice. Examining justice in Hong Kong's housing policy study may incorporate this interesting dimension of occidental-oriental cultural integration, enriching the discussion of equity in the housing arena.

Before any fruitful discussion of Hong Kong's housing sector, it will be worthwhile to establish some background information about Hong Kong.

Background

Hong Kong is a city on the south-eastern coast of China, with an area of about 1,096 km^2 and a population of 6,708,389 in 2001[1]. Hong Kong's population is very homogeneous, with 98% Chinese in origin. Before 1997, Hong Kong was a British colony. China resumes the sovereignty of Hong Kong on 1 July 1997. Since then, Hong Kong has been a Special Administrative Region (SAR) of China.

The immediate post-war years saw the greatest exodus of immigrants from China to Hong Kong. This influx reached its height in 1949 when the Communists took over China. The population rose nearly 400% from an estimated 600,000 in 1945 to an estimated 2,360,000 in 1950 (Hopkins 1969, p. 2; Hopkins 1972, p. 200). Since that peak, there has been continuous small-scale immigration from China (Hopkins 1972, p. 201). From 1950 onwards, natural increase has replaced immigration as the predominant source of population growth, though net migration is still considerable (Chan 1989, p. 15). Between 1951 and 1961, natural increase contributed 63% of the population growth (Chan 1989, p. 15).

Politically, the whole of Hong Kong became a British colony by stages in the nineteenth century, according to three treaties concluded between the British government and the Chinese government at that time:

1. the Treaty of Nanking, signed in 1842 under which Hong Kong Island was ceded in perpetuity;
2. the Convention of Peking in 1860, under which southern Kowloon peninsula and Stonecutters Island were ceded in perpetuity;
3. the Convention of Peking in 1898 under which the New Territories were leased to Britain for 99 years from 1 July 1898 (Ngan 1989, p. 92).

The head of Hong Kong's colonial government was the governor, who was not elected. Instead, he[2] was appointed by the British monarch, after being chosen by the secretary of state for Foreign and Commonwealth Affairs (Ngan 1989). The governor of Hong Kong was directly responsible to the British Crown, not to the people of Hong Kong, who neither had the power to remove him nor had the right to exercise a vote of no-confidence over him (Ngan 1989). The governor was responsible for Hong Kong's internal affairs only, while Hong Kong's foreign relations and defence were in the hands of the British Government (Ngan 1989.)

For more than a hundred and forty years, there were few significant changes in Hong Kong's system of government. All members of the Executive and the Legislative Councils — the centre of governmental authority — were appointed upon the nomination of the Hong Kong governor. Power was concentrated with the governor himself. Elections were not held until 1985, when 24 unofficial members were elected to the Legislative Council. However, the election was not by universal suffrage, but through functional constituencies and by an electoral college (Ngan 1989, pp. 90–91). It was not until 1991 that there were directly elected seats in the Legislative Council. However, the directly elected seats in the Legislative Council only accounted for 18 out of a total of 60 seats in 1991 (Miners 1991, pp. 27–28).

From 1 July 1997, Hong Kong became a Special Administrative Region (SAR) of China, enjoying a high degree of autonomy under the "One Country, Two Systems" arrangement. The life-style, social and economic system of Hong Kong were to remain unchanged until 2047, 50 years after the transfer of sovereignty. The head of the Hong Kong SAR is now called the Chief Executive. S/he is not elected by universal suffrage, but is appointed by the Chinese Central People's Government on the basis of a "small-circle" local election by an 800-member Selection Committee (Ngan 1989, p. 92; Miners 1991, pp. 23, 81).

In economic terms, Hong Kong has been primarily an entrepôt, facilitating trade between China and the West. Entrepôt trade thrived after 1949 (when the Communist took over China) to the early 1950s as Hong Kong became China's only window to the non-socialist world. However, in 1951, when China entered the Korean conflict, the United Nations, and the United States in particular, imposed an embargo on trade between China and the Western world. Entrepôt trade (which largely involved re-exports to/from China) in Hong Kong, thus, ground to a halt as a result of the embargo that limited the flow of goods to and from China, thereby largely reducing the passing of such goods through Hong Kong (Chau 1993, p. 1; Smart 1992, p. 17). In the early 1950s, a large inflow of immigrants from China brought capital, labour and entrepreneurship. Hong Kong began focusing on export-oriented industrialization. The expanding manufacturing sector was the main engine of Hong Kong's economy throughout the 1950s and 1960s. The manufacturing labour force accounted for an estimated 36% of the working population in 1954. This share continued to grow until it peaked in 1971, when it represented about half of the working population. In that same year, the manufacturing sector contributed about 30% to Hong Kong's GDP. From 1980 onwards, more and more factories began relocating northward to China's Guangdong province, decreasing the importance of the secondary sector in Hong Kong (Chau 1993, p. 6) By 1987, manufacturing employment began declining.

With the relocation of manufacturing industries out of Hong Kong to China, Hong Kong's service industries took ascendancy. The finance and business sectors expanded rapidly throughout the 1970s and 1980s. Its proportion in the city's employment quadrupled over this period (Chau 1993, p. 6). The adoption of the open-door policy by China in 1978 stimulated economic growth in Hong Kong and entrepôt trade has become apparent to be a major activity again. In the 1980s, re-exports grew annually at a rate of 20% or more, most accounted for by trade with China (Chau 1993, pp. 20–21).

Hong Kong experienced economic growth from the post-war period through mid-1990s, changing from an entrepôt to primarily service-based financial centre. In the twenty years between 1961 and 1981, economic growth was more accelerated in Hong Kong than in any other Asian country, surpassing that of Western industrialized countries (Chau 1993). Despite a slowdown in the 1980s because of political uncertainties, the increase in GDP still averaged more than 6% per year (Chau 1993). The rate of inflation was low, averaging less than 5% a year from 1961 until 1980, except in 1973–74 and 1979–81 because of oil crises (Chau 1993). Per capita income in Hong Kong doubled every 12 years and quadrupled in one generation during the same period (Chau 1993).

This successful story of the Hong Kong economy ended in late 1997 when the Asian Economic Crisis struck. The property market collapsed, and the economy entered a period of recession which persisted until 2004. The economy was plagued by deflation and a high unemployment rate, which reached 7.8% in mid-2002, whereas from the 1950s until the early 1990s, the unemployment rate had been negligible.

With this brief overview of Hong Kong's history complete, we will concentrate our attention on Hong Kong's housing policy; it will serve as a background for the discussion of justice in Hong Kong's housing policy in the latter part of the book.

Historical Development of Hong Kong Housing Policy

Pre-1954

Before massive government intervention in 1954, the colonial authorities mainly adopted a laissez-faire housing policy (Fong and Yeh 1987, p. 18; Fong 1986, p. 4; Kwitko 1986). Before World War II, Hong Kong's population remained small and mobile. However the post-war era saw a great wave of immigrants from China, resulting in overcrowded private tenements and widespread squatting (Chau 1989, p. 28; Hopkins 1971, p. 276). There was still no alternation to the laissez-faire housing policy on the part of the government, since it believed that once the political situation normalized in due course, the immigrants would return to China (Hopkins 1969, p. 2; Keung 1981, p. 5), thereby solving the housing problem as a consequence.

Though the government did not intervene to provide housing directly to the populace, it gave assistance by setting up agencies which directly provided housing. In 1951, the colonial authorities established Hong Kong Housing Society to provide housing to lower-middle and middle-income families. Also, the Hong Kong Settlers' Housing Corporation, partly financed by the government, was set up in 1952 (Fong 1986, p. 5; Fong and Yeh 1987, p. 19). The government also intervened slightly in 1951, through the establishment of certain "approved area" and "tolerated areas" for squatters to build their cottages and huts (Fong 1986, p. 5; Fong and Yeh 1987, p. 19). However, these designated areas only resettled one-tenth of the total squatters by the end of 1953 because of the small scale of such intervention (Hopkins 1969, p. 2).

On the whole, the government mainly adopted a laissez-faire approach to housing before 1954. This approach was sufficient before the post-World War II period. Yet it became increasingly problematic after 1945, with the great influx of refugees from China which necessitated actions, though limited and indirect, on the part of the government, especially in the early 1950s.

1954–1972

The Shek Kip Mei squatter fire in 1953 made 53,000 people homeless (Fong 1986, p. 16; Fong and Yeh 1987, p. 19; Chan 1999, p. 177). The government responded by providing homes for the fire victims in resettlement blocks. According to the Commissioner for Resettlement, it was more efficient to resettle the fire victims in resettlement blocks than paying them direct relief subsidy (Drakakis-Smith 1979, p. 44). This started off the whole resettlement policy, with the setting up of the Resettlement Department in 1954. One of the main aims of resettling the squatter was to free land for economic development (Hopkin 1969, pp. 2–3). Thus, only squatters occupying land needed for development were resettled, while those occupying land with little developmental value were neglected (Dwyer 1970, p. 610; Hopkins 1971, p. 293; Hopkins 1969, p. 8; Chan 1999, p. 178). When a piece of land was required for development, all squatters occupying the land were resettled without a means test (Dwyer 1971, p. 46; Dwyer 1970, pp. 610, 612; Wong and Liu 1988, p. 2) in order to facilitate the taking over of the land.

The resettled ex-squatters did not live in comfort in the resettlement estates. Each adult was allocated 2.2 m^2, while children under ten were only allocated half that area. All washing and toilet facilities were communal in order to reduce cost, with no kitchen facilities provided (Fong 1986, p. 6). Thus, there were problems of overcrowding as well as poor management and maintenance on the resettlement estates.

Government intervention in this period mainly focused on squatter resettlement, neglecting the housing plight of those living in private tenements (Keung 1981, p. 6), which were often even worse than those living in squatter areas (Drakakis-Smith 1972, p. 158; Drakakis-Smith 1970, p. 115; Hopkins 1972, p. 204; Golger 1972, p. 33). This may be explained by the fact that the slums in private tenements were less visible, while squatter areas, posed a more obvious blot.

In 1961, at last, the government provided public housing with the explicit objective of serving the poor in the form of introducing the Government Low Cost Housing Programme. However, this housing programme was extremely small when compared to the resettlement programme (Hopkins 1972, p. 204).

The government direct intervention into the housing arena was triggered by a fire disaster, and was sustained by the need to reclaim land for development. Despite such great governmental efforts, the housing plight of the people in Hong Kong remained serious in this period.

1973–1986

In 1972, the new Governor, Sir Murray MacLehose, launched the Ten-Year Housing Programme to tackle the slum and squatter problem, as well as the housing plight in resettlement estates. The target was to re-house 1.8 million people in permanent, self-contained public rental housing with good facilities and a clean environment; the project was scheduled for completion within ten years. The Housing Authority was set up in 1973 to be responsible for the policy formulation for this programme (Fong 1986, p. 12; Fong and Yeh 1987, p. 22). In 1976, the Ten-Year Housing Programme was expanded to include the Home-Ownership Scheme, which sold public housing units at a discount price to lower-middle and middle income families (Fong and Yeh 1987, p. 22)

In 1980, the government announced the failure of the Ten-Year Housing Programme. Between 1973 and 1981, it had achieved less than 40% of its intended target (Chan 1999, p. 179). This failure was due to the recession resulting from the oil crisis and the continual inflow of immigrants from China (Hong Kong Government 1981[3]; Fong and Yeh 1987, p. 23). Public rental housing after 1973 was allocated to two categories of household. The first was made up of households on the waiting list, whose income fell below a certain income limit, and who did not own any housing. The second was made up of those re-housed after catastrophes (such as fires), squatter clearance, or urban renewal. Families in the latter category were not required to undergo means-testing (Yeh 1990, p. 447; Li and Yu 1990, p. 108; Lau 1997, p. 100). During this period, once a tenant was granted a public housing unit, lifelong tenure was guaranteed, regardless of the income increase of his/her household (Li and Yu 1990, p. 110) In addition, the right of tenure was hereditary, even though the next generation might be very well-off (Hong Kong Housing Authority 1984, p. 1; Li and Yu 1990, p. 110).

This period saw a great attempt, on the part of the government, to relocate people into adequate quarters. Yet, the efforts failed in the view of unpredictable and changing circumstances, despite being ambitious and well-intended.

1987–2002

The Long-Term Housing Strategy was promulgated in 1987. It relied mainly on the private sector to satisfy housing demand (Chan 1991, p. 181). The promotion of home-ownership was adopted as an overt aim of housing policy. The 1998 White Paper on Long-Term Housing might be fairly described as a continuation of its 1987 predecessor: home-ownership remained a target of governmental policy. The government provided various measures to achieve this aim. It introduced the Home Purchase Loan Scheme in 1988, the Sandwich Class Housing Loan Scheme in 1993, the Sandwich Class Housing Scheme in 1994 and the Home Starter Loan Scheme in 1998. The Tenant Purchase Scheme had the effect of extending subsidized home-ownership to grass-root levels, even though usually only the comparatively better-off sitting public housing tenants could afford to buy.

Another aspect of housing policy in this period was the rational allocation of public rental housing resources. The "rich-household policy", introduced in 1992 (which was subsequently slightly revised) required well-off public rental households to pay higher rents or even to vacate their flats (Lau 2002, p. 71). From 1998 onwards, the government required both income and asset means-testing for *all* public housing applicants, whereas before 1998, households re-housed due to clearance, compassionate or emergency grounds were not required to undergo means-testing. In addition, the inheritance of public housing tenancy by the next generation without means-testing was cancelled in 1998.

In short, there were mainly two trends of development of housing policy from 1987 to 2002. The first was the promotion of home-ownership, and the second was the more rational use of public rental housing resources.

2002 onwards[4]

The property market collapsed after the Asian Economic Crisis in late

1997. Housing prices decreased drastically and negative equity became widespread. In 2002, the government responded by introducing what were unofficially known as "Suen-Nine Measures", which saw the government reduce its intervention within Hong Kong's housing market. The main change was abandoning the promotion of home-ownership as a policy goal. The main focus of housing policy would be to provide subsidized rental housing to the needy. The government stopped all scheduled land auctions, and the supply of new land would only be triggered from the Application List. The production and sale of Home-Ownership Scheme flats would cease, (except for a small number of unsold flats). The Tenant Purchase Scheme was abandoned. However, the Housing Authority still provided Home Assistance Loans to eligible families to buy private property. All these measures were aimed at stabilizing and boosting the property market. Some excess Home-Ownership Scheme flats were changed into public rental housing. These moves reduced the waiting time of public rental housing to just under three years in 2002.

Thus, as the 21st century began, the government becomes less interventionist within the housing arena, as compared to two decades ago. Yet with its massive provision of public rental housing, though, it remains intrusive by world standards.

Book Synopsis

This book will attempt to answer the following research questions:

1) What is social justice?
2) What is justice in public policy?
3) What is a just housing policy?
4) Is and was Hong Kong housing policy just?
5) What are the stakeholders' views on justice in Hong Kong housing policy?
6) What should be the role of justice in public policy?

Various research methods will be used to answer these questions. For example, philosophical analysis will be used to answer question 1 ("What is social justice?"), while I will draw on policy analysis to examine justice in Hong Kong's housing policy, and use qualitative interviewing techniques to find out the common people's idea of justice. The whole research is mainly founded upon the philosophical reasoning on the concept of "social justice" in an attempt to define it. The conclusions of such philosophical analysis are applied to build up theories and suggestion concerning just public policies and a just housing policy. The policy analysis (focused primarily on the development of justice in Hong Kong housing policy), will also hinge on the philosophical clarification of the concept of "social justice" in this book's early chapters. The social science research method of conducting qualitative in-depth interviews will be used to collect Hong Kong residents' definitions of social justice. One should distinguish between what social justice *ought to be* and what it *is considered* to be by the common people. The former is should be logically consistent, while the latter is collected by empirical methods, and may be not just inconsistent but even contradictory at times. (In an ideal world, of course, human beings would be rational and consistent in their thinking.) Data collected from in-depth interviews may or may not coincide with earlier philosophical conclusions; one of the main aims of my research was to pinpoint the degree of overlap between the philosophers' abstract world and the world as experienced by Hong Kong's residents. In this way, we may understand how far the actual world fits with, or deviates, from the theoretical world. I hope the art of philosophizing, in concert with empirical social science research methods, will bring about new enlightenments.

Chapter Outline

In order to examine justice in public policy, we should first analyze the controversial concept of social justice. Chapter 2 will treat this issue. I will examine theories of justice from the ancient (Aristotle) to the contemporary (Young and Fraser). There will be an evaluation of needs-based, rights-based and deserts-based theories of justice. The relation between equal opportunity and social justice will be discussed. Chapter 2 will conclude with a comparison between Western and Chinese concepts of justice, paving the way for an examination of justice in Hong Kong's housing policy, which involves the blending Eastern and Western cultures.

The philosophical conclusions on the concept of social justice in Chapter 2 will be applied to the discussion of public policy in Chapter 3. There are three main types of public policy: the economic, social and political. We will examine relations between social justice and these three public policy types. Privatization has been a trend in public policy. In Chapter 3, there will be an investigation of whether privatization is just or not. Chapter 3 will end with an evaluation of the implications of Confucian concept of justice on public policy.

The aim of Chapter 4 is to examine what a just housing policy is. We will investigate the relation between the private housing market and social justice, followed by an examination of the relation between housing need and justice. Government promotion of home-ownership has become an international trend. Chapter 4 will examine whether it is just to promote home-ownership. Moreover, there will be a discussion on a just tax policy on housing. This chapter will end with by discussing how the Confucian concept of justice applies to the public housing sector.

In Chapter 5, I will discuss the chronological development of justice in Hong Kong's housing policy. Generally, the historical development of justice in Hong Kong housing policy can be divided into five periods, with different concepts of justice playing a dominant role during each period. I will further examine the interplay between Western and Chinese concepts of justice in Hong Kong housing's policy.

Chapter 6 is an account of the analysis of in-depth interviews. I will examine different views of housing justice, on the part of different stakeholders in Hong Kong's housing policy. Roughly, I have separated these into five distinct groups: representatives or members of institutions (including government officials and property developers); private renters; public housing tenants; private home-owners; and people who achieved home-ownership through government assistance. We will examine whether people holding similar stakes agree with one another on housing justice, and learn whether they believe that government housing policy has been just or unjust towards them.

Chapter 7 is the conclusion, which will discuss the philosophical implications of the interviews. Hong Kong's housing policy was and is not purely just; it requires that compromises be made with other policy objectives, such as efficiency, public acceptance, low administrative cost etc. As with housing policies outside of Hong Kong, a purely just housing policy does not and never did exist. We will close the book by discussing the question of what role justice should play in public policy.

2

Social Justice — An Intricate Concept

Ancient Greek philosophers were first to consider the concept of justice, although they never arrived at a consensus about its precise meaning. The question of justice (be it distributive justice, retributive justice, judicial justice) occurs only if two or more persons' interests are in conflict. Thus, justice is essentially social (in contrast with private or personal) in nature; it must involve more than one person. Therefore, the terms "justice" and "social justice" are used interchangeably in this book. Before examining justice in public policy in general, and justice in Hong Kong housing policy in particular, we must arrive at a clear understanding of the controversial concept of justice. In this chapter, various theories of justice will be examined, through them I hope to illuminate justice as a concept, thereby laying a foundation for the discussion of justice in public housing policy in later chapters. Justice is largely a Western concept. In order to pave the way for the examination of justice in Hong Kong housing policy in later chapters, in this one, we will compare Chinese and Western concepts of justice, as Hong Kong is predominantly a Chinese society that embraces various strands of Confucianism and Taoism, yet historically was ruled by a Western-style government, a legacy that still resonates today.

* * * * * *

We will embark on our discourse of social justice by analyzing insights from classical Greek philosophy. We will begin by considering Aristotle's views, followed by those of more contemporary philosophers, hoping that we may derive a comprehensive overview of the issue. Aristotle defines justice as a system that awards equals equally and unequals unequally.

"... The unjust is unequal, the just is equal ... if they are not equal, they will not have what is equal, but this is the origin of quarrels and complaints — when either equals have and are awarded unequal shares, or unequals an equal share" (Aristotle 1998, p. 112). Intuitively, this is quite convincing. If Students A and B are equally outstanding, a just teacher should give both of them one-hundred marks. However, Student C works less hard and is less intelligent. Thus, C only deserves to get eighty marks from the teacher, less than both A and B. If family X and Y both consist of 4 members (a couple and their two young children), it would be just if both families are allocated a 400 ft^2 (about 37 m^2) public housing flat each, since this allotment would be giving equals an equal share. If family Z consists of 6 members (a couple and 4 children), it should be allocated a bigger flat than family X and Y. If all families X, Y and Z are allocated a public housing flat of the same size, then we may find that there is injustice because unequals are given what is equal.

In fact, Aristotle's concept of justice (awarding equals equally and unequals unequally) may be regarded as the underlying principle of social justice. This formal principle provokes two questions. The first question is: by what criteria should people be classed as equals or as unequals according to the principle of justice? The second question is: what kind of equal treatment are equals entitled to by the principle of justice? Concerning the first question, it is not true that people equal in just any aspect should be treated equally by the principle of justice. Justice only requires people equal in *certain* aspects to be treated equally. Let's consider an example. A landlord treats potential tenants of the same race equally by asking all black potential tenants $10,000 per month as rent, while asking all white potential tenants (trying to rent the same flat) $8,000. In short, the landlord is treating all those equal in race equally and treating those of different races unequally. Is the landlord just in doing so? Obviously not. "Even in the case of human beings, however, justice does not call for similar treatment of every similarity or for dissimilar treatment of every dissimilarity. We do not think it necessarily unjust, even if other things are equal, to deal similarly with people of different colors or dissimilarly with people of the same color ... That is, it seems to be part of the concept of justice that not all similarities justify (or justicize) similar treatment, or all differences different treatment" (Frankena 1962, p. 10). Then, people equal in which aspect or aspects justif(ies) equal treatment? Aristotle's formal principle of justice fails to account for the whole of social justice. Other substantive principles of justice must be accounted for in the definition of social justice, namely: what kind of equality deserves equal treatment, and what kind of difference deserves unequal treatment? Only a satisfactory answer to this question can provide a complete definition of social justice. In short, substantive rules of justice must be identified for a thorough examination of the concept.

As for the second question about the formal principle of justice — what kind of equal treatment are equals entitled to by the principle of justice — we will argue that there are two types of equal treatment: *equal result* and *equal opportunity*. Consider the following case. A housing manager pays the estate's security guards, whether European or Asian, a salary of $7000 per month for doing the same job, disregarding their race. This is to give equal reward to equals (individuals doing the same job); this amounts to equal results. If the housing manager wants to promote one of the security guards to be supervisor, s/he considers the performance of all the guards, European and Asian alike. The boss is giving equal opportunity to all the guards of the housing estate, regardless of race, in being promoted to the post of supervisor; the post is then allocated to the employee with the greatest merit. This is equal opportunity to unequal reward according to desert. In order to have a thorough examination of the concept of social justice, we need answers to the following questions concerning the formal principle of justice: people equal in which aspect(s) are to be given equal results? People equal in which aspect(s) are to be given equal opportunity?

Equality of Results

We will first consider how utilitarianism throws light on the concept of substantive justice, in answering the two questions: "People equal in which aspect(s) are to be given equal results?" and "People different in which aspect(s) are to be given unequal results by the principle of justice?" According to J. S. Mill, justice rests upon utility or the Greatest Happiness Principle (Mill 1987, p. 335). "Utility, or the Greatest Happiness Principle, holds that actions are right in proportion as they tend to promote happiness, wrong as they tend to produce the reverse of happiness. By happiness is intended pleasure and the absence of pain; by unhappiness, pain, and the privation of pleasure" (Mill 1978, p. 278). Right actions are those which lead to greatest happiness according to the utilitarian principle; and justice as part of utility means to distribute resources in a way which maximizes utility or happiness.

The utilitarian concept of justice rests on the outcomes, or the consequences of actions, namely whether the greatest amount of happiness can be produced as a consequence of an action. Hayek (1976), however, disagrees and stresses that to talk about social justice in terms of outcome is meaningless, especially in a market economy. According to Hayek (1976), justice "is not concerned with the results that a particular action will in fact bring about. The observation of a rule of just conduct will often have unintended consequences which, if they were deliberately brought about, would be regarded as unjust" (p. 39). Hayek emphasizes that it is only meaningful to consider justice of the *processes* rather than the *results* of an action. In other words, Hayek suggests that a person is not responsible for the unintended "unjust" results of his/her action if they occur as a by-product rather that the object of intention. However, it seems that one should be held responsible also for unintended by-products of one's actions. Suppose A intends to burn some old newspaper in his own flat. Yet by doing so, A accidentally causes a large fire, which guts the whole building. Though A only intended to destroy some old newspapers (not the block of flats), A should be held responsible for destroying the entire building. While his/her responsibility is lighter than if s/he were a deliberate arsonist, still the big fire was a predictable consequence of A's primary action. Analogously, the unintended "unjust" consequences of an action are part of the responsibility of the doer, especially should they be highly probable, predictable and foreseeable. The justice of an action rests partially on the processes and partially on the consequences of the action, and so Hayek's argument cannot fully negate the utilitarian concept of justice which defines justice in terms of consequences.

Nevertheless, the utilitarian concept of justice is itself problematic. What is so-called "just" by the utilitarian principle may be counter-intuitive. Consider the following case. While driving to the venue of his performance, Pop Singer A knocks down B. B is hurt and desperately needs A's help. However, if A helps B, s/he may not be able to reach the concert venue to perform. A's fans will be very unhappy if A does not appear to perform. According to utilitarianism, it will be just for A to leave B unattended so as to make his/her fans happy as only B will be unhappy in such case. Is it just for A to leave B to die? A rigid application of J. S. Mill's theories would give a "yes" answer to this question, and B would be left injured and unattended while the singer drove off. From the example, it seems that the concept of need is highly relevant to the discussion of justice. To each according to his/her needs — those equal in needs should be given equal results and those unequal in needs should be given unequal results seems to be a substantive rule of justice.

Let us consider another case. Suppose a rich person has a lot of estates. S/he has so much that s/he even forgets the existence of some possessions. Comparatively, his/her relative is much "poorer" than him/her, though s/he still enjoys a decent standard of living. According to the utilitarian principle, it will be "just" for the relative to "steal" and occupy one of the estates of the rich person illegally, without permission from the rich person, so that s/he may enjoy the luxury of living in a grand estate. His/Her happiness will increase, while the rich person's happiness will not decrease as s/he has forgotten the existence of some of his/her possessions. It seems absurd to say that it will be "just" to steal possessions from someone, disregarding the property rights of the person concerned. From this case, we may derive that the concept of rights is important to the concept of justice. To each according to his/her rights — those equal in rights should be treated equally; those unequal in rights should be treated unequally seems to be a substantive principle of justice.

Besides needs and rights, it seems that justice is also related to the concept of desert. For example, in a rural community, all the people in the community earn a living by tilling the land. A is a very efficient farmer and works very hard. Besides growing crops, s/he also keeps farm animals. Thus, A earns more than others in the community. Gradually, A accumulates more wealth than others in the community and buy more land and housing for rental purposes. The people in the community want the government to confiscate A's land and housing which A has earned by desert and redistribute A's land and housing among them. In this way, the majority will be happier, with only A suffering. According to the utility principle, it is just to do so, as A is the only one who suffers, while the happiness of all others will increase, thereby maximizing total happiness. Such an outcome is counter-intuitive. Taken to extremes, the utilitarian concept of justice can violate a substantive principle of justice — to each according to his/her deserts, with those equal in desert gaining equal results and those unequal in desert getting unequal results.

From the above examples, it seems that the utilitarian concept of "justice" is absurd, violating the normative substantive principles of justice. The crux of the problem arises from the fact that the utility principle concerns the *aggregate* of happiness, while disregarding the *distribution* of it (Savueseu 1998, p. 214; Rawls 1971, p. 23). According to a utilitarian, it would be "just" to distribute in any way as long as the *total* happiness is maximized, disregarding how such total happiness is distributed among individuals concerned. Thus, a utilitarian distribution may be very unjust (in the normative sense), with some suffering gross unhappiness as long as aggregate happiness is maximized.

So far, three substantive principles of justice have been identified, namely, the need principle, the right principle and the desert principle. Most philosophers' concept of justice concerns one of the three principles of justice. After examining the utilitarian concept of justice, let us consider other concepts of justice so as to have a clearer understanding of the concept and to explore more deeply the exact relation of the three principles of justice that we have identified.

Needs-based Theories of Justice

Not all needs are relevant to the discussion of social justice. Only basic needs essential for survival are relevant. "[T]he problem of satisfying non-basic needs is beyond the scope of principles of social justice" (Sadurski 1985, p. 163). Basic needs are "closely related to a minimal level of subsistence, to the fundamental conditions of biological and social life ... basic needs are related to "those things which we require if we are to survive and to have any sort of life worth living" (Sadurski 1985, p. 159). Some examples of basic needs are food, shelter and security, while some examples of non-basic needs are needs for leisure, self-realization, satisfaction, and cultural self-development (Sadurski 1985, p. 164).

Marx's concept of justice is solely needs-based. Marx envisages that in a communist society, there would be no need for distributive justice, as there is no scarcity of resources which are the circumstances that necessitate distributive justice (Buchanan 1982, p. 57). However, Marx does suggest a principle of distributive justice in a communist society which is summed up in the slogan, "from each according to his ability, to each according to his needs" (Marx 1959, p. 22). Judging from the slogan, the contribution principle recognizes unequal individual endowment and thus productive capacity. Every individual is to contribute to the best of his/her ability. As for the need principle, it also recognizes that people have unequal needs which are to be fully satisfied in a communist society (Geras 1985, p. 61).

Marx did not intend the slogan to be a principle of distributive justice in a communist society. "How are we to reconcile Marx's use of this slogan with his charge that talk about justice and rights is obsolete verbal rubbish and ideological nonsense and his view that scarcity and conflict be greatly reduced in communism? The answer... is that Marx is not offering the slogan as a communist principle of distributive justice, but rather as a description of the way things will in fact be in communism" (Buchanan 1982, p. 58). Though Marx may be denying that the slogan is a principle of justice, "[i]t is in substance a principle of distributive justice, even if its attainment is envisaged together with the death of the state" (Geras 1985, p. 60).

Since Marx's concept of justice is solely needs-based, injustice may result as social justice is more than the principle of needs. Consider the following case. Suppose A and B are builders of houses. Both A and B have similar needs. Thus, they should be given monetary reward (equal results) for the satisfaction of equal needs, according to Marx. However, A and B differ tremendously in efficiency and ability. A can only make one house within one year, while B can build three in a year. As B is a more efficient builder, it seems unjust that B gets the same monetary return as A, though they have equal needs. Intuitively, B should be given more than A in return for his/her greater effort and ability, so that B may enjoy some luxuries of life as reward. To give B greater reward than A is to distribute according to deserts rather than basing distribution on the need principle alone. To distribute according to needs alone may bring about injustices as deserts are neglected.

Furthermore, it is questionable whether solely distributing according to needs will bring about a society in which each performs "according to his best ability". If everyone is to have their needs satisfied, and those who contribute more do not have a greater share, then there would be no incentive for anyone to work to the best of his/her ability. Working in a lazier way, after all, will bring about the same result in distribution, namely, each getting what one needs.

Marx might rebut that in a communist society, individuals are transformed and will work to the best of their ability, even though there is no corresponding greater share in distribution. "According to Marx, the communist mode of production will unfetter the tremendous productivity latent in capitalism. At the same time, it will transform the individual into a cooperative, communal being, who finds work itself intrinsically satisfying and whose need for human association will dwarf his needs for things" (Buchanan 1982, p. 58). However, it is doubtful whether communism can really transform the individual from a self-interested state: a worker tends not to try his/her best without any corresponding incentives. If such a transformation is not forth-coming, "to each according to his needs" will serve as an inadequate motivation for individuals to work according to his/her ability.

Marx's slogan would also create injustice by disregarding rights. Suppose A has ten flats. A only needs one flat to accommodate his/her family. With ten flats, A may rent the extra nine flats and earn more than enough to survive. From the money s/he gets by renting the surplus flats, A and his/her family live luxuriously and save a lot of money. According to Marx's slogan, it would be right to confiscate the savings and the surplus nine flats from A, as A only needs one flat for family use. Anything more than A's needs should be taken away from A, since goods are distributed according to one's needs in a communist state. However, is such a confiscation just? It seems not. A has property rights over his/her savings and his/her nine flats. Confiscating them violates A's property rights. Marx's slogan seems unjust as it is solely needs-based, and disregards the principle of rights. The principle of needs is part of social justice, but it cannot account for the whole. The principle of rights is also relevant to social justice.

Rawls, an "egalitarian liberal" philosopher (Graham 2007, p. 13), proposes a theory of justice which arouses hostility from both the Marxist left and the libertarian right, but a sympathetic responses from the social democratic (Graham 2007, p. 8). Rawls' concept of justice may be classed as needs-based. Rawls asserts that the principles of justice are those principles that would be agreed to in a purely hypothetical situation which Rawls described as "the original position" (Rawls 1999, p. 19). In the original position, everyone is under "the veil of ignorance". "No one knows his place, his class position or social status, nor does any one know his future in the distribution of natural assets and abilities, his intelligence, strength and the like ... This ensures that no one is advantaged or disadvantaged in the choice of principles by the outcome of natural chance, or the contingency of social circumstances. Since all are similarly situated with society, and no one is able to design principles to favor his particular condition, the principles of justice are the result of a fair agreement or bargain" (Rawls 1999, p. 11).

Rawls asserts that people in the original position would agree to two principles of justice. Rawls' first principle of justice concerns political justice. Rawls' second principle of justice, the difference principle, is related to social justice. It states that "[s]ocial and economic inequalities are to be arranged so that they are both (a) to the greatest expected benefit of the least advantaged and (b) attached to offices and positions open to all under conditions of fair equality of opportunity" (Rawls 1999, p. 72). By the least advantaged, Rawls refers to "those who are least favored by each of the three main kind of contingencies. Thus this group includes a person whose family and class origins are more disadvantaged than others, whose natural endowments (as realized) permit them to fare less well and whose fortune and luck in the course of life turn out to be less happy ..." (Rawls 1999, p. 83). As the least advantaged tend to have the greatest needs and Rawls asserts that social and economic inequalities are to be arranged to benefit the least advantaged most, Rawls' theory of social justice may be considered to be needs-based.

Rawls supposed that the principles agreed upon by people in the original position will be rules of justice that should operate in society in reality. Why should it necessarily be so? Rawls is asserting this theory, without providing an argument to support it. "Critics of the theory have tended to take issue with Rawls over what principles would be chosen in the original position, but it is also necessary to examine those features of the position that are thought to support the most controversial choices and to ask why the results of a decision taken under highly specific and rather peculiar conditions should confirm the justice of the principles chosen" (Nagel 1975, p. 2). There are many principles which may be agreed upon in the original position, for example, to distribute according to deserts, not to kill, not to lie under oath. Some of these may be related to justice, while some are not. Why does Rawls only highlight two chosen in the original position? Furthermore, why do principles agreed upon in such hypothetical situation *necessarily* confirm rules of justice in reality? Why are principles agreed upon in a hypothetical situation binding upon people in reality in which circumstances differ tremendously? Rawls does not provide an answer to these questions, but merely asserts his argument is so without supporting it.

Rawls has special regard for the least advantaged, saying that social and economic inequalities are to be arranged so as to bring the greatest benefit to that group (Rawls 1999, p. 72). It may be just that income is to be redistributed to the needy or least advantaged to cater for their basic needs. However, it may not be just that there is *continuous* redistribution of income that brings the *maximum* benefit to the least advantaged, making their living standard comparable to or even higher than those who gain by deserts. Justice requires that there is redistribution of income to the least advantaged or the needy up to the level that they have a decent standard of living in which their basic needs are satisfied. "A maximum strategy would (and in Rawls does) yield principles of justice according to which it would always be just to impose any loss, however great, upon a better-off group in order to bring a gain, however small, to the least disadvantaged group, however affluent the latter's starting point. If intuitions are to be used, this is surely counter-intuitive, [since] not many of us are as egalitarian as that" (Hare 1975, p. 107).

Rawls makes no specification of the kind of social and economic inequalities considered to be just as long as it brings maximum benefit to the least advantaged (his model also prescribes that there are equal opportunities). However, it is obvious that not all types of inequalities which bring maximum benefit to the least advantaged are considered just. For example, in society X, social and economic benefits are distributed in accordance with laziness, with the laziest being the richest and the most hardworking the poorest. Those who are rich (the laziest) pay taxes, which are then limitedly redistributed to the poor (i.e. those who are the most hardworking. According to Rawls, society X will be just, as it distributes in a way that benefits the least advantaged (i.e. the poor who are the most hardworking in Society X) and there are equal opportunities. However, do we consider society X as just? By intuition, it seems that society X is very unjust as it distributes in a way that counteracts the principle of deserts, with the most hardworking being the poorest in society. Thus, it seems that not all types of social and economic inequalities are considered just. It seems that inequalities arising out of the principle of deserts will be considered just rather than the contrary, in addition to Rawls' conditions of bringing maximum benefit and equal opportunities to the least advantaged.

Besides the principle of deserts, the principle of rights is also relevant to social justice. For example, two men, one British and one Chinese, work for a company in a similar position for a month. It is specified in their employment contract that each will get $10,000 after working for a month. However, the boss is a racist and discriminates against the Chinese employee by giving him/her only $8,000 after the Chinese employee has worked dutifully for a month, violating his/her rights as stipulated in the employment contract. The Chinese employee is less well-off than would be, if the employment contract had been honoured. However, s/he is not the least advantaged in society as s/he receives his/her income and pays tax, which will be redistributed to the needy. There are still equal opportunities for a Chinese person to get a job in the company, though the pay for the Chinese worker may be lower than the British, due to racial discrimination on the part of the boss. According to Rawls, this situation will be considered "just" as economic inequalities arising out of racial discrimination (lower pay for the Chinese), benefits the least advantaged and there are equal opportunities to be employed by the company. However, it is absurd to consider such a situation as just, since it violates the principle of rights (as stipulated in the employment contract) and the formal principle of distributing to equals equally and unequals unequally. The British and the Chinese have the same employment contract, so it would be just that they should be given the same pay after working dutifully for a month in the company. This will be considered just as there is the respect of rights and equality of results for equals. Thus, it seems that rights are relevant to social justice.

From the arguments cited above, we may conclude that both the Marxist and the Rawlsian concepts of social justice can lead to very unjust outcomes. Marxist and the Rawlsian concepts of justice are needs-based, paying special attention to the satisfaction of needs. Yet though the principle of needs is part of social justice, it does not make up the whole of it. The principle of rights and the principle of deserts also form a part of justice. Focusing on needs alone would define justice too narrowly, thereby creating further injustices.

Rights-based Theories of Justice

According to Miller, "rights generally derive from publicly acknowledged rules, established practices, or past transactions: they do not depend upon a person's current behaviour or other individual qualities" (Miller 1976, p. 26). Miller distinguishes three types of rights: first, legal rights, (such as the rights of a property owner and those that arise from a contract; second, moral rights, those that arise from promises or agreements; and finally, institutional rights, such as an individual's rights as a university teacher (Miller 1976, p. 52).

Hume's concept of justice is a rights-based theory of justice. According to Hume, there are three fundamental rules of justice — the stability of possession, its transference by consent and the performance of promises (Hume 1739, p. 618). Hume suggests five rules for stability of possession, which underpin his concept of justice. Hume's five rules of establishing stability of possession are essentially rules of establishing private property rights. They are:

a) present possession – when society is first established, everyone continues to enjoy what he[1] at present possesses (Hume 1739, p. 555).

b) occupation – assigning property rights to the person who has first possession of the thing (Hume 1739, pp. 556–557).

c) prescription – something becomes one's property by virtue of one's long possession of it (Hume 1739, pp. 558, 560).

d) accession – objects are acquired as property "when they are connected in an intimate manner with objects that are already our property, and at the same time are inferior to them. Thus the fruits of our garden, the offspring of our cattle, and the work of our slaves, are all of them esteem'd our property, even before possession" (Hume 1739, p. 560).

e) succession – ascribing the son a title to his father's possessions after the parent's decease (Hume 1739, p. 561).

Hume's concept of justice, besides establishing property rights, also incorporates the rule of transference of property by consent (i.e. transfer of property rights by consent). Hume's third rule of justice is the performance of obligations arising from promises, i.e. the satisfaction of corresponding rights arising from promises. "When a man says *he promises any thing*, he in effect expresses a *resolution* of performing it; and along with that, by making — use of this *form of words*, subjects himself to the penalty of never being trusted again in the case of failure" (Hume 1739, p. 574). From the above, it may be concluded that Hume's conception of justice is solely rights-based, focusing only on certain rights, namely, property rights and their transfer as well as rights arising from promises.

Hume's definition of justice is essentially rights-based. No doubt, Hume's rules of justice concerning the establishment of private property and their transfer as well as rights arising from promises are some of many just rules. However, strict following of Hume's rule of justice in every case may not necessarily leads to a just distribution, especially when there are simultaneous conflicting demands based on needs as well as rights at the same time. For example, a person borrows money from a wealthy miser and promises to return it next week. By the end of the following week, the person plans to return the money to the miser. But a stranger collapses in front of his/her door because of starvation. It will be just for the person to use the money to buy food for the stranger, satisfying demands from needs, rather than returning it to the miser (who definitely will refuse to help the stranger), satisfying the demands arising from rights. Returning money to the miser as fulfillment of his/her obligations arising from his/her promise, while allowing the stranger to starve to death, may cause injustice. Thus strict adherence to Hume's rules of justice may bring about injustices, since Hume's definition of justice is a very restricted one. Hume's conception, based solely on rights, is too narrow to take into account the whole of justice. It does not provide for complex circumstances and contingencies which should also incorporate claims made on the basis of deserts and needs.

Besides being solely rights-based, what makes Hume's conception of justice even more problematic is his basing of the theory upon a few selected rights while disregarding other types of rights relevant to the discussion of justice. Hume's discussion of justice only narrowly focuses on property rights and rights arising from promises. In fact, rights arising from contracts are also related to justice. Institutional rights (rights arising from being a member of an institution) should be considered in a just distribution. In addition, there are non-property related human rights, such as the right to life and to freedom, which are highly relevant to the concept of justice. That is the reason why slavery and suttee are considered unjust: these two past institutions respectively deny human beings the basic right of freedom and the right to life. In short, Hume's already restricted concept based solely on rights is made even narrower by his limited focus on mainly two justice-related rights, while neglecting other relevant and important ones.

Hume's first rule of justice (on the stability of possession) focuses on rules governing the *process* of acquiring private property, based on antecedent relations: continual possession, first possession, long possession, product of our present possessions, father-son relation in the case of inheritance. These rules of establishing property rights give the status quo a privileged position (Barry 1989, pp. 174–175) and in fact reinforce it. However, we may still legitimately ask whether the resulting distribution is just, even though all Hume's five rules governing the process of allocating property rights are strictly followed. Following such a process of allocating property rights in accordance with Hume's five rules might still lead to an unjust resultant distribution if the antecedent status quo being perpetuated by this process is itself unjust. For instance, private property may be over-concentrated in the hands of a few, while the majority are left to starve to death. There is no guarantee that Hume's just process of allocating private properties may necessarily lead to a just resultant distribution of properties.

Hume's rules of justice have certain inherent problems beyond being too restrictive. Not least, Hume's system consists of many rules that are potentially in conflict with each other. Thus, the rule of first possession may conflict with the rule of long possession. The situation becomes even more complicated if the person claiming property rights over a property on the basis of first possession dies with a son to inherit it, while the person claiming property rights over the same property on the basis of long possession consents to transfer the property to another person. Who owns the property right in such a case? How are we to administer justice in such a situation, which involves four of Hume's rules of justice? Hume does not provide an answer, seemingly assuming that his rules of justice will never come into conflict. Thus, in outlining a few rules of justice, without setting priorities among them, Hume's system is not very constructive in justice theory-building.

Hume's rules of justice are largely a story of allocating properties basing on antecedent relations (present possession, long possession, first possession). But how are we to allocate possession if there is no existing antecedent relation? That is, how is the property right of a new possession to be acquired? For example, a mother makes a cake and plans to divide it among her six children. How is she going to do so? None of the children has yet possessed the cake, either in part or in whole. The mother may operate on Hume's rule of transfer by consent. But what proportion of the cake should the mother agree to transfer to each child? Based on what principle? Hume's model does not provide an answer, as his whole system of justice rests upon antecedent relation alone. Thus, it cannot resolve the distribution or the allocation of properties and resources that have no antecedent relation. In cases without antecedent relation, distribution in accordance with needs or deserts may be relevant considerations. Hume's inflexible definition of justice prevents him from giving an exhaustive system that would even establish property rights, much less a complete concept of justice.

Another thinker, Nozick, a critic of Rawls, proposes a theory of justice which is related to rights. Nozick distinguishes between patterned and unpatterned theories of justice. Patterned theories are slogans like "To each according to their needs", and "To each according to their merits", that is, just distribution is based on "some natural dimension, sum, or ordering of dimensions" (Wolff 1991, p. 77). Nozick claims the almost all principles of distributive justice are patterned, while his entitlement theory is *not* patterned.

Nozick's theory of justice may be pared down to his entitlement theory. According to Nozick, the subject of justice in holdings consists of three topics: the first is the original acquisition of holdings, which is related to the appropriation of unheld things. The second concerns the transfer of holdings from one person to another. Nozick argues that a transfer is only legitimate if it is a voluntary exchange, or a gift. The third topic is the rectification of injustice of holdings by compensation (Nozick 1974, pp. 150–152). Nozick asserts that:

1. A person who acquires a holding in accordance with the principle of justice in acquisition is entitled to that holding.
2. A person who acquires a holding (in accordance with the principle of justice in transfer) from someone else entitled to the holding, is entitled to the holding.
3. No one is entitled to a holding except by (repeated) applications of 1 and 2. (Nozick 1974, p. 151)

Nozick asserts that "a distribution is just if everyone is entitled to the holdings they possess under the distribution. A distribution is just if it arises from another just distribution by legitimate means" (Nozick 1974, p. 151). Nozick has given examples of illegitimate means. "Some people steal from others, or defraud them, or enslave them, seizing their product and preventing them from living as they choose, or forcibly exclude others from competing in exchanges. None of these are permissible modes of transition from one situation to another" (Nozick 1974, p. 152).

Voluntary transfers, according to Nozick, upset any pattern (be it "to each according to his/her needs" or "to each according to his/her deserts"). Thus, the only way to maintain the original patterned distribution is to prevent or nullify those voluntary transfers: this stipulation implies limiting or interfering with people's liberty. Nozick defends his entitlement theory as the only one which respects liberty — allowing people to transfer resources according to their own choice (Nozick 1974, p. 152).

Nozick claims that his theory of justice is not patterned. Yet his entitlement theory is, in fact, also patterned, in accordance with the patterned principle "to each according to his/her rights". Since rights can be transferred voluntarily through exchange or gifts, the pattern based on rights is volatile. Nozick could rebut that if rights-based patterned distribution is constantly changing, it is not patterned at all. However, other patterned distributions are also unstable. For example, as people's needs change, the needs-based pattern also alters accordingly. The same applies to other patterned distributions. It is arguable that rights transfer is comparatively more frequent than that of other pattern-criteria, (for instance, transfer according to needs, or to deserts). However, the variability of rights as compared to other pattern-criteria is a matter of degree rather than a difference in kind. In this way, Nozick's entitlement theory is no different from other patterned distribution: it is also patterned upon a distributive principle, namely, "to each according to his/her rights", even though, at times that system is subject to more frequent alternations and adjustments.

Furthermore, Nozick claims that his entitlement theory is "superior" to other patterned theories of justice, since it alone takes liberty into consideration. However, is liberty the sole and most important intrinsic value? Can there never be overriding competing values in a case of conflict? Let's consider the following Kohlberg's dilemma as an illustration. Lab technician A works for a medical researcher who invents a special kind of medicine to cure disease X. The medical researcher has the liberty to do anything with his invention; he charges a very high price for the new medicine, which ordinary people cannot afford. Suppose A's wife is suffering from disease X and is on the verge of death, but cannot afford to buy the new medicine from the medical researcher. If A steals the medicine to save his wife's life, his actions will not be considered unjust. That is, in the case of justice, A's wife's right to life is more fundamental than respecting private property rights and the freedom of the medical researcher (to handle his own property as s/he desires) in the case of justice. The transfer of the new medicine from the medical researcher to A is not voluntary, and violates the former's liberty to dispose of his/her invention and property, yet it may not be considered unjust. Taxation and redistribution of income to the poor is involuntary and limit one's liberty to use what one earns, yet it is considered just by most in society, as the needs of the poor are satisfied. Nozick disagrees and equates taxation as a kind of forced labour. Thus, the principle of needs is relevant to the discussion of justice: it is more fundamental than both the principle of rights, and the liberty to dispose of one's property as one wishes.

Nozick's entitlement theory is a theory of the process of the establishment of private property rights and their transfer. It is thus classed as a rights-based theory of justice. Nozick argues that a transfer of property is just, but only as long as it is voluntary. Yet consider the following example. A boss grants a bonus to his/her employees. S/he transfers the greatest amount of bonus to X, who is the laziest and most inefficient employee in the company. Whereas Y, the hardest working employee, brings the greatest profit to the company but gets the smallest bonus. Such a bonus distribution would be very unjust, though the transfer is voluntary. Thus, the principle of deserts is also relevant to a just transfer if one is to transfer property rights to more than one person. That is, the principle of deserts is relevant to justice, in addition to the principle of rights and the just transfer of rights.

In conclusion: Hume's and Nozick's theory of justice are essentially rights-based, and the principle of rights is of critical importance to the concept of justice. However, blinkered application of Hume's and Nozick's theory of justice can lead to very unjust situations because the principle of rights accounts for only part of, rather than the whole, of justice. The principle of needs and the principle of deserts must also play a part in a just distribution. By solely concentrating on the principle of rights alone, Hume's and Nozick's theory of justice leads to absurdity.

Deserts-based Theory of Justice

According to Miller, "desert" means rewarding behaviour which arouses admiration and approval by most people in society. "The range of possible desert bases coincides with the range of possible bases for appraising attitudes ... The existence of appraising attitudes make intelligible the connection between a desert judgement and its basis" (Miller 1976, p. 89). Desert does not only apply to qualities voluntarily acquired, but also to inborn qualities. "When we admire the superlative skill of a musician, we do not ask about the conduct which led to its acquisition before granting our admiration. The attitude is held directly towards the quality as it now exists, and the question "voluntarily acquired or not?" is simply not considered" (Miller 1976, p. 96).

Aristotle's principle of justice is also based on deserts according to one's merit. "This is plain from the fact that awards should be "according to merit"; for all men agree that what is just in distribution must be according to merit in some sense, though they do not specify the sort of merit ..." (Aristotle 1998, p. 112). Aristotle takes an extreme relativistic stand in his definition of merit, saying that it varies with different political society. "[T]he democrats identify it with the status of freemen, supporters of oligarchy with wealth (or with noble birth) and supporters of aristocracy with excellence" (Aristotle 1998, p. 113). Thus, to Aristotle, "what is just is proportional [to one's merit as defined in the society one is in]; the unjust is what violates the proportion ... for the man who acts unjustly has too much, and the man who is unjustly treated too little, of what is good" (Aristotle 1998, p. 114).

According to Aristotle, justice means awarding people in accordance with their merit or deserts: those with equal deserts are to be awarded equally. However, in some instances, individuals have no merit or deserts of any sort. They may be physically weak, unintelligent, not of noble birth, not exceptionally morally virtuous or disabled and may be unable to work or contribute to society. According to Aristotle's theory of justice, they should not be allocated any share by the principle of deserts. Are they to be starved to death? If this is so, Aristotle's concept of justice will lead to a type of inhumane meritocracy, with the disadvantaged suffering. Can we call such a society just, if the disadvantaged suffer, without any share of prosperity? By humanitarian standard, such a society is unjust; concepts of justice should take into consideration the needs of the disadvantaged, rather than hinging on deserts alone.

Let us consider another case. A father promises to buy a toy car for his son as a Christmas present. Thus, the son has a right arising from the promise of his father. However, the son fails all subjects in his examination. By the principle of deserts, he does not deserve to receive a Christmas present from his father. When Christmas approaches, by the principle of rights, it would be just for the father to give his son a toy car as promised (though his son does not deserve it) since when he made the promise, the boy's father did not attach the condition that this son would have to pass his examination before receiving his Christmas present. The son's right to the Christmas present — arising from the "unconditional" promise — should be respected. Thus, the principle of rights is also relevant to the concept of justice. Strict adherence to the principle of deserts when calculating all distributions may lead to injustices.

All in all, Aristotle's concept of justice rests on one criterion only, namely that of deserts. It is true that to distribute according to deserts might lead to just distribution in some cases. However, the strict adherence to the principle of deserts in every case would lead to injustices, as the concept of justice is a complex one, incorporating more than one principle. The principle of needs and the principle of rights are also relevant to the concept of justice.

Three Principles of justice

Hayek, as a critic of theories of social justice, points out that the appeal to social justice is illusory. He argues that it is impossible to agree on the criterion of social justice which could guide public policy, because there may be many possible criteria of just distribution, e.g. deserts, needs etc. Thus, different definitions of justice will be used to disguise interest-group competition for resources which governments can distribute. Instead, Hayek tries to justify the market and its "free" exchanges (as opposed to distribution models based on any arbitrary just criterion) (Plant 1994, p. 167). Hayek thinks that injustice occurs only when there is *intentional* interference of another person's life. As markets are producing *unintended* outcomes with various "free" acts of exchange between different actors, the resulting poverty of some (in a market) is a misfortune, rather than an injustice, because it is an outcome not intended by any person's act. This is different from the case when private property has been intentionally removed (Plant 1994, p. 165). However, though poverty among certain groups within society is an unintentional consequence of free market exchange, it is still a foreseeable and predictable consequence: (Plant 1994, p. 169) those with fewer skills and property will lose out naturally in the market. Intuitively, we are also held morally responsible for the foreseeable, but unintentional results of our actions. If we were not, manslaughter would not be a crime (Plant 1994, p. 170). Thus, all actors — not just individuals — in the market should be held morally responsible for the unintended poverty of some members of society. A government (acting on behalf of all) is therefore justified in redistributing wealth from rich to poor according to a criterion other than that of "free" market exchange. The question remains: what are the appropriate just criteria for distribution?

So far, the theories of justice discussed are based solely on a single criterion, whether needs, rights or deserts. Yet such single criterion theories are fairly criticized as overly simplistic. Miller's theory of justice is different from all others by stating that justice essentially incorporates three conflicting principles: deserts, rights and needs (Miller 1976). By intuition, normative justice is connected to all three. However, none, by itself, suffices to stand alone as the normative principle of justice. If justice is to allocate solely by deserts, then those without any merit will be starved to death. Because that model is very unjust, needs must be added as a criterion of allocation if justice is to exist in a meaningful way. Justice based solely on deserts also implies that allocation does not have to take into consideration rights arising from established contracts. Does this mean that an employer does not have to pay the monthly salary as stipulated in the employment contract if the worker turns out to be not very competent in his/her work, though s/he has worked hard for the whole month? It seems that allocation according to rights does have some weight in the theory of justice, in addition to allocation by deserts and needs. Similar unjust situations may arise if allocation is done solely by the other two criteria, needs and rights.

Miller points out that the three principles of justice may necessarily or contingently conflict with each other (Miller 1967, pp. 27–28). A normative theory of justice, often leading to conflicting and incompatible conclusions, may be a sufficient reason to dismiss it as an adequate theory. Thus, to say that justice incorporates all three conflicting principles, different priorities must be given to each of them in a normative theory of justice so that in a conflict between them, one is definitely sure which of the conflicting principles should be given priority.

Which of the three principles of justice should be given priority? Let us consider Miller's example. "You may promise to meet a friend, and it happens that on the day in question your neighbour falls ill. The neighbour has no right (against you) to be taken care of, yet he may badly *needs* your assistance, so it may be just to break your promise and violate your friend's rights" (Miller 1976, p. 77). From the example, it seems that when the principle of needs and the principle of rights are in conflict, justice demands that the principle of needs takes priority over that of rights.

Consider another example. Suppose a dying person has promised to pay all the educational fees for his/her niece who comes from a poor family. This dying person is extremely well-cared for by a devoted nurse before his/her death. It will be "just" for the dying person to leave some of his/her properties to the nurse in accordance with the principle of deserts. However, his/her promise to the niece is another "just" claim on his/her properties by the principle of rights (arising from promises). In this case, it will be just to satisfy what is demanded by rights first by paying off all the educational fees of his/her niece, before giving anything over and above the nurse's rights (his/her salary as stipulated in the employment contract) as a reward s/he gains by deserts for his/her extremely great devotion to his/her work. From this case, it seems that whenever the principle of rights and deserts are in conflict, rights take priority over deserts.

Let us use another case to illustrate. In the Olympic games, the marathon runner who is the first to break the line at the destination has the right to get the gold medal. If a runner from Algeria is born with very appropriate physical abilities to run a marathon and has devoted extremely great effort to training in preparation for the Olympics, it may be said that s/he deserves to get the gold medal by the principle of deserts. However, during the race in the Olympics, s/he unfortunately twists his/her leg and is forced to withdraw from the race. Another runner from the U.S. who is less physically fit and less devoted to training reaches the finish line first, thereby earning a gold medal. In such a case, it would be just to give the U.S. runner the gold medal according to the principle of rights, rather than giving it to the Algerian runner, even though s/he "deserved" to get it by the principle of deserts. Again, this scenario indicates that the principle of rights takes priority over that of deserts whenever they come into conflict.

To summarize, social justice incorporates three principles: to each according to his/her needs, rights and deserts; people equal in needs, rights and deserts should be given equal results. These three principles may come into conflict with each other. In the case of conflict, the principle of needs should be given first priority, the principle of rights should be given second priority, followed by the principle of deserts.

So far, we have identified three principles of justice. Which principle of justice are we going to apply in the distribution of a good in question? It is apparent that any arbitrary application of any principle of justice, namely, the principle of needs, rights or deserts, to the distribution of a good may create the very injustices a just society seeks to avoid. For example, it is just to award a scholarship to the most brilliant student in class, according to the principle of deserts. It would be unjust to divide the scholarship equally among all students in class according to the principle of rights, with each student (as a member of the class) having equal rights. Based on which criteria are we going to select the appropriate principle of justice in the allocation of a specific good?

In a recent book, Miller (1999) sketches his theory of justice by appealing to the "modes of human relationship". "Human beings can stand in different kinds of relationship to one another, and we can best understand which demands of justice someone can make of us by looking first at the particular nature of our relationship" (Miller 1999, p. 25). In a solidaristic community where people share a common identity as members of a relatively stable group with common ethos (examples include a family, village community, club, or professional association), Miller suggests that the relevant principle of justice is distribution according to needs (Miller 1999, pp. 26–27). In an instrumental association, one defined by economic relations, "people relate to one another in an utilitarian manner; each has aims and purposes that can best be realized by collaboration with others" (Miller 1999, p. 27); therefore the relevant principle of justice is distribution according to deserts. The third mode of association is citizenship, in which "anyone who is a full member of such a society is understood to be the bearer of a set of rights and obligations that together define the status of citizen" (Miller 1999, p. 30). The just distributive principle of a citizenship association is equality[2].

Yet Miller's assertion that the justice principle selection criterion is the mode of human relations is unconvincing. There is no necessary relation between the justice principle and a particular mode of relation. A particular mode of relation may have more than one relevant just principle, making conflicting claims. For example, in a family which Miller classifies as a solidaristic community, a mother intends to divide a cake among her six children. The mother may give the biggest piece to the child who misses lunch, according to the just principle of needs. Alternatively, the mother may give the biggest piece to the child who did the best in a recent examination, according to the just principle of deserts. In the latter case, the relation between the mother and children remains the same (solidaristic community), yet another relevant justice criterion may apply in addition to Miller's sole need criterion for such mode of relations.

Similarly, it is also problematic to assert that for a certain justice criterion to be met, it must involve a particular mode of human relations. Miller asserts that the just principle of deserts is related to instrumental association. We tend to agree that it is just for a teacher to allocate the highest mark to the best student, one who excels in the examination, according to the principle of deserts. However, it would be degrading to characterize the teacher-student relation as an instrumental association in which the desert principle is relevant. Again, the flaw in this model underscores the fact that there is no necessary connection between the relevant just principle and the connected mode of human relations.

If the mode of human relations is irrelevant to determining the justice criterion, then how are we to determine which just principle should be applied for a given situation? The answer rests on the presence or absence of the justice-related elements: needs, rights or deserts. If a justice-related element is present, then the corresponding just principle should apply. For example, if a mother is to divide a cake between her six children and only one justice-related element, namely, needs, is present, then it will be just to distribute the cake to the children according to the just principle of needs. According to the principle of needs, it would be just to distribute the biggest pieces to those children who missed both breakfast and lunch, with smaller pieces doled out to those children who missed lunch only and the smallest pieces to those children who had both breakfast and lunch.

In a similar way, if another justice-related element, namely, rights, is involved in a distribution, then the principle of right should be the just criterion in the distribution. If A promises to pay B $8,000 for renting his/her flat for a month and promises to give C $10,000 for renting C's flat for a month in a contract, then it will be just for A to pay B and C accordingly in light of the just principle of rights, with rights arising from the rental contract. In the same way, if the third justice-related element, namely, deserts, is present in a distribution, then the just principle of deserts should apply.

If more than one justice-related element are involved in a distribution, then the priority among the three principles of justice discussed earlier should apply. For example, if A promises to meet B at three o'clock, then right arising from a promise is involved. A, on the way to meet B, passes a wounded man, C, who desperately needs A's help. That is, another justice-related element, namely, the needs of C, becomes relevant to the distribution of A's time. It will be just for A to stop to care for C's needs, instead of meeting B. The principle of needs should have priority over the principle of rights which has priority over the principle of deserts according to earlier discussion.

The three-principle concept of justice discussed earlier is an end-result concept. That is, justice is determined by the structure of the distribution concerned. Le Grand (1991) suggests that the equity or justice of a situation generally depends on how it comes about, namely, whether free choice is involved. According to Le Grand, distribution resulting from factors beyond individual control are generally considered inequitable or unjust (for example, lower incomes for black employees doing the same job) while distributions that are the outcome of individual choice are not (for example, lower income for those who choose to work part-time) (Le Grand 1991, pp. 86–87). Consider the following cases. A distributes bonuses to his/her employees according to the contribution of each employee made to the firm, with the one contributing the most receiving the most bonus. This allotment will be just, according to the principle of deserts. B distributes bonuses to his/her employees, giving most to the laziest employee of his/her firm, while giving least to the most hardworking employee. Intuitively, B is very unjust. In both A's and B's case, the question of choice is not involved. Yet, one may still determine whether it is just or not. From the above, one may determine that whether a distribution results from free choice is not a necessary and sufficient condition of justice, even though it may be involved in some cases of justice.

Equality of Opportunity

According to Aristotelian formal principle of justice, justice means treating equals equally, and unequals unequally. Equal treatment is classed in two types; equal results and equal opportunity. After discussing equal results — justice involves equal results for those with equal needs, rights or deserts, let's focus on equal opportunity. What is equality of opportunity? What must be equal for opportunities to be equal in the case of social justice? Let's consider a case. For example, Country X is a colony in Africa, occupied and ruled by a Western power. All the members in the civil service are whites. This also applies to other high positions in society, such as lawyers, doctors, judges etc. The selection of civil servants and other high position is hereditary, passing the position to the eldest son. Thus, all those in high positions are white males. One may say that there are injustices in Country X since there is no equal opportunity for women and the Africans to compete for high positions, leading to racial and sex discrimination. Furthermore, there is inefficiency in Country X since the eldest son of officials and those occupying high positions may not possess competence in relevant aspects to take up the positions they inherit from their father. It is quite unjust for the competent to be barred from high positions which are selected by blood rather than by merit.

How can we make Country X more just? More equal opportunities may be created by applying the principle of merit. According to Fishkin (1983), the principle of merit, requires widespread procedural fairness in evaluating job applicants; that is a common liberal approach to equal opportunity (pp. 21–22), and thereby social justice. Country X can be made more just by instituting an examination for the selection of civil servants and other senior government positions; that test would impartially rate candidates' skills and knowledge relevant for the position. Only those who excel in the civil service examination would be selected as civil servants, satisfying the principle of merit.

But are such selection examinations enough to bring about equal opportunity, and thereby social justice? It depends on whether the examinations are open to all, disregarding sex and race. If the examinations are open to whites and males only, while indigenous people and women are barred from participating, injustices will persist. Essentially, there is still no equal opportunity in the selection of candidates for high positions and the civil service in Country X. There is only the superficial implementation of the merit principle, since women and

Africans with comparatively more merits are barred from competing. Roemer (1998) points out that one of the pillars of equal opportunity is the nondiscrimination principle, which states that "in the competition for positions, all individuals who possess the attributes relevant for the performance of duties of the positions in question must be included in the pool of eligible candidates, and that an individual's possible occupancy of the position be judged only with respect to those relevant attributes" (p. 1).

If the principle of merit is an important principle of equal opportunity, then we should define what counts as merit. If one excels in the civil services examination with relevant merits, it may be a result of the interplay of his/her natural ability, his/her environment and his/her effort. It seems that equal opportunity requires that merit is to be a result of the interplay of one's natural ability and effort, demanding the equalization of the environment. Let's go back to the example of Country X. Even if the examinations for the civil services and other high positions are open to all, males and females, Africans and whites alike, we still cannot conclude that there equal opportunities exist in Country X. It may be possible that the Africans in Country X are all poor and cannot afford education for their children. In fact, the indigenous people are so poor that most are undernourished. As for the women, they may be barred from receiving an education. How can the Africans and women compete in examinations for high positions even though they are officially allowed to join the examinations for selection? According to Fishkin (1983), the equality of life chances which requires "that the prospect of children for eventual positions in society should not vary in any systematic and significant manner with their arbitrary native characteristics" (p. 32), such as race, sex, ethnic origin or family background. In short, this demands that the government "level the playing field" of the competitors (Roemer 1998, p. 1), that is, that it minimize environmental effects on the performance of competitors in the competition. This will involve background fairness for the indigenous population and for women in Country X. For example, welfare should be provided for the citizens so that they will not be undernourished, and will live healthily. With good health, the natives may compete on equal terms with whites for high position. Furthermore, education should be provided for all inhabitants, regardless of class, colour or sex, so that they can compete on equal terms with the white males in the selection examinations. In fact, the indigenous people and women are from a disadvantaged background. For example, the African children must support their families by working part-time even while they are still attending school; the girls are discouraged to excel in their studies even though they have a chance to receive education. In order to provide equal opportunity for the Africans and women in Country X to compete with white males, there should be comparatively more resources devoted to the education of the indigenous people and women to make them as prepared for the examination as their white male counterparts. This is to equalize the impact of circumstances on the competitors in the competition. If a one-legged man enters a race with a healthy person, without doubt, the healthy person can be predicted to win the race before even the race starts. Sen (1990) points out that "[s]ince the conversion of primary goods and resources into freedom[3] to select a particular life and to achieve may vary from person to person, equality in holdings of primary goods or resources can go hand in hand with serious inequalities in actual freedom enjoyed by different persons" (footnote added, p. 115). Sen further suggests that the assessment of justice should not be based upon resources or primary goods people actually hold, but upon the actual freedoms to choose or opportunity to live different ways of living (Sen 1990, p. 115). Thus, the disadvantaged requires the provision of more primary goods or resources in order to have the opportunity to achieve the same successes or lifestyle (i.e. the freedom to choose between different ways of living).

According to Bowie (1998), "equal opportunity exists when persons with the same ability and talents, and who expend roughly the same effort, have roughly the same prospects for success. Race, religion, sex and family background should not be relevant to one's success or failure in the competitive struggle" (p. 3). In short, Bowie advocates the interplay of natural ability and effort as the determination of merit in the competition. Roemer disagrees with Bowie by proposing that equal opportunities involve the allocating of offices according to their propensity to expend effort — if two persons exert the same degree of effort, they should receive equal rewards (Roemer 1998, pp. 15–16). Roemer, in other words, asserts that only effort, but not natural abilities, should be the measure of merit that decides equal opportunity for unequal position. However, if A has low IQ but studies very hard, s/he may still fail the qualifying examination to become a doctor. We will not conclude that A is suffering from unequal opportunities, if A's achievement is less than B's, since B has a high IQ and needs only a little effort to pass the qualifying examination. That is, A has less merit than B in the competition for the position of doctor. If equal opportunity only requires the measurement of effort, with natural abilities as a circumstances to be equalized as Roemer advocates, then some sort of genetic engineering will be required before equality of opportunities can be said to be genuinely applied. However, this is counter-intuitive and we are not prepared to accept that equal opportunities require genetic engineering in order to level the playing field or equalize the circumstances of the competition for certain positions. Thus, Bowie's definition of merit as the interplay of natural abilities and degree of effort is a more appropriate reflection of our common concept of what equal opportunity requires.

Having discussed what equal opportunity is, let us examine who deserves to have the treatment of equal opportunity. Justice involves treating equals equally, unequals unequally. Who is to be considered as equals for enjoying equal opportunity? It seems that justice requires equal opportunities to all, disregarding one's race, family background, age, sex etc. If "equal opportunity" is only limited to the male sex, then there is, in fact, no genuine equal opportunity, as the female sex does not have equal opportunity to compete. The principle of merit and the equality of life chances as the requirements of equal opportunity are not satisfied. If equal opportunity does not apply to all, without discrimination, then, in fact, there is no genuine equal opportunity at all. According to Rawls, justice requires that "offices and positions [are] open to all under conditions of fair equality of opportunity" (Rawls 1999, p. 72).

If justice involves equal opportunities to all, what must be equal for opportunities to be equal? All people are equal as an individual is the basis of equal opportunity for all. "All people should be given equal opportunities" is another substantive principle underlying the formal principle of justice "to treat equals equally".

Nature of Justice

So far, we have argued that the four-principle[4] concept of justice is universal in nature, in the sense that it applies to all distribution over time and space. Communitarians assert that justice is what the community defines as just. Yet because what is defined as just may vary from community to community, the communitarians are in fact claiming that justice is relative rather than universal in nature. According to MacIntyre, "there is no place for appeal to a practical-rationality-as-such or a justice-as-such to which all rational persons would by their very rationality be compelled to give their allegiance. There is instead only the practical-rationality-of-this-or-that tradition and the justice-of-this-or-that tradition" (MacIntyre 1988, p. 346).

Walzer (1983) asserts that principles of justice are pluralistic in form — different social goods should be distributed for different reasons, through different procedures, for different reasons (p. 6). In Walzer's view, distribution is "just or unjust relative to the social meanings of the goods at stake" (Walzer 1983, p. 9). In light of the fact that social meaning varies from place to place and over time, Walzer is in fact asserting that justice is not universal in nature, but rather is relative in time and place, that is, being relative rather than universal in nature. However, the fact that one may criticize a certain widely accepted distribution in one's own society as unjust, shows that we apply certain normative universal notions of justice when we evaluate certain well-established institutions within our society. For example, Lincoln recognized the well-entrenched institution of slavery as unjust, even though most people in his society considered it as unproblematic and just. Lincoln in doing so, must be relying on a universal criterion of justice rather than the societal standard of justice which was largely accepted by people of his time. Thus, there is a distinction between "*what justice ought to be*" and "*what is considered just by society*". The former is universal while the latter is relative in nature. The four-principle concept of justice discussed earlier is "*what justice ought to be*" which is universal in nature.

Bell criticizes the communitarian concept of justice. According to Bell (1993), "[m]ore fundamentally, perhaps, many liberal theorists have objected to "communitarian" methodology on the grounds that it has conservative implications and endorses moral relativism. If what is just is defined only in terms of a community's deepest understandings, does that mean I can never criticize what is approved in my community, or what is approved in other communities, no matter how abhorrent the practice and the justification for it" (p. 11)?

Our earlier discussion of justice implies that the question of social justice is mainly a distributive issue. Young argues that social justice is more than a matter of distribution. According to Young (1990), contemporary theories of justice "are dominated by a distributive paradigm, which tends to focus on the possession of material goods and social positions ... [Instead], oppression and domination ... should be the primary terms for conceptualizing injustice ... Actually as a family of concepts, oppression has five aspects: exploitation, marginalization, powerlessness, cultural imperialism and violence. Distributive injustices may contribute to or result from these forms of oppression, but none is reducible to distribution and all involve social structures and relation beyond distribution" (pp. 8–9). Okin (1989) stresses that contemporary Anglo-American theories of justice have patriarchal assumptions, neglecting the fact that "marriage and the family are unjust institutions, rendering women vulnerable to dependency, exploitation and abuse" (pp. 110, 135–136). Young (1990) suggests that "social justice requires not the melting away of group differences, but institutions that promote reproduction of and respect for group differences without oppression" (p. 47), that is, a "politics of difference" which argues that "equality as the participation and inclusion of all groups sometimes requires different treatment for oppressed or disadvantaged groups" (p. 158). Democracy, according to Young, is an element and a condition for social justice as the voices of the disadvantaged groups can be heard in the decision-making process, thereby ensuring a just outcome (Young 1990).

It is true that Young is correct that social injustices are rooted in oppression and domination. However, even acknowledging inequalities in society does not preclude that social justice is not distributive in nature. The distributive paradigm, suggested by different theories of justice, is not merely limited to the distribution of tangible goods, (income, wealth, and social positions), but also includes the distribution of intangible goods/desirables, such as rights, power, respect, and prestige. The existence of domination and oppression reflects the unequal distribution of rights and power. For example, an unequal distribution of rights and power in a family leads to the oppression of women in the family, leading to injustices.

Young claims a distributive paradigm, that focuses attention on distributive outcome alone without accounting for the processes that gave rise to these outcomes, neglects the main issue of social justice. Miller, who views social justice as largely a distributive issue, argues that Young's charge simply misses the point. Miller claims that the main aim of focusing on distributive outcomes is not to label a certain distribution as just or unjust, but rather to indict the institutions and practices that give rise to unjust distributive outcomes (Miller 1999, p. 15).

Young suggests that the remedy for social injustices is through the implementation of democracy, rather than through redistribution, upon which the distributive paradigm focuses. Young claims that democracy allows the disadvantaged to be heard in the decision-making process, thereby eliminating oppression. However, even democracy has its flaws: it has been described as a system that allows what Tocqueville termed as the "tyranny of the majority" over the minority. Even though the disadvantaged's voices are heard in a democracy, they are often the minority. Though they may vote, their interests may still be unrepresented. When some citizens are more "equal" than others, even democracy cannot guarantee a just outcome. The acknowledgement of the equal distribution of rights, so central to the distributive paradigm, is more fundamental than the mere implementation of democracy; with oppression eliminated, social justice may be achieved.

Like Young, Fraser asserts that social justice is more than a distributive issue. Fraser distinguishes two types of injustice. The first is socioeconomic injustice which is rooted in the political-economic structure of society. Some examples of socioeconomic injustices are: exploitation, economic marginalization and economic deprivation. The second type of injustice is cultural or symbolic, being rooted in social patterns of representation, interpretation and communication. Examples include cultural domination, non-recognition and disrespect. The remedy for economic injustice is redistribution, while the remedy for cultural injustice is recognition involving some sort of cultural or symbolic change (pp. 13–15). Fraser's economic injustices largely deal with the distribution of tangible goods (e.g. wealth, income and social positions); while cultural injustices largely concern the distribution of intangible "goods" or desirables, (e.g. respect, power and rights). Fraser suggests that the remedy for cultural injustice is not redistribution, but recognition. However, recognition may still be viewed as the redistribution of respect, power and rights. Thus, Fraser's non-distributive aspect of justice may still be interpreted as a distributive issue, if one considers both tangible and intangible elements in distributions.

On the whole, both Young and Fraser fail to show that social justice is more than a distributive issue because they only focus upon the distribution of tangible goods, while failing to acknowledge the distribution of intangible "goods" or desirables. The unjust distribution of both tangible and intangible "goods"/desirables reflects the unjust functioning of institutions and practices underlying such a distribution which a distributive theory of justice aims to tackle.

Chinese versus Western Concepts of Justice

The Confucian Concept of Justice

Scholars are divided among them as to which concept in classical Confucian literature corresponds to the Western concept of justice. Some scholars believe that the Confucian literature does not have a single concept that can readily translated into justice in the Western sense of "giving everyone their due" (Lee 1995, p. 125; Fan 1997, p. 427; Peerenboom 1990, p. 17; Fan 2003, p. 145). According to Fan (2003), "given that we follow Rawls to understand social justice as involving establishing fundamental moral principles to guide the structure of society, such principles are already implicit in classical Confucianism" (p. 145). Other scholars believe that *yi* (義) can be understood as the Western concept of justice (Cheng 1997, p. 417; Roetz 1993, p. 111). However, *yi* and justice do not coincide in all accounts. According to Cheng (1997), "a Confucian philosopher would call the following cases as "not-*yi*" ... a: the betrayal of a trusting friend; b: seeking self-interest at the expense of a friend; c: ignoring evidence in order to persecute the innocent. We can also see that to a Western philosopher a/b/c as instances of injustice. On the other hand, the following are cases of *yi* which are cases of justice: d: keeping one's promise even if there is no witness to the vow; e: defending the innocent against a persecuting and vengeful ruler's persecution; f: rendering correct and rational/fair judgement even to the point of hurting one's own personal interests. But we need not think that the two terms "*yi*" and "justice" coincide on all accounts. For example, as in some Chinese stories, a person may sacrifice his own son in order to provide help or welfare for his brother or friend's child. This is *yi* for the Chinese, but not necessarily justice for the modern Westerner" (Cheng 1997, p. 417).

Fan (1997; 2003), in comparing Rawls' theory of justice with Confucian concept of justice, points out that the former concerns the distribution of instrumental goods, while the latter concerns the pursuit of intrinsic virtues. Rawls' theory of justice concerns the distribution of instrumental goods (e.g. liberty, opportunity, wealth and income) which are useful for or instrumental to the pursuit of one's life plans. That is, his principles of justice are independent of what may be described as the good life. However, Confucians are concerned with intrinsic goods which are valued for its own sake, forming part of good life, such as *ren* (仁; benevelence) and *yi* (義; righteousness). "What is the point of mentioning the word 'profit'? All that matters is that there should be benevolence and rightness" (*Mencius* 1A:1). Confucian social justice concerns the promotion of intrinsic goods which constitute the good of humans in the fundamental sense. "[T]he ultimate concern of Confucian general justice is loving humans by pursuing intrinsic goods, rather than distributing instrumental benefits" (Fan 2003, p. 148) as stressed by Rawls' theory of justice.

Implicit in the Western theories of justice is the treating of people as equals. Everyone's needs, rights and deserts count the same, without the preference of one individual's over that of others. Though the Confucian principle of *ren* requires loving all humans, it does not require that one should love all humans equally and similarly (Fan 2003, p. 150). "Confucianism always requires that there ought to be a clear and definite order, distinction, and differentiation in the application of love" (Chan 1995, pp. 8–9). It is not that one should not love all; it is one should love all with differentiation and relativity of importance" (Fan 2003, p. 50). This spirit is summed up in the Confucian slogan "love with distinction" or "care by gradation". It is not correct for a person to love a stranger as much as his parents. Similarly, it is inappropriate for a person to love a sage as an ordinary man (Fan 2003, p. 150). Confucianism stresses that different human relations have different moral significance in the practice of *ren*. According to Roetz (1993) who equates *yi* in Confucianism with justice, "What is just for man? The father is kind and the son is filial, that the elder brother is good to the younger brother and the younger brother respects the elder brother, that the husband is just (*yi*) and the wife is obedient, that the elder are gracious and the young are docile, that the ruler is humane and the subject is loyal — these ten things are called the just for man" (p. 113). The Confucian general concept of social justice is to treat people harmoniously, but not equally as in the Western world; the principle of *ren* directs naturally unequal humans to live harmoniously among one another (Fan 2003, p. 152).

As discussed earlier in this chapter, the Western concept of justice incorporates the need principle ("to each according to his/her needs"). This principle of need is also present in a Confucian society, however, its satisfaction is done by multiple performers. In a communist state or a Western welfare state, it is mainly the state which distributes in accordance with the principle of needs. However, in a Confucian state, there is a multi-layer of provision of care or welfare in which the family, the village and the government all play a role (Chan 2003, p. 238). When a person is in need, the family is the first tier to ask for help: the family is the most basic and important tier to distribute according to need. The village or the commune serves as the second tier of help. "If those who own land within each *jing* [or village] befriend one another both at home and abroad, help each other to keep watch, and succor each other in illness, they will live with love and harmony" (Chan 2003, p. 239). It is only after the first two tiers of help fail, that assistance from the government is sought — and then only as a last resort. Thus, in a Confucian society, "to each according to his/her needs" is the responsibility of the family, then the village and only lastly the government, whereas in the Western world, this is mainly catered for by the government. Thus, in a Confucian society, the government is a small one, as the family and village assume most of its welfare functions.

Besides the need principle, the Western concept of justice also incorporates the principle of rights. Hume's theory of justice stresses the establishment and transfer of property rights. In Western society, it is the individual who has exclusive use of income and property. By contrast, in a traditional Confucian society, "property was considered owned by the family, not the individual. The family clan lived together and pooled family property, and it was assumed that economically productive members of the family would fulfil their duties of care for needy family members within this context" (Bell 2003, p. 230). The needy family members refer to members of the extended family. It especially refers to the need to care for elderly parents. "Mencius said, 'What is the most important duty? One's duty towards one's parents ... There are many duties one should discharge, but the fulfillment of one's duty towards one's parents is the most basic'" (*Mencius* 4A:19). Confucius also stresses filial piety in the *Analects*: "Meng Wu Po asked about being filial. The Master [Confucius] said, 'Give your father and mother no other cause for anxiety than illness' " (2:6).

In addition to property rights, the Western concept of justice incorporates the idea of human rights which is an entitlement universally given to every individual as a human, irrespective of sex, age, class, and race. The just principle of rights emphasizes to each according to his/her rights, underscoring the equal distribution of human rights. Westerners tend to think in terms of rights, whereas Confucians tend to think in terms of obligations (Wu 1987, pp. 42–43). "It seems that a Chinese lives in a society of obligations, obligations to serve the ruler, obligations to work for the family, obligations to obey parents, obligations to obey elders, obligations to help relatives, obligation to do well to glorify the name of ancestors, obligations to oneself to cultivate one's own virtue.

It would also seem the rights belong only to one individual — the Son of Heaven [i.e. the ruler]. He alone has rights; he alone is outside and above the law; he alone has everything because he is the Son of Heaven who has the Mandate of Heaven. Such has been the tradition in Chinese civilization" (Wu 1987, p. 41). One may argue that one's obligations towards others, such as parents, involve the corresponding rights on the part of those whom one is obliged to, for example, the rights of elderly parents to be taken care of by their adult children. However, in Confucianism, "people in close personal relationships should not even think of themselves as subjects possessing rights upon which they make claims against each other. Rather, they should think of themselves as participating in a relationship of reciprocal commitments and mutual caring" (Fan 2003, p. 153).

The principle of deserts is an important principle of justice in Western society. It would be useful here to define what, in the Western world, counts as merit? And who deserves reward according to the principle of deserts? Talent and striving for accomplishments are the most important criteria. Those who have more talent and who strive hardest deserve greater rewards, both tangible ones (like income), and intangible ones (like power, respect and prestige). In a Confucian society, what counts as merit is one's effort in practicing virtues, not one's talent or diligence. Such merit will accrue intangible rewards, like love and respect, though it might not bring material rewards. The main concern of Confucianism is the practice of virtues, rather than the pursuit of income and wealth. "Human individuals differ from one another in the degree to which they possess and exercise the virtues ... It is the Confucian conviction that, other things being equal, those who are more sincere, make greater efforts, or accomplish more than others in practicing virtues, should receive more love and respect than others" (Fan 2003, pp. 149–150).

The Rawlsian concept of justice stresses equality of opportunity. However, Confucians emphasize the autonomy of family which forms the basic unit in a Confucian society. A family's autonomy implies that the state should not interfere with the development of children in a family. Families can give children special advantages such as private schools, an advantaged peer group and role models which in turn may enhance children's opportunity to seek high positions in society (Fan 2003, p. 151). "Given that the existence of such advantageous family opportunities is unlikely to be beneficial to the least favored children in society, Rawls' social justice, with its requirement of fair equality of opportunity, would have to restrict them in order to equalize life prospect for every child (or at least for those with similar natural endowments). But these family opportunities are alright and even encouraged by the Confucian principle of *ren* ... Confucian social justice wants opportunities autonomously provided by families, rather than the so-called "fair" equality of opportunity imposed by the state" (Fan 2003, p. 151). The Confucian principle of *ren* requires one to love one's family members (children in this context) more than others, and give preferential treatment to them. Parents strive to provide the best opportunity for their children and thus children from better families enjoy better and more opportunities. This is considered appropriate or "just" in a Confucian society, with state intervention to provide equal opportunity by violating the autonomy of families as "unjust" or inappropriate.

Western scholars such as Okin (1989) point out that marriage and family are unjust institutions, oppressing women. However, in a Confucian society, the dominance of male over female is considered the norm and is not considered unjust; on the contrary, it is considered an appropriate model for the two sexes. According to Mencius, "When a girl marries, her mother gives her advice, and accompanies her to the door with these cautionary words, "When you go to your new home, you must be respectful and circumspect. Do not disobey your husband". It is the way of a wife or concubine to consider obedience and docility the norm" (3B:2). From this, we can conclude that dependent and submissive role of women in a Confucian family is considered appropriate. Yet, this relationship may be considered unjust in a Western modern society.

The Taoist Concept of Justice

Besides Confucianism, Taoism is another important philosophical school of thought underlying Chinese culture. In essence, the two complement each other, with Taoism helping the Chinese to harmonize the Way of Humanity to the Way of Nature, while Confucianism emphasizes the development of the Way of Human Morality (Fu 1997, p. 553). "For more than two thousand years the traditional Chinese have managed to perform a delicate balancing act that allows them to be simultaneously Confucian and [T]aoist ... appropriate to changing situations" (Fu 1997, p. 553).There is no Taoist concept which directly corresponds to the Western concept of justice. However, the Taoist concept of *wu-wei* (無為; non-action) may have some implications on the issue of justice. ".... [T]he idea of *wu-wei* is that you achieve things because you do nothing, but travel with the force of Way or Tao.... *Wu-wei* is the art of being. It is the art of being in such harmony with the Tao that everything happens as it should — not forced, not sought after, not planned, not bought, not desired — it just happens" (Palmer 1991, p. 49). According to Shen, *wu-wei* means ruling according to the Tao — "that is, no particular action or no action of particular interest but universal action, acting for all things, no artificial action but spontaneous action" (Shen 2003, p. 360). Thus, the concept of *wu-wei* implies impartiality and universality according to Shen: acting for all, instead of particular groups, in accordance with what is "naturally" should or is appropriate. The Western world considers what is just as what is appropriate. In the sense, the Taoist concept of *wu-wei* and the Western concept of justice converge, yet the latter may — and often does — involve positively taking actions to achieve justice which diverges from the former.

Confucians consider government intervention to be only a last resort in the satisfaction of needs. Taoists also recognize the importance of the satisfaction of needs, on the part of the government; the model thus has characteristics in common with the Western principle of justice, "to each according to his/her needs". According to Lao Tsu, "Therefore in governing the people, the sage empties minds but fill their bellies, weaken their wills but strengthens their bones. He always keeps them innocent of knowledge and free from desire ..." (*Tao Te Ching* 3:9). "Filling bellies" in the Chinese context implies the satisfaction of basic needs. Lao Tsu stressed that the sage government should keep the people free from desire, implying that the satisfaction of anything besides basic needs might be beyond government's role. Thus, the ideal state has only a minimal government apparatus, with the wise ruler governing with minimal interference in accordance with the Tao or the Way (Clarke 2000, p. 31). The Taoist state is in essence a laissez-faire government in modern Western terms, which calls for little governmental interference and strong local autonomy (Clarke 2000, pp. 107, 108). The Taoist supports light taxation. According to Lao Tsu, "The people are hungry: it is because those in authority eat up too much in taxes [t]hat the people are hungry" (*Tao Te Ching* 75: 181). Heavy taxation is an evil, since it will keep the basic needs, on the part of the people, unsatisfied, with the government failing to fulfill its basic mission.

The Western concept of justice incorporates the idea"to each according to his/her rights". One of the most prevalent rights is property rights. The Taoists do not advocate the pursuit of property (as well as the assertion of its related rights): instead they stress the adoption of a "simple life which rejects the conventional trappings of wealth and power, and advocated living modestly and selflessly in harmony with the processes of nature" (Clarke 2000, p. 100). This spirit can be summarized in Kwang-tze's writing, which advises, "the small man pursues wealth; the superior man pursues reputation ... Do not be small man; — return and pursue after the Heavenly in you. Do not be a superior man; — follow the rule of the Heavenly in you" (Kwang-tze, 29: 3.7.2).

The Taoists not only do not emphasize property rights, but rights in general. In fact, they commend a kind of altruism, putting others' interests before one's own rights and interests. The concept of *wu-wei* is sometimes translated as "non-selfishness", doing things for altruistic reasons (Palmer 1991, p. 9). According to Lao-tsu, "Therefore the sage puts his person last and it comes first, treating it as extraneous to himself and it is preserved. Is it not he who is without thought of self who is able to accomplish his private ends?" (*Tao Te Ching* 7: 19–19a) Lao-tsu also advised, "Make the small big and the few many; do good to him who done you an injury"(*Tao Te Ching* 63: 148). In this, Lao-tsu does not press for one's rights, but altruism.

Confucians stress obligations, rather than rights, in contrast to Westerners. Taoist Kwang-tze also shared such views. According to Legge (1968), Kwang-tse pointed out that "a man has his place among other man in the world, he is a member, while he lives, of the body of humanity and as he has a place in society, so also he has his special duties to discharge, according to his position, and his relation to others. Taoist writers refer to This Book [Book IV *Zan Kien Shih*] as proof of the practical character of the writings of Kwang-tze" (p. 131). Thus, the stereotypical picture that Taosim advocates the abandoning of social and political obligations is being questioned (Clarke 2000, p. 103).

The Western concept of justice involves the deserts principle "to each according to his/her deserts". The Taoists also share a similar perspective. "Under the government of sages, all offices are distributed to the fitness of their nature; all appointments are made according to the ability of man ..." (Kwang-tze, Bk.7, Pt.2 Sect.5:12). By deserts in the Western context, both innate talent and effort may count. However, Taoists emphasize the former, while downplaying the latter. Taoists also diverge from the Confucians by not referring to moral qualities or virtues in the assessment of deserts, but merely counting natural endowment. According to Kwang-tze, "When I pronounce men to be good, I am not speaking of their benevolence and righteousness; — the goodness is simply (their possession) of qualities (of the Tao). When I pronounce them to be good, I am not speaking of what are called benevolence and righteousness; but simply of their allowing the nature with which they are endowed to have its free course" (Kwang-tze, Bk.8 Pt.2 Sect.1.3).

As for the Western just principle of equal opportunities, the Taoists also give due regard to this objective. While Western thinkers focus on equal opportunities when evaluating who should achieve high position, wealth or other benefits, Taoists emphasize the equal opportunities in understanding and seeking happiness in the Tao. According to Legge (1968), "Kwang-tze illustrates his thesis first by the cases of creatures, the largest and the smallest, showing that however different they may be in size, they should not pass judgment on one another, but may equally find their happiness in the Tao" (p. 127). Since the finding of happiness in the Tao is the main focus for Taoists, equal opportunities do not only apply to all human beings, but to all creatures as stressed by Legge. According to Lao Tsu, "... The Way [the Tao] gives them [myriad creatures] life and rears them; brings them up and nurse them; brings them to fruition and maturity; feeds and shelters them" (*Tao Te Ching* 51:115). Thus, the Tao treats every creature equally, without discrimination, providing equal opportunities for each to be nurtured.

Though every creature, including every human being, has equal opportunities in finding happiness in the Tao which nurtures all, not everyone will appreciate It equally. Their degree of reverence will depend on each individual's merit. Thus, the principle of merit in the Western concept of equal opportunities also applies within a Taoist context. "When the best student hears about the Way [or the Tao], he practices it assiduously; when the average student hears about the Way, it seems to him one moment there and gone the next; when the worst student hears about the Way, he laughs out loud. If he did not laugh, it would be unworthy of being the Way" (*Tao Te Ching* 41:90).

* * * * * *

We have established, in this chapter, that justice as understood by Western thinkers is an intricate concept, involving four principles: the principle of needs, rights, deserts and equal opportunity for all. The Chinese perspective on these just principles has also been highlighted in this chapter. Having clarified the concept of justice, the stage is set for an examination of justice in public policy in general and justice in housing policy in particular.

Different Theories of Social Justice

Thinker(s)	*Nature of Theory*	*Main Principle(s) of the Theory of Justice*
Aristotle	i) Formal Principle ii) Deserts-based	i) To award equals equally and unequal unequally ii) Awards should be "according to merit".
J.S. Mill	Utilitarian — aggregate-based	Rests upon utility and the Greatest Happiness Principle — "To distribute in a way that maximizes happiness".
Marx	Needs-based	"From each according to his ability, to each according to his needs".
Rawls	i) Needs-based ii) Equal-opportunity-based	"Social and economic inequalities are to be arranged so that they are both: i) Promote the greatest expected benefit to the least advantaged and ii) Offices and positions are open to all under conditions of fair equality of opportunity".
Hume	Rights-based	i) Stability of possession — 5 rules of establishing private property rights ii) Transfer of possessions by consent iii) Respect of rights arising from promises
Nozick	Rights-based	i) Acquisition of holdings in accordance with the principle of justice ii) Voluntary transfer of holdings iii) Rectification of injustice of holdings by compensation
Miller	Three-principled	i) Incorporates three conflicting distributive principles: deserts, rights and needs ii) The appropriate application of the distributive principle rests on the "modes of relationship".
Le Grand	Process-oriented	Distributions resulting from factors beyond one's control are unjust, while those that involves free choice are not.
Fishkin	Equal-opportunity-based	The principle of merit is to be considered in the evaluation of qualification for positions under equal opportunities.
Roamer	Equal-opportunity-based	Respect the non-discrimination principle by which only relevant attributes for the performance of duties of the position in question will be judged.
MacIntyre	Communitarian	What is just varies from tradition to tradition.
Walzer	Relative	"All distributions are just or unjust relative to the social meanings of the goods at stake."
Young	Feminist	"Oppression and domination should be the primary terms for conceptualizing injustice", rather than the "distributive paradigm".

Different Theories of Social Justice *(continued)*

Thinker(s)	*Nature of Theory*	*Main Principle(s) of the Theory of Justice*
Fraser	More than distributive	i) Injustices may be socio-economic or cultural (or symbolic) in nature ii) The remedy for economic injustice is redistribution, while that for cultural injustice is recognition (involving some sort of cultural or symbolic change).
Confucian	Intrinsic-virtue-oriented	i) Multi-layered welfare provision to satisfy "to each according to his/her needs". ii) Think in terms of obligations, rather than assertion of one's rights. iii) Measurement of deserts rests on one's effort in the exercise of virtues, rather than talent and effort in doing things as in the West. iv) Preferential treatment of one's family members rather than the Rawlsian concept of equal opportunity for all.
Taoist	Nature-oriented	i) The government is to "fill the bellies": satisfy the basic needs, not the desires, of the people. ii) Instead of the pursuit of property and the assertion of one's property rights and other rights in general, Taoists advocate a simple life in harmony with nature and altruism, emphasizing obligations. iii) Emphasis on one's in-born talents and nature, slighting effort, in the assessment of desert. iv) Equal opportunity measures in terms of opportunities in understanding and seeking happiness in Tao, not in terms of opportunities to high positions.

3

Social Justice in Public Policy

We have established in Chapter 2 that the concept of justice is multi-principled. In this chapter, we will apply the clarified concept of justice to the discussion of public policy. Broadly speaking, public policies can be categorized into economic, social and political policies. We will examine the relation of these three types of public policy with social justice in turn. In this chapter, it will be argued that a capitalist-socialist hybrid model, rather than a pure form of either system will be more in line with social justice. Privatization has been a trend in the arena of public policy. Whether privatization is compatible with social justice will be discussed. In addition, the implications of the Confucian concept of social justice on public policy will be examined at the end of this chapter.

* * * * * *

Critics of a public policy often point out that a policy is a bad policy because it is unjust. When asked to articulate why a policy is unjust, a critic may cite very diverse reasons:

1) Policy A is unjust because the poor are made worse-off.
2) Policy B is unjust since it discriminates against minorities.
3) Policy C is unjust as it disregards people's rights.
4) Policy D is unjust as it does not treat equals equally.
5) Policy E is unjust because the rich and the poor pay the equal amount.

Yet that list of of factors implicating injustice in public policy is not exhaustive. From the above five examples, we can conclude that social justice in public policy means many things, some of which are quite different from one another. We may conclude that justice in public policy involves making the poor better-off; that it means treating everyone as equals; respecting people's rights; or that the rich and the poor should bear different burdens.

In the arena of public policy decision-making or evaluation, justice is not the only consideration. There are other considerations as well; for example, whether the policy is efficient, effective, has political support, and whether the administrative costs involved are prohibitive. Sometimes, among these different policy considerations, there may be conflicts that will require compromises. Thus, social justice may sometimes be slightly compromised by a policymaker's need to consider other questions (like efficiency), since "social justice is not the only valuable end in politics" (Weale 1978, p. 3). Though social justice may be compromised to a certain extent in public decision-making, it cannot be totally disregarded, as it is one of the most important criteria for public policy evaluation:

> The role of the idea of justice is, therefore, to evaluate social institutions. There are, of course, other ways of evaluating them. Are they efficient? Are they popular? But what makes them better or worse as a whole is whether they are just or unjust. That is the point of calling justice "the first virtue" of social institutions. (Loizou 1997, p. 166)

Economic Policy and Social Justice

The economic policy of a government determines its involvement and role in the economy and society, affecting the content and the scope of its public policy. In a socialist society, with the government pursuing socialist or communist economic policy, there is public ownership of the "means of production" and property. There is central planning in the production and distribution of goods and services, necessitating active and widespread governmental involvement in the economy and society, thereby giving rise to a large scope for public policy. Essentially, central planners operate according to the Marxian principle "from each according to his ability, to each according to his needs". Is such a socialist economy just? As discussed in Chapter 2, justice is an intricate concept, involving various principles. Socialist economic policy is just by certain concept of justice; yet it may be unjust when weighed against other concepts of justice. A socialist economic policy is just when considered from the point of view of the just principle of needs. That is, it is just by the Marxian concept of justice because essentially socialism is a Marxian construct formed to combat the injustices of capitalism. The needs of everyone in a socialist economy are catered for because goods and services are distributed according to the principle, "to each according to his needs".

Besides the need principle, the concept of justice also incorporates the principle of rights. Rights include property rights and their transfer, rights arising from promises, institutional rights, and human rights. Theories of justice concerning rights essentially focus on the most popular type of rights, namely, property rights. Hume's and Nozick's theory of justice are examples of these theories. In contrast, socialism emphasizes public ownership, without paying heed to private ownership. Socialist economic policy involves the confiscation and nationalization of private property, involving the confiscation of land from landowners or the nationalization of factories. These socialist confiscation policies violate property rights, taking away property without consent, and thereby are unjust according to the Humean and Nozickian theories of justice, which focus on the respect of private property rights and their just transfer by consent.

Besides slighting the rights principle, a socialist economic policy also does not give due regard to the just principle of deserts, thereby violating the Aristotelian concept of justice which stresses distribution according to deserts, and the need to treat unequals unequally. In a socialist economy, goods and services are distributed solely by the principle of needs. If two persons have similar needs, they will be given similar amount in a socialist distribution system, even though one of them is twice as productive (in doing his job) as the other. The one with higher productivity will not be given more as a reward in a socialist system. Intuitively, this violates the just principle of deserts, treating unequals (in deserts) equally, violating the Aristotelian concept of justice.

Since those with higher productivity will not be rewarded accordingly in a socialist economy, people will not work to their best ability, thereby diminishing the total production of the economy as a whole. That is, the socialist ideal "from each according to his ability" will not be achieved in reality, since those with higher abilities will not be given more in a socialist economy. Those with higher abilities will be given the same as those with lower productivity if they have similar needs, in accordance with the socialist ideal. A Marxist might rebut that people would be transformed after a socialist revolution: so in the new state people would work to the best of their ability, even without extrinsic rewards or incentives. However, judging from history, there is no sign of such transformation of human nature in a socialist state, such as in past China after the Communist Revolution[1]. Thus, the productivity of a socialist state is lower than it would be if people worked to the best of their abilities; under such a regime, the people are less well-off in that they are able to enjoy less goods and services. This outcome is unjust according to the utilitarian concept of justice, which stresses the maximization of happiness, assuming that increased productivity and abundance will bring about greater happiness and utility to people in general.

In a socialist state, there is a large scope for public policy, with the government involved in the central planning of the production and distribution of goods and services. The government is actively involved in many aspects of people's life, from food rationing, assigning jobs, setting the production targets of factories, to allocating housing. Thus, the government has power over its populace in nearly all aspects of their lives, without a counter-balancing force. The power of the government officials is enormous in a socialist state. Thus, it is easy for government officials to abuse their already extensive power and oppress the people, thereby violating Young's concept of justice, which emphasizes that injustices arise from oppression, rather than merely unjust distribution. Since the government in a socialist state controls many aspects of people's life, governmental oppression seems likely to occur, causing injustices in Young's sense.

Having concluded that a socialist society is unjust by different theories of justice, (aside from Marxist theory) , then let us consider its diametric opposite, capitalism. Is capitalist economic policy more just than the socialist? In a capitalist society, a market system operates. "The market system is characterized by three main features: (1) *private ownership* of resources and the goods and services produced in an economy; (2) *voluntary exchange*, in which individuals are free to enter into mutually advantageous trades; (3) the *profit motive*, whereby people engage in trading solely to advance their own well-being. In a market system ... individuals trade with each other, giving up things they own in exchange for other things they need or want. The motive of these economic actors is to improve their lives" (Boatright 1993, pp. 107–108). In a capitalist or a market system, the allocation of resources in the production and distribution of goods and services operate automatically without governmental intervention. For example, if a property developer sells several 400 ft^2 (about 37 m^2) flats at $10 billion each, nobody will be willing to buy from him/her. As no one buys these flats, the developer is "forced" to decrease the price of the flats until the price is \$2 million. At this price, people will be willing to buy flats from the developer until all the flats are sold out. If the property developer sells his/her 400 ft^2 flats at \$10,000 each, there would be a lot of people "fighting" to buy them. Thus, they are willing to pay more to buy the property developer's flats. Therefore, the property developer finds out that s/he may raise the price. This continues until the developer raises the price to \$2 million each and all the flats are sold out.

The labour market in a capitalist economy operates in the same way as other markets. "... Labour is a market commodity, in that workers must sell their labour in order to make a living" (Sainsbury 1996, p. 30). Similar to the property developer's selling flats, Clerk A may not be able to find an employer (i.e. sell his/her labour) if s/he demands \$100,000 per month as salary. Thus, Clerk A has to lower his/her demand for salary. When Clerk A demands \$8,000 per month as salary, s/he may successfully get a job. Likewise, if Clerk A demands \$100 per month, s/he will find employers "fighting" to employ him/her. Clerk A may thus ask for more as salary until s/he demands \$8,000 per month and at the level of \$8,000 per month, Clerk A will be successfully employed by an employer.

In a capitalist or market system, there are private ownership rights and the free transfer of property rights by consent. Thus, a capitalist economic policy is judged to be just according to Hume's and Nozick's theory of justice, since both models emphasize the importance of respecting private property rights and their just transfer by consent. "To critics who fear that unregulated markets would lead to great disparities between rich and poor and a lowering of the overall welfare of society, Nozick has a reply. The point of justice is not to promote human well-being or to achieve a state of equality; it is to protect our rights. Because a market system does this better than any other form of economic organization, it is just" (Boatright 2000, p. 94).

Besides the just principle of rights, a capitalist economic policy may be considered as just according to the Aristotelian just principle of deserts in theory. If occupation A is remunerating its workers at a pay level below what the workers deserve, the workers will leave occupation A. The supply of labour in occupation A decreases; thus the reward will increase up to the level that its workers deserve and its workers will therefore stop leaving occupation A, gaining a reward that they deserve at the new equilibrium pay level. If occupation B is rewarding its workers more than their deserts, workers from other occupations will switch to this high-reward occupation. This will increase the supply of labour in occupation B, thereby decreasing the pay level to the level justified by deserts. Thus, the market system operates in a way that indirectly satisfied the Aristotelian just principle of deserts. However, this only applies in an ideal free competitive labour market. In reality, there is no perfect mobility of labour between different labour markets. Workers in below-desert level reward occupations may not be informed of other alternative occupation openings. Some, especially unskilled workers, may have low educational levels. Thus, it is difficult for them to learn new skills so as that they can switch to another occupation which rewards its workers as they deserve. Also, non-monetary factors, such as cordial working relations, job satisfaction, good working environment, or working in a particular preferred city, may encourage workers to stay in their jobs, even though the monetary reward is far below the desert level. Thus, in practice, there may be cases where remuneration does not correspond to deserts in a market system. However, in general, there is rough justice according to deserts in a capitalist society: there is no perfect justice.

The operation of the labour market leads to unequal income among members of society. Some may earn more than $100,000 per month, while some may earn only $3,000 per month, not enough to satisfy even the most basic living expenses. It must be pointed out that unequal income in society does not necessarily incorporate injustices, though no doubt, some may. Suppose A earns $70,000 per month, owning a luxurious flat; while B earns $7,000 per month, renting a small simple flat. A is a medical doctor who has spent many years of hard work in the medical school in order to gain the qualification to be a doctor. A has to work shifts and while working, A has to put in a lot of effort as s/he is handling the life and death of his/her patients. Comparatively, B earns less, as B works as a receptionist. B successfully finishes his/her secondary school education with a bare pass. B works from nine to five. B does not have to put a lot of effort in his/her work as his/her mistakes will only lead to the disconnection of a few phone calls, delays or other inconveniences. It seems not unjust that A earns more than B, as A deserves to earn more by the just principle of deserts, given his training, effort and work ethic. "It should be emphasized that inequality *per se* is not necessarily unjust or unfair ... Much depends on the mechanisms that produce inequalities. Some people work harder, educate themselves, and make better use of their resources. Therefore, it is justifiable that some people deserve more than others do" (Kangas 2000, p. 520).

Let's consider another example. X, Y and Z work as typists at firm F. X earns $7,000 per month, while Y and Z earn $4,000 per month. Y earns less as Y is an Asian person, while X is a white person. The employer of firm F discriminates against Asians. Thus, s/he pays Y less than X because of his/her racial discrimination mentality. As for the case of Z, s/he earns less than X, as s/he treasures leisure more than X and chooses to work part-time, while X works full-time. Thus, Z earns less than X. It seems that Y earns less than X represents a kind of injustices while Z earns less than X does not represent injustice as free choice is involved in the latter case, but not the former. This example is in line with Le Grand's theory of justice, as he points out that justice or equity involves choice. Thus, not all cases of income inequality represent injustices. It depends on whether the principle of deserts or choice is involved in the case concerned. "... Most people accept, as we do, that some inequalities are just. There is, however, a question about justifiable *extent* of an inequality, even if we accept that inequality *per se* is not unjust" (The Commission on Social Justice 1998, p. 44).

In a capitalist or market economy, only producers who make efficient use of productive resources to produce goods and services that consumers demand can make a profit. Motivated by the desire to maximize profits, the producers have to make the best use of resources in production. If not, the consumers will not buy from them since their price will be higher than their competitors. Though individuals are self-interestedly motivated, the highest possible level of welfare results (Boatright 2000, p. 86) since there is the most efficient use of limited resources through the operation of the market. Though the level of benefit people get from the market differs, the overall efficiency of production is maximized in a market system. This is just by the utilitarian theory of justice which stresses the total rather than the distribution of welfare in society. "After all, historically in Western Europe, Japan and North America, capitalism, with its staggering inequalities, has been the agent of economic growth and development" (Nielsen 1980, p. 265).

The market system tends to favour equal opportunity in society, thereby being just in this aspect. If firm A discriminates against black people or women, the black and the female employees will not be motivated to work to the best of their ability, thereby making the firm inefficient. The better black and female employees of firm A will leave firm A, leaving those inefficient employees behind. Also, firm A is unlikely to attract the best black or female applicants. Eventually, firm A will lose in face of competition from other similar firms that do not discriminate against the black and female employees. Thus, indirectly, capitalism discourages discrimination, fostering more equal opportunities, thereby justice.

Capitalist economic policy is unjust when judged by Marxian and Rawlsian theories, since it pays little attention to the needs of the most disadvantaged. By the market mechanism, each worker may sell his/her labour in return for a salary to support himself/herself and his/her family. However, there are some workers whose productivity is so low that the wage that s/he gets from the labour market is too meagre to support himself/herself, not to say his/her family. That is, his/her basic needs and that of his/her family are left unsatisfied by his/her selling of his/her labour alone in the labour market. Besides inadequate income, there are people who cannot participate in the labour market because of illness, old age, unemployment, disability, or the need to take care of children or elders at home. These people are barred from selling their labour in the market. "The market's failure to provide incomes for all does not represent an efficiency failure. It is a failure to meet the distributional goal, however defined. There can be very different definitions of equity, but the fact that there are differences on how much redistribution there should be does not preclude against that some redistribution is necessary" (Wilkinson 1997, p. 17). In short, relying on the market alone to satisfy basic needs creates injustice: in the most extreme cases, some people would starve to death as the market failed to satisfy their basic needs. The market thus fails to deliver justice, by falling short of the just principle of needs, especially that of the most disadvantaged.

Besides disregarding the just principle of needs, capitalism violates the Aristotelian just principle of deserts in a specific aspect, with regard to the institution of inheritance. The market system of the capitalist society respects private property rights and their transfer by consent. The controversial type of transfer of property rights by consent is inheritance which may involve the transfers of large amount of wealth. Hume considers inheritance as legitimate and just (Hume 1738, p. 561). However, inheritance entitles the beneficiary to large sums of wealth without requiring his own effort or contribution. This is against the just principle of deserts. "The transmission of wealth through the family line was profoundly unfair, because it conferred upon people advantages which bore no relation to their personal merit, or their services to society" (Parkin 1992, p. 60).

It has been pointed out that distribution resulting from market mechanisms cannot be said to be just or unjust, as the market is impersonal and its outcomes are likewise unintentional (Forrester 1997, pp. 147–8; Plant 1998, p. 62; Plant 1991, p. 76). Just as the destruction of crops by bad weather is a matter of bad luck rather than injustice (as this is not an intentional outcome of any deliberate action), the distribution resulting from market operation is irrelevant to the question of justice, as it is also unintentional. "… Hayek argued (1) that the very idea of social justice is meaningless in the context of a market economy [since in a market economy, the distribution of wealth is neither deliberately brought about nor foreseen by anyone]; (2) that any attempt to achieve social justice is bound to fail; and (3) that any attempt fully and consistently to attain social justice must inevitably lead to totalitarianism" (Freser 1997, p. 583; quoted by Johnston 1997, p. 608). Johnston points out that we often ascribe responsibility for acts of injustice while treating misfortune in which no one is responsible as accidental (Johnston 1997, p. 610). However, not all acts of injustices are deliberately or intentionally brought about, with responsibility ascribing to the performer. Johnston gives an example to rebut Hayek. "Suppose a man is wrongfully convicted of murder in a trial in which all parties, including prosecution attorneys, defense attorneys, witnesses, the presiding judge, and the members of the jury acted in accordance with proper legal procedures and in good faith, just because crucial exculpatory evidence never came to light. We might describe the man's conviction as the result of an accident in which no one could reasonably be accused of a wrongful or unjust action, but the conviction would still be an injustice" (Johnston 1997, p. 610).

Though the destruction of crops by bad weather is a misfortune, it is far from being true that no acts of injustice are involved. According to Macleod (1983), a situation can be described as just or unjust if (a) it was brought about by human action, or (b) it could have been prevented by human action, or (c) human actions can contribute to its perpetuation or transformation (p. 576). In the twenty-first century, weather has become more predictable, as we have accurate weather forecasts. The destruction of crops by bad weather is sometimes alterable or preventable (by human action), if warning of the coming bad weather are given to farmers so that they may harvest their crops before the coming bad weather, with losses being reduced to a minimum. If what is foreseeable, alterable, preventable by human action has not been done to the unintentional coming bad weather, then injustice may be said to have occurred to the losing farmers. Similarly, the great income disparity between rich and poor as the result of market operation is both foreseeable (Forrester 1997, p. 148; Plant 1998, p. 67) and alterable

(Plant 1991, p. 83) through human action. If something is not done to redress the distribution by a market so as to prevent poverty, for example, through governmental redistribution, then injustice may be said to occur.

In conclusion, it is apparent that neither a pure capitalist nor a pure socialist economic policy is totally just. While they may be just from the point of view of certain models of justice, they are unjust according to other concepts of justice. However, in reality, no pure form of capitalism or socialism exists. Economies are usually a hybrid of the two, with differing emphasis on the balance of capitalist and socialist elements. If neither capitalism nor socialism are fully just in their pure forms, then would a hybrid of both be more just? We will therefore start with the capitalist model and try to examine ways to make the capitalist or market system more just by introducing socialist elements to it.

Social Policy, Taxation and Social Justice

The market in its purest form would leave the basic needs of some people unsatisfied by the pure operation of the market. By the Marxian just principle of "to each according to his needs", money and goods are distributed among those whose basic needs the market fails to satisfy, thereby introducing socialist elements to the capitalist system. Justice incorporates redistribution to those with unmet basic needs. "Poverty is what philosophers describe as a *categorical need*, that is, a need which must be met in order for a person to develop properly as human being ... The essence of a categorical need is that it gives the poor a moral claim for action. As fellow human beings, we have an obligation to meet the needs of the poor" (Bradshaw 1999, p. 11).

Redistribution may be done on a voluntary basis. However, voluntary transfer to the needy or the poor may not be very effective in a large impersonal society. "No doubt voluntary redistribution will be a significant factor only in closely integrated groups where one individual perceives his well-being as being intimately tied in with the well-beings of others and where one individual is, in fact, aware of the well-being or of the sadder state of other individuals. With a larger group, voluntary redistribution is likely to become less efficient or effective because individuals may not have information about the well-being of others" (Boulding and Pfaff 1972, p. 4). Indeed, voluntary redistribution from the rich to the needy (in the form of charity) does enable some unmet basic needs to be satisfied. However, in a large and impersonal society, it is difficult for voluntary redistribution to meet all the basic needs of every single person in need. Some unsatisfied basic needs may be unnoticed by the donors. Sometimes, charitable donations are simply not equipped to meet the needs of the poor. Donations may not be well distributed among the needy, so some basic needs of the poor are left unattended. In short, we may not rely solely on voluntary redistribution to deliver social justice in society in meeting basic needs.

If voluntary redistribution is not effective in eliminating poverty (or meeting needs), government intervention in the face of market failure to provide a decent income to all is deemed necessary. Non-voluntary redistribution required by the government to deliver justice will be more effective in handling the needs of the poor. "... A few major redistributive measures on an egalitarian basis effected through the fiscal and benefit systems could in a relatively short space of time more or less solve the problem of poverty and establish social justice, provided that there was the political will to wage such a war on poverty for the sake of the health of society as a whole" (Forrester 1997, p. 90). Thus, a just government is to facilitate the redistribution of income from the rich to the poor as well as life-cycle redistribution (from the stage of life in which income is high and needs are less to the stage at which there is no income and needs are great).

Social justice requires the government to guarantee a minimum income to all those whose basic needs cannot be satisfied in the labour market. The minimum income should be high enough to satisfy the basic needs of the poor: food, shelter, transport, and utility payments. Non-basic needs or wants would not be catered for by the minimum income[2]. Some examples of non-basic needs or wants are: travelling abroad on holidays, luxurious flats, and expensive wines. Luxuries of life have to be earned by one's effort or hard work. This is in line with the just principle of deserts. Thus, those receiving a minimum income only have the basic necessities of life. They have a living standard comparatively lower than those who earn their own income in the market, since the minimum income is only intended to serve the basic needs on the part of the poor or needy. Anything in excess of basic needs must be earned by hard effort. Since the basic needs of people vary, the minimum income also varies from individual to individual. For example, a disabled person may need a wheelchair for mobility and s/he may need special type of transportation. The minimum income should cater for such special basic needs so as to fully implement the just principle of "to each according to his/her needs".

The minimum income standard is selective, rather than universal, in nature. It must be targeted towards those whose basic needs cannot be satisfied in the labour market. Those who can be successfully employed in the labour market and thereby earn a decent income, are ineligible to receive the minimum income, since their own earned income is enough or more than enough to satisfy their basic needs. In short, the minimum income is to be means-tested, targeted at the poor or the needy.

The minimum income may be calculated in cash or in kind; for example, the free provision of medical care and housing to the poor should be considered part of the minimum income. Social justice requires that the poor be provided with benefits in kind (such as government subsidized public housing), with those earning more paying more for these benefits and those who are rich have to pay for the full cost for public services such as medical services. Just like minimum cash income, benefits in kind should also be means-tested. This policy is in line with the formal principle of justice,"to treat equals equally and unequals unequally". Those who can pay to satisfy their needs are to be distinguished from those who cannot afford to meet their basic needs through the means-test. Benefits in kind are to be distributed to the poor according to need. "If external benefits and efficiency do not justify state provision, then equity may do so: the provision of health, education and housing services represent income distribution according to need. This redistribution in kind, the provision by the state of **merit goods**, is justified in a variety of ways, including the belief that taxpayers prefer to make "gifts that are earmarked" rather than pay cash benefits which recipients may spend as they please" (Wilkinson 1997, pp. 79–80).

It has been argued that if justice may be defined as distributing according to need, then a basic income will satisfy the requirement of "justice":

> A basic income is essentially an income which (1) everyone receives unconditionally: that is, regardless of current work, past work, willingness to work, or a condition of need; and (2) is sufficient to cover one's basic needs. It is not necessary for a basic income to be set at the same level for everyone; indeed, its explicit reference to need suggests that it is likely to vary accordingly. (Baker 1992, pp. 122–123)

Allegedly, the unconditional basic income will meet the needs of those not in employment (Norman 1992, p. 15), raise the standard of living of the worst-off, and reduce inequality (Baker 1992, p. 124), serving the end of justice.

However, the institution of basic income violates the formal principle of justice "treating equals equally and unequals unequally". The underlying assumption of basic income is that the basic needs of everyone in society are to be treated similarly. However, those who are gainfully employed should be able to satisfy their own basic needs; while poor people often fail to satisfy their own needs. Those who can satisfy their own basic needs should do so themselves; whereas the impoverished should be helped so that their basic needs are paid for by the government. The policy of basic income implicitly treats self-satisfiable basic needs of the rich and the non-self-satisfiable basic needs of the poor alike, giving an income for the satisfaction of basic needs to everyone, regardless of how much one earns in the labour market. This is to treat unequals equally. This violates the formal principle of justice. Thus, basic income as a public policy is unjust.

Whereas a means-tested selective minimum income treats the basic needs of those who are gainfully employed in the labour market and those basic needs of the disadvantaged differently. Those people who are gainfully employed, earning a decent income, will not be given a minimum income as a means-test would screen them out. Only those who fail to satisfy their own basic needs through employment in the labour market or because they earn too meagre an income through work will be given a minimum income by the government. Essentially, minimum income is a form of social security. Social justice in public policy involves the giving of minimum income to the needy on the part of the government. This is an expression of the just principle of "to each according to his/her needs". (Needs here refer to unsatisfied basic needs.) Those who have unsatisfied basic needs will get aid from the government. Those who are able to satisfy their own basic needs will do so on their own, without interference on the part of the government.

The minimum income policy is just according to the Rawlsian theory of justice, as the plight of the most disadvantaged, namely, the poor, is alleviated through its guarantee of the most basic standard of living. Redistribution of money from the rich to the poor is also considered just by the utilitarian concept of justice since a dollar sacrificed by the rich yields less loss of utility or happiness than the happiness or utility gained by the poor through the receiving of the same dollar, as the poor will spend it on necessities of life while extra money in the hands of the rich will be used either on unnecessary luxury items or banked as savings. Thus, redistribution maximizes utility or happiness, and is therefore just according to the utilitarian concept of justice.

A just government social policy provides minimum income to the poor in cash or in kind (the provision of public housing); it may also provide a combined cash/ kind package. But such provisions require a great amount of resources. Where does the government get the capital to finance minimum income programmes? The government gets it from the people in society through taxation. It is arguable that taxation violates property rights: do individuals not have property rights over their own income? Thus, taxes are "unjust" because they violate the just principle of rights. Nozick even equates taxation as "forced labour". However, as we have argued earlier, whenever the right principle and the need principle are in conflict with one another, the principle of needs must take priority. Part of the capital that a government raises through taxes is used to satisfy the basic needs of the very poor through provision of minimum income. In this case, the right principle of justice is subordinate to the need principle. Taxation involves compromising the property rights of the rich in order to satisfy the minimum needs of the poor. Thus, taxing the rich to help the poor is a just institution.

Though taxation as an institution of redistributing income and wealth from the rich to the poor is just, it does not mean that every tax system is just. Whether a tax system is just or not depends on the design of the tax system. Consider the following example. A earns $7,000 per month while B earns $70,000. What A earns per month may be just enough to cover his/her basic needs: A is unable to save any part of the salary. On the contrary, B earns quite a lot of money so that s/he may enjoy luxuries of life and has a lot of savings. If A has to pay 20% of his/her income ($1,400) as tax, A will cut back his/her expenditure. What A cuts back to pay tax will be necessities of life as his/her income is barely enough to cover his/her basic needs. Whereas B only has to pay 10% of his/her income (i.e. $7,000) as tax. B may pay the tax easily as s/he has a lot of savings, even when taxed. The tax gained by the government aids those who have no job: the sick, the old and the disabled. Is such a tax system just? Essentially, such tax system taxes the poor more than the rich in order to help the poorest. It disregards the ability to pay on the part of the tax payers, as A cannot afford to pay 20% of his/her income in taxes and must leave some basic needs unsatisfied. Such a regressive tax system[3] seems unjust.

As the marginal utility per dollar earned decreases with increased income, the ability to pay tax increases with increased income. It is more just to tax those with higher income a higher percentage of their income than those with lower income. Those with lowest income ought to be exempt from paying tax. "Most people would agree that the tax system as a whole ought to be progressive. Taxes on the poor cause hardship because they reduce the ability of the poor to pay for the basic necessities of life. Taxes on higher income cut into luxuries rather than necessities. Problems arise, of course, in judging precisely how progressive a tax system ought to be and whether new taxes should make it more or less progressive than it already is" (Pechman 1974, p. 203). Thus, a progressive tax system[4] (together with social provision to the needy) genuinely redistributes income and wealth from the rich to the poor. "To most people — those who favor a progressive tax system, tax justice means taxing according to ability to pay and that means that taxes should be progressive" (Pasquariello, 1985, p. 44).

Besides being progressive in nature, a just taxation system should give due regard to the Aristotelian formal principle of justice: "to treat equals equally and unequals unequally". This is expressed in two types of equity within a tax system — horizontal equity and vertical equity. Horizontal equity demands that equals be treated equally — people with similar income should be taxed equally and income from all income sources (e.g. interest, salary, rent) should be taxed equally. Vertical equity demands an appropriate differentiation among unequals — people with different level of income should be treated unequally, with those receiving higher income paying more tax, that is, to tax according to the ability to afford.

In a capitalist society, there is one source of income or wealth earned not by one's own effort, namely, the institution of inheritance. This is considered unjust by the Aristotelian just principle of desert. Thus, a just tax system should try to devise a remedy by charging heavy inheritance taxes on property the younger generation receives from its parents. This model respects the just principle of deserts by reducing the unjust effect of gaining great wealth without striving for it.

Political Policy and Social Justice

The political policy of a government affects its people to a very great extent. The most important political policy of a government is the type of political system it enforces in society which affects the distribution of political power and rights among the members of the state. There are many types of political systems, each with its own manner of distributing political power among the people. Let us examine them in turn. One of the most common types of political system, especially in the past, was the monarchy: political power and rights were concentrated in the hands of one person. This model also includes the modern one-man dictatorship. From a procedural point of view, the monarchy or one-man dictatorship is unjust, for although public policies affect all people of a state, only one person (and that individual's coterie) can influence the decision-making processes. Thus, the monarch or dictator may impose his will upon the common people who have no political right and power. What is the justification of such a concentration of political power? By desert? Definitively not. Historically there have been many monarchs and dictators who were incompetent and only ruled the country for their own benefit. All one-man rule political system are unjust according to the principle of rights: political rights and power are concentrated in the hands of one person arbitrarily and without rational justification, while the subject population has neither political power nor rights.

The monarchy or one-man dictatorship is also unjust by the Aristotelian concept of justice, which stresses distribution according to deserts. Political power in such political systems is usually passed down by heredity. There is no guarantee that the descendents of a monarch or a dictator has the political acumen to rule a country. Yet a commoner who is a potentially competent ruler has no chance of gaining power in such a political system, even though s/he deserves to do so. In short, there is no equal opportunity to gain political power, making the political system unjust. Political merit counts little and heredity decides all in determining the transfer of political power.

If decision-making procedures and the source of political power of one-man rule are unjust, does it bring about just outcome? Responses to this question are inconclusive. It is possible that the monarch or dictator may be a benevolent one who rules with political acumen, ensuring just outcomes in his/her decision-making. S/he may maximize the happiness of his/her people, thereby satisfying the utilitarian concept of justice. Yet the monarch or dictator may be a tyrant or an incompetent person with regard to political decision-making, thereby resulting in unjust policies. S/he may maximize his/her own happiness at the expense of that of the populace, an outcome that creates injustice in the utilitarian sense. In short, a monarch or dictator may still bring about just policies, even though all political power is concentrated in his/her hands, while the common people have none. However, there is no guarantee that s/he will necessarily do so. There is a great possibility that s/he will rule the people for his/her own benefit at the expense of the common people, leading to unjust public policies.

If autocracy is unjust when measured by various perspectives of justice, then what about a political system in which political power resides in the hands of a few? In a meritocracy, for example, political power and rights are concentrated in the hands of those with merit in some sense — whether those with higher educational levels or those who pay tax. Spencer suggests that "there should be no representation without (direct) taxation" (Miller 1978, p. 6). A meritocracy is just according to the Aristotelian just principle of deserts, since those with relevant merit are given political power. However, the system is considered unjust when viewed from a procedural point of view. Public policy affects everyone. Yet only some are involved in its decision-making, namely, those with merit. Those with or without relevant merit are also members of the political society. They should be allowed to participate as political equals in decision-making processes. However, in a meritocracy, only those with merit are given political power and right of involvement. This is unjust according to the principle of equal rights.

Will a meritocracy ensure a politically just outcome? It depends on what kind of defining criterion the meritocracy involves. If the merit criterion requires political acumen, wisdom and skills, then such a meritocracy will tend to bring about just outcomes. Such a meritocracy may maximize the happiness of the people, leading to just outcomes in accordance with the utilitarian concept of justice. However, if the merit criterion rests on criteria that ignores the necessity of political acumen and wisdom, unjust political outcomes may result. For example, if those educated have political power, with education as the merit criterion, then those with political power may decide to preserve the privileges of the educated at the expense of the uneducated. If paying taxes is the merit criterion, then those with political power may try to manipulate the system by cutting protection (social security) for the lower strata so they do not have to pay higher taxes to fund the social security system. Since the uneducated and the lower strata of people belong to a less advantaged group, any meritocracy resting on education or the payment of tax might lead to injustices according to Rawls' sense of justice, which stresses benefits for the least advantaged in society.

Having determined that meritocracy can result in an unjust system, let us now consider democracy. Democracy refers "to a form of government, namely one in which ultimate control rests in the hands of the people rather than in hands of a single man or a small minority ... [T]he crucial element [of a democracy] is political equality. Each member of the society whose political institutions are in question is to have an equal share in political power ... [T]he notion of political equality resolves itself into two parts: first, each person is to have an equal say in the election of representatives; second, the representatives thus chosen are to carry out, in broad terms, the wishes of those they represent" (Miller 1978, p. 13).

Political equality of democracy is judged to be just by Rawls's first principle of justice. According to this model, "each person is to have an equal right to the most extensive scheme of equal basic liberties compatible with a similar scheme of liberties for others" (Rawls 1999, p. 53). In a democracy, each citizen is entitled to equal liberty to participate in the political decision-making process through equal right to vote and stand for elective office (Gould 1995, p. 197), thereby being just according to the Rawlsian concept of justice.

When judged by its procedures, democracy may be classed as just. As citizens of a society, all people enjoy equal rights and the power to participate in decision-making (Gould 1995, p. 213). Thus, democracy is just by the just principle of rights, because democracy allows for equal consideration of interests in the decision-making process in a democracy; therefore, a just solution to the conflict of interest is more likely (Christiano 2003, p. 194). Thus, democracy, allowing equal access to decision-making processes, has a greater possibility of resulting in just outcomes, since it encompasses views from various groups in decision-making.

However, democracy does not necessarily lead to just outcomes in all circumstances. In fact, democracy means "rule by majority". There is a chance that it leads to what Tocqueville termed as the "tyranny of majority over the minority", even when the minority's views are represented in democratic decision-making processes. "Collective decisions can violate the rights of individuals in a whole variety of ways. For instance, if a democratic assembly votes to enslave a minority of its population, or if it simply severely restricts the rights of a minority, it seems that this is unjust" (Christiano 1993, p. 175).

To ensure justice prevails in a democracy, there should be a recognition of equal individual rights for all, including minorities, as a constraint on democratic decision-making process. "The protection of individual rights as a requirement of justice and the protection of minority rights against potential injustices by majority rule are seen to be essential constraints on democratic decision-making, which is taken to be embodied in a constitutional framework" (Gould 1995, p. 194).

A democracy gives equal political power and rights to everyone in society. This is unjust by the Aristotelian concept of justice, which emphasizes distribution according to deserts. In a democracy, everybody, with or without merit of any kind, may enjoy same political rights and power. This is against Aristotle's formal principle of justice, as the democratic model treats those with unequal merit equally. However, democracy is just in the sense that it provides equal opportunity for all to participate in politics (through the equal right to vote and stand for election for public offices).

In conclusion, no political system would be considered just when measured against all concepts of justice. In pursuing a just political policy when adopting a political system for society, a government must strike a balance between different concepts of justice.

Equal Opportunity and Public Policy

Justice incorporates equal opportunity for all. The right to equal opportunities is considered just by the utilitarian principle of justice, since it maximizes welfare, and thereby total happiness, for the whole of society. Equal opportunities make the most efficient use of human resources, further maximizing the production of goods and services for human consumption, thus maximizing happiness or utility. Thus, the equal opportunity principle is supported by utilitarians.

One may think that the passage of equal opportunity legislation would be enough to guarantee equal opportunities to all in society. However, this only brings about equal opportunities in name. Consider the following example. In colony X, people from the colonizing country are Europeans, while the indigenous colonial people are Chinese. There is equal opportunity legislation in colony X. In order to be a civil servant in colony X, one has to sit for civil service examination. Because of the equal opportunity legislation, the civil service examination in colony X is open to all, Europeans and Chinese alike. Therefore, it appears to be a just institution. However, education in colony X is a "luxury". There is no free education for the poor. Education in colony X is so expensive that only Europeans can afford it, while nearly all Chinese are illiterate. Though the civil service examination is open to all, only the Europeans can successfully pass the examination, while the Chinese are barred from the civil service because they are illiterate. Thus, all the civil servants in colony X are Europeans though there is equal opportunity to civil service examination. This is equal opportunity *de jure* but not *de facto*. All the important administrative positions and professional roles in colony X are occupied by Europeans, (despite nominal equal opportunity) since only the Europeans are educated. The indigenous Chinese people are "barred" from high positions as they are illiterate. As a result, the Chinese people in colony X concentrate in doing manual work, earning only meagre incomes. As the Chinese people live in poverty, they cannot afford to educate their children, who thus cannot occupy high positions in future. There is a vicious circle, leading to cross-generational poverty.

Genuine equal opportunity (and thereby justice) should involve the provision of free basic education for the poor by the government. With free basic education, the poor may compete with the rich for professional jobs within society on fairer basis. Not only should the basic education for the poor be free, it should also be compulsory, as the drop-out rate of children from poor families tends to be high since the children will likely be required to work to assist their family in earning a living. In order to be just, a government must provide minimum income to poor families to satisfy their basic needs, thereby releasing children from the necessity of earning a living for the family. Justice does not incorporate free basic education for all. Free education for all involves the treating of unequals equally, violating the Aristotelian formal principle of justice. The cost of education should be borne by the families according to their ability. Children from poor families should be given free education while the cost of education of children from rich families should be borne by families themselves. Justice demands that there should be some sort of means-test for free education.

Besides free education for the poor, the equal opportunity principle has many implications for public policy. "In a just society [with equal opportunities] ... , every effort should be made to eliminate differences that result from the accidents of birth and social conditions, in order to give people roughly equal prospects to fill positions in society. Thus, the principle of equal opportunity would lead to heavy inheritance taxes, child-care support, comprehensive free education [for the poor], training programs for the unskilled, and effective measures to prevent discrimination" (Boatright 1993, p. 105).

Equal opportunity may be viewed from the perspective of the "capability approach" suggested by Sen and Nussbaum. Equal opportunity should be concerned with equal capabilities for all; opportunities should reflect one's "actual ability to achieve various valuable functionings" (Sen 1993, p. 30). "*Functionings* represent ... various things that he or she manages to do or be in leading a life. The *capability* of a person reflects the alternative combinations of functionings the person can achieve, and from which he or she can choose one collection (Sen 1993, p. 31). People have varying needs, thus having "different abilities to convert resources into functioning. A person in a wheelchair will need more resources to become mobile than a person with unimpaired limbs ..." (Nussbaum 1999, p. 34). Thus, equal opportunity will involve providing more resources to the disabled, so that they may have similar capabilities and functionings as other non-disabled people. Both Sen and Nussbaum suggest that the central goal of public policy "should be the *capabilities* of citizens to perform various important functions" (Nussbaum 1999, p. 42), implying the idea of equal opportunity through provision of more resources to the disadvantaged who may then enjoy similar capabilities and functionings as others.

New Right Policies, Privatization and Justice

Traditionally, in a welfare state, the government is involved in the direct provision of a large range of goods and services, particularly the necessities of life, ranging from health, public transport and educational services to utilities (gas, electricity, telephone, and water). In such a state, there is a big government, with great governmental intervention into the economy. The citizens are very dependent on the government. There is a chance for the government to attach excessive rules and regulations for the use of services and goods under its direct provision, with no alternative substitution. This may lead to governmental oppression, which violates Young's concept of justice. For example, a government may threaten to withdraw government-provided goods and services necessary to life, if a person is involved in anti-government activities.

In such a state, with big state enterprises, the provision of these public services is largely done through public monopolies, which dominate the whole of the market. There is a lack of choice on the part of the users, as they can only obtain services and goods from the government through public monopolies run by bureaucrats. Such lack of choice is unjust according to Le Grand, who stresses that justice involves choice.

These public monopolies are protected by the government. Even though they are inefficient or run at a loss, they will not close down because there is a lack of competition. They will be financed through taxation if they run at a loss. There is also injustice because there is no equal opportunity for potential market entrants to compete with these public monopolies, which are financed and run by the government. "State action is monopolistic. Monopolies are inefficient. Managers of public services have no incentives to efficiency because neither they nor their services are exposed to the disciplines of the market. Therefore they are inefficient" (Wilding 1990, pp. 22–23). As there is a lack of competition, the production cost of these public monopolies is high (due to inefficiency); the shortfall is financed by taxation, or borne by the users. This is unjust as the citizens have to bear more financially than they would if the government allowed market competition.

The late 1970s and 1980s saw the rise of a so-called New Right ideology in welfare states such as the United Kingdom under Margaret Thatcher government and in the United States under Ronald Reagan. The New Right ideology "championed the cause of the free market and called for a significant reduction in the size and role of the government" (Ashford 1993, p. 19). One of the most significant aspects of the New Right model involved the privatization of public services. "There is ... a core element which appears in all various manifestations of privatization — the desire to strengthen and expand the market at the expense of the state and increase the exposure of the public sector to market forces. Privatization is therefore about denationalization and liberalization of public enterprises. It is about aid to the private sector as a deliberate policy to attract it to certain fields of work. In relation to welfare state policies, privatization is about reductions in state provision, reduction in state subsidy and reductions in regulation" (Wilding 1990, p. 19). According to Ashford (1993), there are four main kinds of privatization: the transfer of state assets to the private sector; the abolition of government subsidies, grants and loans; contracting out of publicly funded services; provision of opportunities for "exit" from public services — such as private pensions (p. 39).

With privatization, many formerly public services provided directly by the government are offered by private companies. "The UK consumer was promised a great deal from privatization. The government raised the spectre of the "dead hand" of state control and stressed the need to release companies to allow them to fulfil their potential. It was argued that private control of these stagnating publicly owned industries would make the companies responsive and efficient. Most importantly, competition from new, dynamic and imaginative market entrants would force prices down" (Meek 1998, pp. 100–118). The Consumers' Association of the U.K. believes that privatization and the competition it invites benefits consumers. "Competition brings choice; it promotes efficiency within companies and provides the strongest possible incentive to keep retail prices as low as possible" (Meek 1998, p. 100). Privatization brings choice arising from competition between private firms or from potential entrants into the market. This is just in accordance with Le Grand's theory justice which emphasizes the necessity of choice in just arrangements.

With the implementation of New Right policies, the offering of many public services were transferred from the state to the hands of private companies or individuals. For example, the sale of public rental housing to tenants, and private firms could provide water, transport, and telephone services. Privatization makes the citizens less dependent on the government, reducing the power of the government over the people. The state thus has less opportunity to oppress its citizens. This is more just by Young's standard, which emphasizes that injustices arise from oppression, rather than the failure to distribute justly.

After privatization, private firms may compete to provide services formerly offered by public monopolies. With privatization, there is an equal opportunity for private firms to enter and compete in the market. This is more just as there is equal opportunity to enter the market, gaining profits if they prove themselves efficient and competitive.

The policy of privatization has an impact on the labour market. "Most of the savings from contracting out arise because contractors offer poorer conditions of employment" (Whitfield 1992, p. 269). However, this does not apply to all employees in privatized companies, but to those in lower positions, doing mainly manual work. "Policies were intended to shift the balance of power even more towards senior management. Not only has this been used to impose job and wage cuts in the name of "efficiency" and "savings" but senior management in privatized companies have used the opportunity to award themselves massive pay rises and lucrative share option schemes. There could not be a sharper contrast than that between the treatment of cleaners in privatized companies and that of the directors" (Whitfield 1992, p. 279). Thus, privatization adversely affects the manual workers, while benefiting the senior management. This is unjust according to Rawls' concept of justice, which stresses that social and economic inequalities have to bring greatest benefits to the least advantaged, rather than to those occupying senior positions.

Privatization brings competition, choice and efficiency. However, this does not hold true in every instance. In some industries, economies of scale is important for efficient production, for example, the provision of water and electricity. In such cases, a monopoly is the most efficient form of production. Privatization of such industries, in fact, means changing public monopolies into private monopolies. Public monopolies may serve aims beyond profit-making: social equity, for example. As for private monopolies, their main aim is profit-maximization. Thus, they may raise prices and cut quality, thereby maximizing profits. The consumers have no choice, since the privatized firm is a monopoly. In such a market, the poor are most severely affected; the model is thus unjust according to Rawls' concept of justice. For such monopolistic privatized firm, government regulation in the form of franchise is necessary. Though the privatized firm is a monopoly, it is subject to potential competition, since the government may threaten to withdraw its franchise and give it to another firm. Thus, the monopolistic firm must take into account the interest of the clients and provide high quality services. Otherwise, it may be forced out of business, should the government withdraw its franchise.

Confucian Concepts of Justice and Public Policy

The Confucian concept of justice stresses one should love everyone (though with differentiation, depending on different human relations or social positions), according to the practice of *ren*. One of the important human relations with moral significance is that between the ruler or the monarch and the subjects. It is just for the ruler to be humane and the subject to be loyal. A humane ruler should be like a father to his subjects in a Confucian state. "The Confucian ideal of a government is a family-state. In a family-state, the ruler acts as patriarch, taking care of a big family. A patriarch, as his principal duty, strives for the well-being of his family members. The same is true of a ruler who, with a benevolent heart, operates for the benefit of the people" (Kwong 2002, p. 100). Such type of Confucian parental government requires the monarch or ruler to treat his people as he treats his children. However, "even though he has the children's well-being in mind, it is the father who is the sole decision-maker, not the children. The decision-making power of the father does not come from the children, and the king's power comes from Heaven, not from the people … . This kind of government is at most 'for the people'. It is highly questionable whether it is 'of the people'. It is not 'by the people' " (Li 1999, p. 170). Thus, the Confucian just relation between the ruler and his subjects implies a monarchy, rather than a democracy, with power concentrated in the hands of one person. The

Confucian concept of justice leads to the political policy that political rights and power are not to be distributed equally among the people, but being held in the hands of a benevolent ruler. Confucians stress rule by moral example. "[T]he common people always look up to their betters and if those in position of authority set an example, this will be imitated even if the people are not ordered to do so" (Lau 1979, introduction to *The Analects*, p. xxx).

As for a just government, the most important task is to reduce suffering and help people to pursue material welfare according to Confucians. It is only after the people's material well-being is improved that their education becomes important:

> Ranyou drove the Master's [Confucius'] carriage on a trip to Wei. The Master remarked, "What a teeming population!" Ranyou asked, "When the people are already so numerous, what more can be done for them?" The Master said, "Make them prosperous." "When the people are already prosperous," asked Ranyou, "what more can be done for them?" "Teach them," replied the Master. (*The Analects* 13:9)[5]

Even though the Confucians emphasize the securing of material welfare of the people, they do not envisage "a nanny state that takes care of every aspect of people's lives from the cradle to the grave. The government's job is rather to provide the conditions in which people can make a living so that they can help their families and relatives if they are in need" (Chan 2003, p. 237). Thus, Confucian social policy does not imply the implementation of a welfare state (as the term is understood in the West), but rather a small government to aid the most worst-off, with the family and the village taking up some of the welfare functions normally performed by the state in a western welfare state. As stated in a previous chapter, in a Confucian state, aid from the government is sought as a last resort, only after the family and the village fail to provide help. The state is to help the most worse-off who are those without a family to turn to for help. "Old men without wives, old women without husbands, old people without children, young children without fathers — these four types of people are the most destitute and have no one to turn to for help. Whenever King Wen put benevolent measures into effect, he always gave them first consideration" (*Mencius* 1B: 5).

In economic terms, the Confucian concept of justice envisages a private property market economy, with the working of a price mechanism. This is inevitable because of the division of labour:

> To trade grain for implements is not to inflict hardship on the potter and blacksmith. The potter and the blacksmith for their part also trade their wares for grain. In doing this, surely they are not inflicting hardship on the farmer either. Why does Hsu Tzu not become a potter and a blacksmith as well so that he can get everything he needs from his own house? ... 'If we follow the way of Hsu Tzu there will only be one price in the market, and dishonesty will disappear, for no one will take advantage of him. For equal lengths of cloth or silk, for equal weights of hemp, flax or raw silk, and for equal measures of the five grains, the price will be the same; for shoes of the same size, the price will also be the same.'
>
> That things are unequal is part of their nature. Some are worth twice or five times, ten or hundred times, even a thousand and ten thousand times, more than others. If you reduce them to the same level, it will only bring confusion to the Empire. If a roughly finished shoe sells at the same price as a finely finished one, who would make the latter? ..." (*Mencius* 3A:4)

A private property market economy is also considered as just by Hume, with his emphasis on the establishment of private property rights and their transfer. Thus, there is a point of convergence between Humean and Confucian concept of justice in economic policy. However, the Confucian just economic policy does not imply a pure laissez-faire policy. It also incorporates a limited state intervention in the distribution of land, the most important "means of production" in an agrarian society. Mencius advocates the well-field system:

> Benevolent government must begin with land demarcation. When boundaries are not properly drawn, the division of land according to the well-field system and the yield of grain used for paying officials cannot be equitable. For this reason, despotic rulers and corrupt officials always neglect the boundaries. Once the boundaries are correctly fixed, there will be no difficulty in setting the distribution of land and the determination of emolument ... A *ching* [well-field] is a piece of land measuring one *li* square, and each *ching* consists of 90 *mu*. Of these, the central 100 *mu* belongs to the state, while the other eight plots of 100 *mu* each are held by eight families who share the duty of caring for the plot owned by the state. Only when they have done this duty do they dare turn to their own affairs (*Mencius* 3A.3)

In a Confucian society, landed property is not traded freely between the people. Instead, it is distributed by the government. "The most important point is for the state to maintain a relatively equitable distribution of land at the local community, to allow individual households to make productive use of land for their families, and to qualify farmers' right to the produce of the land in order to ensure that enough food is supplied to the nonfarming classes. These principles, Mencius suggests, will secure basic material welfare for all members of the state"(Bell 2003, p. 225). Thus, a just Confucian economic policy is a hybrid of both market and socialist economic principles.

In a Confucian society, a just taxation policy is to tax the people lightly so as to make them prosperous and to allow enough resources for the family to take care of the elderly parents and children:

> Mencius said, 'Put in order the fields of the people, lighten their taxes and the people can be made affluent ...' (*Mencius* 7A:23)
>
> If your Majesty practises benevolent government towards the people, reduces punishment and taxation, gets the people to plough deeply and weed promptly, and if the able-bodied men learn in their spare time to be good sons and good younger brothers, loyal to their prince and true to their word, so that they will, in the family, serve their fathers and elder brothers, and outside the family, serve their elders and superiors, then they can be made to inflict defeat on the strong armour and sharp weapons of Ch'in and Ch'u, and armed with nothing but staves. (*Mencius* 1A:5)

In a modern Confucian state, besides low taxation, the tax policy should also give due regard to the Confucian obligation to support one's elderly parents through the introduction of tax allowance or relief for the support of parents, as in the Hong Kong taxation policy.

Confucianism emphasizes equal opportunities in public policy. Confucius advocates the ideal of universal education. "All humans, according to Confucius, are born with the ability to be moral. A primary goal of education is to develop that morality. Therefore, according to Confucius, education should be for all people. Confucius said, "In education, there should be no class distinctions." ... Confucius made it clear that no group of people should be denied an equal opportunity for education. Confucius says, "I have never denied instruction to anyone who, of his own accord, has given me so much as a bundle of dried meat as a present"" (Spring 2001, p. 25). Though Confucians argued for the implementation of universal education as a means of achieving a harmonious and peaceful society, this ideal was never achieved under

Confucian leadership, because of the government's unwillingness to provide the funds (Spring 2001, pp. 28, 30).

To a certain extent, equal opportunity and therefore justice, is respected in a Confucian state through the implementation of a civil service examination (Spring 2001, p. 28; Lee 1995, p. 134). According to Fan (2003), "... [O]nly those who indicated their abilities in commanding the Confucian classics and virtues by passing a series of examinations could be selected for high governmental positions" (p. 158). However, though it is a Confucian ideal that there should be universal education, only those children lucky enough to have an education in reality had the chance to compete for government positions. In ancient Confucian society, the mere implementation of civil service examinations, without also the actual implementation of universal education, meant that equal opportunities existed only in name, rather than in fact.

In a Confucian state, the ruler rules the people because he has the Mandate of Heaven. The passing of political power from one ruler to another is by heredity. It is a system without equal opportunities for political advancement; by contrast, a democracy theoretically allows any citizen can stand for election and with majority support, can become the head of government. In a Confucian monarchy, the emperor is selected according to bloodlines; he alone enjoys political power over the people. This system is considered appropriate or just, at least not unjust, by the Confucians.

In conclusion, the Confucian concept of justice envisages a monarchy in which political power is concentrated in the hands of one person. It calls for a small government, with some welfare functions taken up by the family and the village. In economic terms, it implies a private property market economy, with government intervention in the distribution of land. It also involves equal opportunities through the pursuit of the ideal of universal education and the implementation of a civil service examination.

* * * * * *

In this chapter, we established that justice in public policy involves a hybrid of capitalist and socialist economic principles. It involves the provision of a minimum income to those who cannot gain sufficient income to support themselves and their family in the labour market. The provision of minimum income is financed by taxation and a just tax system is progressive in nature. The relation of political systems and social justice is inconclusive, with each political system judged to be just by some concepts of justice while judged to be unjust by others. The same also applies to policy of privatization. In the latter part of this chapter, the implications of the Confucian concept of justice on public policy are examined. Essentially, a just Confucian society involves a monarchical family-state, with a private property market economy while the distribution of land lies in the hands of the government. After investigating justice in public policy in general in this chapter, we will examine justice in housing policy in particular in the following chapter, paving the way for a discussion of justice in Hong Kong's housing policy.

4

Just Housing Policy

In Chapter 3, we established that justice in social policy involves the government providing a minimum income to the needy. What does the provision of minimum income mean in the context of housing policy? Does this institution imply that it is just to provide adequate housing to the needy? In short, what is a just housing policy? In this chapter, we will try to provide an answer. This chapter will begin by examining the relation between the private housing market and justice, followed by that between housing need and justice. Governments have been trying to promote home-ownership by different means. This chapter will probe into the question of whether it is just to promote home-ownership. In addition, we will discuss what a just tax policy on housing is. This chapter will end with an investigation into the implications of Confucian ideas of justice on housing.

* * * * * *

Food, clothing and shelter are the basic necessities of life. However, in order to have a healthy life, not just any form or type of food, clothing and shelter will suffice. As for food, an adequate quantity of nutritious food requisite for a balanced diet is necessary for health. As for clothing, appropriate clean garments that keep you warm or cool according to the season are necessary. As for adequate shelter or housing, the necessities are even more demanding. Adequate shelter or housing requires a hygienic environment with appropriate lighting and ventilation; one not overcrowded, that offers physical protection and provides basic amenities, creating a home to which one belongs and can be a physical and psychological refuge. "... Housing is a basic human necessity. It offers physical protection from nature, the elements and the unknown. It provides warmth and offers amenities that allow households to pursue their wider aims. It is possible to suggest that housing has been a necessity in all cultures throughout the history of human civilization" (King 1996, p. 160).

Housing as a good has certain specific characteristics. "Housing is a durable good producing both necessary and luxury flows of consumption services as well as representing a capital asset to its owner. Houses are heterogeneous, immobile and expensive in relation to income ... The market is dominated by the exchange of second-hand houses. New house construction takes time to plan, is labour-intensive, requires significant inputs of materials and land, and is highly susceptible to the economic business cycle ... Finally, housing is not only regarded as a necessity, *per se*, but a certain minimum of housing services is socially demanded, enforced by building and planning controls and public health legislation" (Stafford 1979, p. 39).

According to King (2003), the "right to housing is a natural right and thus is attached to all persons. It is not a relative condition, depending on circumstances and resources, but a *universal* condition (p. 49)". In light of the fact that housing is a necessity for all people and there is a universal right to housing, housing policy is an important public policy. It affects the distribution of housing resources. Since it concerns the distribution of resources among people in society, the question of justice is involved. "Any attempt to create a more just society cannot afford to neglect housing" (Clapham *et al.* 1994, p. 24). Different people may have different views on what a just housing policy is. The upper class may think that they are unjustly treated as they do not receive any housing subsidy from the government. The middle class may think that justice means they should receive the most housing subsidy as they pay the most tax in society. The lower class may believe that they are entitled to greatest housing subsidy in light of justice as they have greatest unsatisfied needs. Are these views justified? Do these views reflect genuine justice in housing policy?

Private Housing Market and Justice

In a private market, private property rights over housing are recognized and respected. Housing may be traded, exchanged and transferred by consent between buyers and sellers at the agreed market equilibrium price.

This is just by Hume's and Nozick's concept of justice, which emphasizes the respect of private property rights and their transfer by consent. "While housing has particular attributes in terms of cost, fixed location, durability, status, security and the services it provides, it is nevertheless a commodity that is produced, consumed and exchanged through the same processes that apply in markets for other goods" (Forrest, Murie and Williams 1990, p. 1). Since housing is a necessity, it has a high use value. In light of the fact it is exchanged in the private market, it also has an exchange value. "... Housing has an exchange value as well as a use value. Consequently, it is affected not only by changes in demand for shelter, but also in its role as an investment. However, changes in its value as a financial asset will have an impact on those seeking to gain access for use" (Forrest, Murie and Williams, p. 12).

How do people get money to pay for housing services provided in the private housing market? Most do so by selling their labour in the labour market. Some excel in the labour market. They thus can afford to live in luxurious housing. While others fare less well; they can only afford to live in medium-sized, ordinary housing. Those who fare even worse may be "forced" to live in small, lower quality housing. As has been discussed in Chapter 3, there is a type of rough (incomplete) justice according to deserts in the labour market in the sense that there is a tendency for those who have talents and who work hard to gain more. As income directly affects housing affordability, rough justice according to deserts in the labour market leads to rough justice in the housing market. There is a tendency for those who fare well in the labour market to fare well in the housing market, gaining return (in terms of the quality of the housing they live in) for their effort and ability, though this does not apply to every case. This tendency is in line with the Aristotelian concept of justice according to deserts. The provision of different types and sizes of housing in the private housing market allows people to choose their own housing according to affordability. This allowance of choice is concordant with Le Grand's concept of justice, which stresses that justice cannot exist without choice.

Housing Need and Social Justice

In the private market, housing is exchanged and allocated according to the ability to pay. Adequate housing can only be enjoyed by those who can afford to pay in the housing market. People work in exchange for an income which pays for the housing they need. However, there are people who cannot "sell" their labour in the market: the sick, the elderly, and the disabled, for instance. There are also people who are unemployed, and others who, though employed, earn a very low income. This group of people may not be able to pay for adequate housing in the housing market. "The high cost of housing and the unequal distribution of income meant that significant sections of the population would have been unable, without assistance, to afford the full economic price of decent accommodation" (Lansley 1979, p. 31). As a result, the poor are forced to live in inadequate housing, with their need for adequate housing unsatisfied.

Living in inadequate housing adversely affects the households concerned as well as society at large. Inadequate housing may create a health risks; a poor quality and weak workforce; high crime rates; and even lead to social unrest (Conway 2000, p. 3; Aaron 1972, p. 12; Lansley 1979, p. 30). Thus, the non-self-satisfiable housing need (i.e. needs that cannot be satisfied fully by one's own effort) on the part of the poor affects not only the poor, but also society as a whole.

One way to alleviate the housing plight of the needy is through voluntary redistribution of income in the form of charity. For example, some non-profit-making housing associations may provide housing at below the market rent. However, since housing is an expensive commodity, it is questionable whether charity would ever be enough to help all the needy to gain decent accommodation. If voluntary redistribution of income cannot solve the problem of inadequate housing, then non-voluntary means have to be sought to assist the needy.

In light of the failure of the market to provide adequate housing for all, government intervention to help the needy to gain access to decent accommodation is deemed necessary in light of the just principle of needs. "A minority of households may not be able to provide adequate housing through the market. Therefore the government should use its tax-raising powers to fund improvements in the housing of those in poverty ... This notion is based on the most obvious criticism of a market, namely, that it does not guarantee all households an income, whilst some households will become wealthy. Thus a market allows, indeed even encourages inequality of resources distribution. The state, it is argued, therefore, has a role in redistributing resources away from those who benefit inordinately from markets towards those who do not" (King 1998, p. 58). According to Angel (2000), "there are two arguments for state support in the form of direct housing subsidies ... The first argument rests on our earlier observation that housing is a "merit good", wherein the state intervenes to ensure that people consume adequate amounts of housing because it is in their best long-term interest and in the public interest. The merit good argument is strengthened by focusing on the externalities associated with the under-consumption of housing — its adverse (or beneficial) effect on the immediate neighbourhood, on the quality of life in the city as a whole, or on social and economic stability ... The second argument in favour of housing subsidies rests on the fact that housing-related poverty exacerbates and multiplies other inequalities ... Inadequate housing is thus a source of poverty, as well as a consequence of poverty. It stands to reason, therefore, that a direct attack on housing ills — as part of a more comprehensive anti-poverty program — would be an efficient way to assist the poor in combating other social ills" (p. 113). Government intervention through the provision of housing subsidies to the needy is just according to the Marxian and Rawlsian concept of justice, which focus on distribution according to need to the least advantaged in society.

In order to institute a just housing subsidy, there should be equal opportunity to apply for, and be allocated, housing subsidy. The allocation of housing subsidy should be in strict accordance with need on the part of the applicant. There should not be discrimination on the basis of race, sex, creed, nationality or religion. Equal opportunity to be allocated housing subsidy basing solely on need without discrimination is part of a just housing policy.

Governmental housing subsidy may take the form of a cash subsidy which allows the poor to rent decent accommodation in the private housing market. However, in such a case, those who receive cash housing subsidy may not spend the housing subsidy on housing. Instead they may spend the housing subsidy on other luxuries while depressing their housing consumption. In this way, the housing problem of having people living in inadequate housing may still remain despite the provision of housing subsidy. As a way of improvement, the government may provide housing subsidy in the form of housing vouchers and rent rebates so as to allow the needy to rent adequate housing in the private market. This may ensure that the subsidy earmarked for housing will be used for its intended purpose, thereby solving the housing problem through the satisfaction of need.

Housing subsidy (in the form of rent allowance or rent rebate) enables the needy to rent through the private property market is more just than in kind provision in Le Grand's sense, which emphasizes that justice involves choice. This is because a household receiving housing subsidy in the form of cash allowance or rent rebate may enjoy the choice to live in a district that it prefers and move whenever it likes, so long as housing is available. It enjoys comparatively more choice and freedom than a public housing tenant has, since the provision of vacant public rental housing is usually limited to certain areas, and any move from one public rental unit to another requires approval from the government. A cash subsidy in the form of rent allowances or rent rebates to rent in the private market allows greater choice than in kind provision: it is thus more just in Le Grand's sense.

However, housing subsidies in the form of direct provision of housing, on the part of the government, is more just in the Marxian and Rawlsian sense, than the provision of housing allowance, as this subsidy benefits the needy tenant directly, rather than benefiting a private landlord. "... In high growth regions where low-income sub-markets are tight, housing allowances would swell up demand and drive up short- and medium term prices. Accordingly, in these conditions, significant portions of the housing allowances would end up as landlord rather than the tenant benefits" (Pugh 1980, p. 107). According to Lansley (1979), "the advantage of the direct public provision of housing is that it guarantees a supply of housing that might otherwise not have been provided, and poses less of a problem with respect to the incidence of subsidies. Such housing can also be allocated on the basis of need rather than ability to pay and rents set at levels which it is felt tenants can afford. By by-passing normal market processes, access to decent housing at reasonable cost is improved" (p. 36).

Public Rental Housing and Justice

According to concepts of justice that emphasize the needs principle (the Marxian and the Rawlsian), the government should provide public rental housing or housing subsidies in kind (if it does not provide a cash subsidy) to those who cannot afford adequate housing in the private market. Thus, public rental housing should be means-tested. Those who can afford to rent or buy in the private market, should do so without aid from the government. Justice does not require universal provision of subsidized housing to all. The Rawlsian concept of justice only requires that the least advantaged, who fail to afford decent accommodation in the private market, be allocated public rental housing by the government. This is benefit in kind, which forms part of the minimum income package as discussed in Chapter 3.

A just public rental housing policy should provide equal opportunity for all those with the same non-self-satisfiable housing need to be allocated public rental housing without discrimination on the basis of sex, religion, or race. The equal opportunity policy should include: equal waiting time for public housing allocation; similar choice of rental unit and rent policy; and being allocated a rental unit of similar age and facilities relative to those with similar housing needs applying for public rental units, without discrimination. Non-discriminatory practices are an important aspect of a just housing policy.

Public rental housing for the needy should mean housing that is adequate without being luxurious. A just government should be responsible for satisfying the basic housing needs of the poor by the Marxian just principle of need. Any luxury is to be earned by hard work in the labour market by the Aristotelian just principle of deserts. Those who gain high income by working hard may afford luxurious housing in the private market in accordance with the just principle of deserts. A just government is merely responsible for providing very basic adequate housing for the needy according to the Marxian just principle of needs.

However, what constitutes adequate housing varies from society to society. For example, in Hong Kong where land is scarce, a small self-contained two-bedroom flat for a family of four may be regarded as adequate housing, while a house with a garden would be considered a luxury. Whereas in Britain, where land is more readily available, a house with a garden is not considered luxurious. A just government is to be responsible for providing adequate housing for the needy in accordance with the standard and expectations relative to the society concerned.

The just allocation of public rental housing is to be based on housing need in addition to time spent on the waiting list, according to the Marxian and the Rawlsian concept of justice. Those with the greatest housing need are to be allocated public rental housing first. Housing need should be measured by the inadequacy of an applicant's present housing: the degree of overcrowding, the lack of amenities, and the degree of resistance to wind and rain. British council housing, which once operated on a kind of point system for allocation, was an example of allocation according to need. "Council housing [was] allocated according to "housing need". This [was] not a sign of poverty in money terms ... To help determine "housing need", most local authorities operate[d] a points system which [took] into account social and environmental factors, such as the number of children in a family, any mental or physical disabilities, the number of rooms they at present occupy, the lack of amenities such as hot and cold water or own w.c., and so forth" (Burke 1981, p. 16).

Le Grand's theory of justice stresses that justice involves choice. For a just allocation system of public rental housing in Le Grand's sense, the prospective public housing tenant should be given a choice from a few vacant housing units, preferably in different districts, available for occupation. In recent choice-based letting of British social housing, "customers are not able to choose *between* landlords, but must accept a limited range of options according to eligibility criteria determined by landlord", thus choice-based letting serves as "a tool for improving managing efficiency of landlords, but not for empowering tenants" (King 2003, p. 15). The allowance of choice in the selection of one's public housing unit (choice based letting), however limited it may be, respects the preference of individual prospective tenant to a certain extent, and is therefore just in accordance with Le Grand's concept of justice.

The government should subsidize public rental housing below market rates. A just rent for public rental housing is to set the rent in accordance with the tenant's ability to pay. Those who do not have an income or those who are extremely poor are to be exempt from paying rent; the government should fully subsidize their housing. Those who are less poor pay a higher rent, receiving less subsidy from the government as their need for assistance is lower. It would be unjust for all tenants of public rental housing to pay the same rent, as their need for assistance varies. By the Marxian and Rawlsian just principle of needs, those with the greatest needs should be given more assistance by the government. Those with lesser needs should play a greater part in being adequately housed; they should receive less support from the government and pay higher rents.

A public housing tenant may become affluent after living in public housing for a period of time. It would be just for him to move out, so as to allow others with greater housing needs to move in. Thus, it would be just to rent public housing on a contract basis. When the contract ends, the tenant must undergo a means test. If he still cannot afford decent accommodation in the private sector, the contract will be renewed. However, if he becomes "rich" enough to afford adequate housing in the housing market, he is not justified in receiving subsidies from the government. It would be just not to renew his contract. The public rental housing he vacates would be allocated to others who have greater housing need by the Marxian and Rawlsian just principle of needs. One may argue that such an arrangement, though just, may lead to other problems. It would result in the so-called "residualization" of public rental housing: the lack of families of differing incomes can create sink estates and lead to stigmatization. Also, the cost of means-testing is high. In addition, if public rental housing provision is immediately withdrawn if the tenant's financial situation changes for the better slightly, this may discourage him from improving his situation by taking up a part-time job; upward social mobility by one's own effort would be thereby discouraged. It has to be pointed out that justice is only one among many considerations in public decision-making. There should be a balance between justice and other considerations in the formulation of a sensible housing policy, which should not rest on the consideration of justice alone.

A public housing tenant may be subjected to more governmental interference over different aspects of his/her life. For example, the tenant may be forbidden to keep a pet, to decorate his/her home as s/he likes, or to put his/her belongings outside the door. All these controls and regulations, on the part of the government, represent the management and maintenance of order in the public housing estates. However, excessive regulation of the behaviour of the public housing tenant may limit the freedom of the tenant, resulting in oppression. A public housing tenant is comparatively more dependent on the government than the tenant of a private landlord. There is a possibility that the government may oppress him/her, for example, threaten to terminate his/her rental contract if s/he is involved in anti-government activities. The provision of public rental housing, on the part of the government, may open the way to governmental oppression of the people, thereby being unjust in Young's sense which regards social justice as more than a distributive issue, involving oppression.

Home-Ownership and Justice

The government may take different measures to encourage home-ownership. The government may provide mortgage interest tax exemption to make home-ownership less expensive than renting. The government may build housing for sale at below market prices. Alternatively, the government may provide interest-free or low-interest loans for paying down-payment for mortgages. Does justice require a government to assist home-ownership? Is a policy for home-ownership just?

Home-ownership is not merely a matter of the satisfaction of the need for shelter. It is an investment decision. "... People buy houses not only for use, but also as an investment to increase their personal assets. The idea that 'bricks and mortar' is one of the most secure areas in which to invest personal savings is a long-standing axiom" (Forrest and Murie 1995, p. 61). As the price of housing increases, home-ownership can be a source and store of wealth (Forrest, Murie and Williams 1990, p. 18; Murie 1983, p. 167; Morris and Winn 1990, pp. 55–56).

A just housing policy should stress the use value of housing. If people are living in inadequate housing, there is a housing need. It is just for the government to give assistance by the just principle of needs. Justice does not require a government to assist in housing investment and accumulation of wealth through home-ownership. If a household cannot afford home-ownership, it does not mean that they are necessarily living in inadequate housing that requires state intervention by the rule of justice. In some cases, the tenants may still be able to afford adequate housing in the rental sector. "Ownership can be seen as a second-order problem, emerging only after progress has been made towards meeting more basic requirements" (Malpass and Murie 1999, p. 3). Home-ownership is more a matter of investment and wealth accumulation than a matter of housing need. Justice in Marxian and Rawlsian sense merely requires the government to intervene for the satisfaction of housing need of the worst-off, not for investment and wealth accumulation. Home-ownership is to be earned by the Aristotelian just principle of deserts.

If justice does not require the government to assist in home-ownership, then why do governments take a series of measures to encourage home-ownership? Though there is no evidence to show that home-ownership contributes to political stability (Forrest, Murie and Williams 1990, p. 166), the belief, on the part of politicians, that home-ownership helps the maintenance of status quo, thereby contributing to political stability, is sufficient reason for politicians to pursue the course of encouraging home-ownership. That is, governments encourage home-ownership for political reasons, rather than for just ends.

Although justice does not require a government to assist home-ownership, it is not unjust to do so. However, injustices may occur if a government puts priority in encouraging home-ownership rather than providing public rental housing or other types of housing subsidy, to shelter the needy. If resources for the latter are diverted to the former, the housing needs of the poor may be neglected. That is, the satisfaction of housing needs required by justice could be compromised for political ends. According to Chiu (2002), "obviously, the [Hong Kong] government gave a higher priority to the policy objective of increasing home ownership than providing more rental housing. Thus, low-income households, which had the most severe housing problems, did not receive the greatest attention from the government" (p. 157). Such a policy of prioritizing home-ownership over addressing the housing plight of the poor is unjust, according to the Marxian and Rawlsian concept of justice, which focus on the needs of the worse-off rather than those who are more well-off and who can afford home-ownership (with or without government assistance). "Subsidies need to be administered justly and to large numbers of those in need, rather to the selected few. If resources are limited, then those in the greatest need should be targeted first" (Angel 2000, p. 114).

It has to be pointed out, however, that justice is merely one among many considerations for public policy. Justice is far from being the sole end of public policy, though undoubtedly, it is an important consideration. Sometimes, justice may be compromised for the sake of the pursuit of other ends in public policy. In the case of governmental intervention to encourage home-ownership, justice in the Rawlsian and Marxian sense is compromised for the sake of other ends, like the assumed end of maintaining political stability.

However, as a society becomes more affluent, the income of the people increases, and the desire for home-ownership may become stronger. This is especially the case in a booming private property market since home-ownership may imply an investment which can yield lucrative returns. In such a society, when there is public favouring of home-ownership, it would be just for the government to adopt measures to assist and encourage home-ownership (even to the detriment of assisting the poor) according to the communitarian concept of justice, even though it may be unjust in the Marxian and Rawlsian sense. The communitarian concept of justice emphasizes that justice is to be defined by the community at large. In a community favouring home-ownership, it will be just for the government to assist and favour home-ownership according to the communitarians.

As a means to increase the home-ownership rate and spread home-ownership to the lower class, the government may sell public rental housing to sitting tenants at a discounted rate. In other words, these sitting tenants in public housing may achieve home-ownership with great government subsidy while private tenants in similar income brackets receive none (Chiu 2002, p. 159). This is unjust according to Aristotle's formal principle of justice of treating equals equally. Those public tenants who can afford to buy their rental units are comparatively better-off. After buying their rental unit, they will stay, instead of vacating their rental unit, which could then be allocated to waiting list households with greater housing needs. Thus, those low-income households on the waiting list must wait longer for allocation of public rental units than they otherwise would. In other words, those comparatively well-off public housing tenants, who have benefited from years of subsidized rents, receive further subsidy to achieve home-ownership, while those on the waiting list receive none to improve their housing plight. This is unjust according to the Marxian and Rawlsian concept of justice, since the needs of the least advantaged are neglected.

In an effort to promote home-ownership, making renting a secondary option with limited choice due to decreased supply, the government may marginalize the rental sector, both public and private. However, there are people who cannot afford to own their home, whether students who seek short-term accommodation, or people who change jobs very often. These people still prefer rented accommodation. As the number of rental units decreases because the government is encouraging home-ownership, those people who prefer to rent may lack choice. This is unjust according to Le Grand's theory of justice which states that justice involves choice.

Just Tax on Housing

Justice involves the taxing of all sources of income (treating all income equally), that is, treating equals equally, the Aristotelian formal principle of justice. Buying property as an investment may create an income stream. Thus, it is justified that there should be tax on the ownership of a property. The ownership of property may generate income in the form of rent. As for owner-occupied housing, the owner obtains rent in kind. There should be tax on rent that may be generated from a property. "... As an investment good, owner-occupier housing should be taxed, thus bringing it into equivalence with the taxed investment income from machines, factories, warehouses and so on" (Pugh 1980, p. 84). For example, A owns a flat which may generate a rent of \$5,000 per month, while B owns a luxurious flat which brings in about \$25,000 per month. The tax rate for A's flat is 10%, which requires a tax of \$500 per month. Whereas the tax rate of B's flat is 5%, which means B has to pay \$1,250 in tax. This is unjust, as B pays only two and a half times as much tax as A, though s/he receives a rent much more than A. As discussed in Chapter 3, a just taxation system should be progressive. Thus, a just tax on housing should be progressive as well, with those owning property capable of generating a higher rent, paying a higher rate of tax, than those owning property of lesser value. This is to treat unequals unequally, in line with the Aristotle's formal principle of justice.

Besides rent, a property owner may gain income by selling the property at a higher price than the price s/he bought it if the price of his/her property increases during the period s/he owns it. This source of income may be very great. Justice requires that this source of income is to be taxed as other sources of income, which is in line with the Aristotelian just principle of treating equals equally. Likewise, a just capital gains tax should be progressive, with those gaining more from the sale of their property paying higher tax rate than those who receive less from the sale of their property.

A property is a very durable good. With good maintenance, a property may last for more than a hundred years. Therefore, it is natural for a property to pass from one generation to another. If a child inherits a property from his/her parents, this may be a great source of income as a property usually worth a lot of money (even though it may not be a luxurious one). Inheritance involves gains not earned by one's effort. This is unjust, according to Aristotle's just principle of deserts. However, inheritance of property is considered just by Hume and Nozick, as it involves the transfer of property rights by consent. To strike a balance between the two conflicting claims of justice, inheritance tax is to be levied on inherited property. Such a tax should also be progressive, with those inheriting property of greater value paying a higher percentage of the property price as tax, while those inheriting property of lesser value paying a smaller percentage of the property price as tax.

In order to promote home-ownership, some governments may provide mortgage interest tax relief. This scheme favours home-owners, while private and public tenants do not enjoy any tax relief. This is unjust according to the Aristotelian formal principle of treating equals equally. Those in the rental sector may be in the same income bracket with some of the home-owners. If the home-owners enjoy tax relief, the renters should also enjoy tax relief so as to be fair.

Confucian Concepts of Justice and Housing

So far, we have been discussing Western concepts of justice, which stress that it is just for the government to provide housing subsidy to the poor. However, in a Confucian society, it is just, or at least not unjust, for the government *not* to provide housing subsidy to the needy, as the needy in a Confucian society are to be taken care of by the extended family first. If the family fails to help, the needy may turn to their social network in their village for help. Seeking assistance from the government is only a last resort. Thus, the housing plight of the needy is to be catered for by the family, rather than the government. In other words, redistribution of wealth and income occurs first within the extended family in a Confucian society, rather than the government redistributing within society as a whole. Thus, a Confucian society allows only for small government, with little or no government housing subsidy to the poor. Relatives in their extended family are responsible for their well-being.

According to Confucian thinking, a family, rather than an individual, owns a house. The economically active family members will finance housing for the family and the property is considered to be family property in a Confucian society, instead of being owned by the individual, as in the West.

In a modern Confucian state, housing policy can be used to reinforce Confucian values, such as the importance of family and filial piety. Singapore, a state that embraces Confucian values, uses its housing policy to strengthen the institution of family which always comprises the basic unit in a Confucian society. "The monopoly of housing [in Singapore] is also used to shore up the family institution. Public housing is only available to households. Only single persons who is presumed will never marry — males more that fifty years old, and single females over forty years old — are eligible to rent; and then only if they share with another person. Young single individuals are as a rule excluded in line with the government's pro-family policies" (Chua 1995, p. 141)

In addition, housing policy can also aid mutual support among members of the extended family which is stressed in Confucianism. In Singapore, "families of siblings or a married child and the family of his/her origin may apply to be neighbours in order to maintain mutual support; these joint applicants are given priority of allocation, and the waiting time for their flats is reduced by as much as two years" (Chua 1995, p. 142). This pro-family policy may reinforce the welfare support among family members, reducing the role of government in the provision of welfare services to the people. This is in line with the spirit of Confucianism.

Housing policy may also be used as a means to reinforce the Confucian value of filial piety in a modern Confucian society. Confucianism emphasizes the support and care of elderly parents by adult children. In Hong Kong, a Chinese society, a young family living with parents will be given priority in the allocation of public rental housing, and have a shorter waiting time. In Singapore, in addition to priority of allocation, the income ceiling for eligibility for public housing is raised substantially for a young family who chooses to live with one of their parents (Chua 1995, p. 142). Such housing measures are meant to encourage adult children to live with their parents even after marriage so that they may take care of their elderly parents in an expression of the Confucian virtue of filial piety.

* * * * * *

In this chapter, we have established that justice in housing policy involves the provision of housing subsidies to the needy according to the just principle of needs. Though many governments are involved in encouraging home-ownership, assistance in home-ownership on the part of the government is not required by the just principle of needs. Governments pursue the course of encouraging home-ownership for political ends rather than for just ones (in the Marxian and Rawlsian sense). We have also argued that a just tax on housing should be progressive. Also, there should be a capital-gains tax levied on properties, as this is a great source of income which should be taxed in accordance with the Aristotelian rule of justice. In the latter part of this chapter, we have established that justice in a Western welfare state demands more government involvement in the housing sector than a Confucian society does. Housing policy may also be used as a means to promote Confucian values. Having defined the concept of social justice, and examined justice in public policy and housing policy, we will turn to justice in Hong Kong's housing policy. We will trace the historical development of justice in Hong Kong's housing policy and investigate how justice is conceived by different stakeholders in Hong Kong's housing policy in following chapters.

5

Justice in Hong Kong's Housing Policy — A Historical Perspective

Having discussed the theoretical framework of justice in public and housing policy, we will turn our attention to the case study of Hong Kong's housing policy. In this chapter, we will examine the chronological development of justice in Hong Kong's housing policy. Roughly speaking, the development of justice in Hong Kong's housing policy can be divided into different periods, with different conceptions of justice playing a dominant role in each. We will examine each period in turn.

* * * * * *

About 50% of Hong Kong's population lives in public housing, receiving government housing subsidies in the form of subsidized rent or discount sales price. Yet despite this figure, a housing problem still exists at the beginning of the 21st Century. In spite of half a century of governmental intervention into the housing market of Hong Kong, there are still people living in inadequate housing: people who are homeless, and those living in bedspace apartments, board-partitioned rooms and non-self-contained housing. Judging from this scenario, one might argue that social injustices exist in the housing sector of Hong Kong. Is the government subsidizing the "wrong" people, while neglecting those inadequately housed? There are numerous conceptions of justice. Based on which conception of justice is this conclusion of the existence of social injustice made? Does it rest on Aristotle's desert-based theory of justice? Do those inadequately housed have common merit that should prompt the government to resettle them in adequate housing? Such common merit among those inadequately housed is difficult to be identified. Thus, it seems that the judgement that the inadequately housed suffer injustices cannot be based on Aristotle's conception of justice, which focuses on distributing according to merit or deserts. How about Hume's conception of justice, based on property rights? It seems absurd to say that these inadequately housed people have property rights over adequate housing that would necessitate the government to provide adequate housing according to rights. If the judgement that inadequately housed people are unjustly treated is not deserts-based and rights-based, then is it needs-based? It seems appropriate to say that what is common among all those inadequately housed is that they have housing needs which they cannot satisfy themselves; thus they are "forced" to live in substandard housing. Therefore, the judgement that those living in substandard housing are suffering from social injustices must rest on a needs-based theory of justice, namely, the Marxian conception, which calls for distributing according to one's needs.

In order to have a comprehensive overview of the development of justice in Hong Kong's housing policy, one has to consider policy issues from the perspective of different theories of justice. Since different theories of justice are so divergent in their content, it is possible that a policy may be just from the perspective of one theory of justice but may be very unjust when viewed through the prism of other theories. In the following analysis, the development of justice in Hong Kong's housing policy will be approached from the perspective of different theories of justice, enabling a deeper understanding of the issues under examination.

When analyzing justice in Hong Kong's housing policy, in addition to taking into consideration of different theories of justice, one has to consider justice on two policy levels — first, justice as an objective of the particular housing policy concerned; second, justice as a by-product (of policy aiming at achieving non-justice goals). Housing policy may be pursued for different policy objectives. If justice is one of the many policy objectives, rather than being the sole objective, sometimes justice may be compromised for other ends. Sometimes, housing policy may be pursued for aims other than social justice, yet the result may be just. That is, justice occurs as a by-product, rather than being the primary objective of the housing policy concerned.

Most of Hong Kong's people are Chinese, yet they were and are governed by a Western-style government both during the colonial period and after the handover of sovereignty to China in 1997[1]. Is Hong Kong's housing policy mainly shaped by Western or Eastern conceptions of justice? Or is it a result of the interplay of the Western and Chinese conceptions of justice? An analysis of this issue seems worthwhile.

We will examine the development of justice in Hong Kong's housing policy. At a general level, the development of justice in Hong Kong's housing policy can be divided into five periods. The five periods are demarcated in accordance with the critical changes in the interplay of different conceptions of justice. Roughly speaking, these five periods coincide with the development of major housing policy changes as the latter lays the foundation for the development of justice in housing policy. It should be noted that such classification largely rests on the consequences of housing policies, rather than on the overt and conscious intentions of the policy-makers. Evidence for each period is chosen on the basis of the extent and significance of a housing phenomenon resulting from certain housing policies through the analysis of official documentation and academic literature.

It should be noted that the following discussion of justice in housing policy is limited to the context of Hong Kong, rather than referring to a global context. According to Pojman (2006), Kant distinguished between perfect and imperfect duties. Perfect duties are "absolute and universally binding", whereas imperfect duties "allow discretion regarding how and to what extent the individual will fulfill them" (p. 98). The Hong Kong government has perfect duties, both moral and contractual (based on the social contract between the sovereign and the governed) towards Hong Kong's people, and thus is responsible for their welfare; while it has imperfect (solely moral) duties towards people (whose plight is perhaps more serious) living in other countries. Thus, according to Kantian precepts, the Hong Kong government's perfect duty (satisfying the housing need of the Hong Kong's people) should take priority over its imperfect duty (satisfying the housing needs of people living elsewhere, though the latter may be even be more serious). The satisfaction of the latter is one of the perfect duties (both moral and contractual) of the world government (if existed), rather than the Hong Kong government. Thus, the following discussion of justice as executed by Hong Kong's housing policy focuses on the perfect duties of the Hong Kong government in bringing about social justice within the context of Hong Kong, rather than its imperfect duties in the global context. A brief discussion of each of the five periods of the development of justice in Hong Kong's housing policy follows.

Clashes between Marxian and Chinese Conception of Justice (Pre-1954)

Before massive government intervention within the housing market in 1954, housing provision in Hong Kong was predominantly left to the private sector. Prior to 1954, the government essentially adopted a so-called laissez-faire policy in the provision of housing, with minimal intervention (Fong and Yeh 1987, p. 18; Fong 1986, p. 4; Kwitko 1986, p. 6). The first attempted governmental intervention within the housing sector occurred in 1903 with the introduction of Public Health and Building Ordinance, which regulated a building's height, depth and other specifications. This ordinance was subsequently revised in 1935. However, due to opposition from powerful unofficial members from the business and property communities within the Legislative Council, the government was reluctant to enforce this Ordinance (Fong 1986, p. 4). The government's adoption of laissez-faire policy did not seem problematic before World War II, when the population in Hong Kong remained small and mobile[2].

After World War II, there was a great influx of immigrants from China. In addition, there was an exceptionally high natural growth rate of more than 3% per year in the 1950s and the early 1960s. In the five years from 1945 to 1950, the population in Hong Kong expanded around fourfold from 600,000 to about 2.4 million (Fong and Yeh 1984, p. 1; Hopkins 1972, p. 200). This sudden increase in population by itself was more than enough to create housing problems in post-war Hong Kong. The situation was made even more serious by the narrow site around the harbour bounded by steep hills in the north and the south, making it even more difficult to build housing for the growing population (Hopkins 1972, p. 201).

The war destroyed an estimated one-fifth of the tenements floors and almost all the European-style housing. In 1946, Hong Kong had accommodation designed to house about 640,000 persons, however, by the end of 1946, the population had risen to 1,600,000, reached 2,360,000 by 1950 (Goodstadt 1969, p. 262). This resulted in overcrowding in private tenements:

> Floors have been partitioned off into cubicles and sublet by a principal tenant; the cubicles themselves have been further subdivided into bedspaces; in extreme cases, bedspaces have been occupied on a shift system by three different sets of inhabitants. Roofs, cellars and lofts

> have been let and before strict official control was instituted, the population still spilled over onto the pavements. (Dwyer 1971, p. 4)

Despite severe overcrowding in private tenements, many more Hong Kong residents had no accommodation at all. After 1947, urban squatting was extremely acute (Dwyer 1970, p. 609). There was extensive squatting on roof tops, stairways, and on hillsides at the margin of the built-up areas. In 1952, it was estimated that about 340,000 people lived in squatter huts; and about 350,000 people lived in substandard conditions in the urban centres (Chau 1989, p. 28; Hopkins 1971, p. 276). This housing shortage was created since the private housing sector failed to respond to the huge inflow of low income immigrants by building affordable housing to accommodate them.

This housing plight created great problems for Hong Kong — "threats to public health, large fires in squatter areas, the danger of riots, the barrier to development of land which had been encroached upon by squatters, and the pressure on wages of high rents" (Wong 1998, p. 5). Despite these problems, the government still adopted the laissez-faire policy before 1954. One of the reasons was that Hong Kong's population had always been mobile — it was believed that once the political situation in China returned to "normal", the population in Hong Kong would go back to China (Hopkins 1969, p. 2; Keung 1981, p. 5). Thus, "in the meantime, there was no point in making visitors too comfortable" (Hopkins 1969, p. 2).

Besides this demographic reason for governmental inaction despite serious housing problems, economic motives also came into play. There was an unwillingness on the part of the government to spend its limited resources on becoming the landlord of the poor, since re-housing a large number of squatters was an expensive business, and the government was reluctant to prioritize the illegal squatters as well as the poor over other social groups and other social objectives (Hopkins 1969, p. 2). After all, according to Hopkins (1969), "[t]he poor have never been particularly favoured in Hong Kong".

According to Chan (1999), another economic reason for government non-intervention within the housing market to solve the housing problem was that intervention would not facilitate Hong Kong's economic development and growth. "In the immediate post-war years, Hong Kong was an entrepôt on the southern coast of China. Hong Kong's labour force consisted primarily of labourers or sailors. Governmental intervention in housing appeared to have little economic rationale. Thus, the government was reluctant to take action" (Chan 1999, p. 177).

The Marxian conception of justice demands "to each according to his needs". There was a great housing need, on the part of the people, in the post-war period, with many living in overcrowded private tenements and squatter areas. The government's inaction — whether due to demographic and economic reasons — left the housing need of the people unsatisfied. This may be regarded as injustice from the Marxian point of view, arising out of government omission or inaction, in sharp contrast to injustices arising from government commission, that is, injustices resulting from governmental active action.

Following the great great influx of refugees from China, the government in 1951 established certain "approved areas" in which squatters could build cottages with fire-resistant materials. "Tolerated areas" were also designated for poorer squatters to build wooden huts (Fong 1986, p. 5; Fong and Yeh 1987, p. 19). Out of a total of 300,000 squatters, only 30,000 had been resettled to "approved or tolerated" squatter sites on the periphery of the urban area by the end of 1953 (Hopkins 1969, p. 2). This form of government intervention did not solve the housing need of the squatters concerned. In the "approved or tolerated areas", the squatters were still living in substandard housing, that is, squatter huts, without any facilities. In other words, the housing needs of the squatters were still not satisfied, even in "tolerated and approved areas". There were still housing injustices according to the Marxian conception, with the housing need of the squatters left unsatisfied.

Although the government refrained from direct provision of housing to the people prior to 1954, it assisted the establishment of housing agencies which provided housing for the people. In 1952, the Hong Kong Settlers' Housing Corporation, a non-profit organization financed partly by the government and partly by subscription from the public, was formed. It constructed 1,500 cottages which were later possessed by occupants who paid monthly rentals for seven years. In 1951, the Hong Kong's Housing Society, an independent voluntary organization, was established to provide housing to lower-middle and middle-income families. The Society was first established, with a government loan of HK$2.5 million. Also, building sites were provided by the government at one-third the market value. Within two years, the Society succeeded in providing homes for 8,000 people (Fong 1986, p. 5; Fong and Yeh 1987, p. 19). Despite the enormous unmet housing needs of the poor, the government failed to intervene. However, the government gave housing assistance to the lower-middle and middle income households through the Housing Society, no matter how small and indirect this assistance was. The Rawlsian conception of justice requires that social and economic inequalities are to be arranged so that there is greatest benefit to the least advantaged. The aiding of the middle income households through the Housing Society in the early 1950s represented a form of injustice according to the Rawlsian concept, since it benefited those with middle income rather than the least advantaged, namely, the poor. To assist the lower-middle and the middle income households, while neglecting the greater housing needs of the poor, represents a form of injustice in Rawlsian sense. This may be regarded as a kind of vertical inequity, giving more assistance to middle income people, while giving none to the poor.

It may be argued that the government just could not handle the housing situation after the post-war years because of limited resources, thus should be excused from being criticized as unjust in the Marxian and Rawlsian sense. Yet, the fact that it could finance the setting of the housing agencies in the early 1950s to assist the middle-income families showed that the government could take some action, however limited it might be, to alleviate the plight of those in sub-standard housing to a certain extent. There was a lack of government motivations (both economic and political) rather than a total governmental incapability to do so. Rehousing the refugees in the light of justice was simply not the government's priority.

The government's handling of housing prior to 1954 can thus be considered unjust according to Marxian and Rawlsian conception of justice, judging from the consequences of housing policies rather than the intention on the part of the policy-makers. That is, it was considered to be unjust by the Western conceptions of justice. However, the majority of the Hong Kong population were Chinese in the post-war period, being influenced by Confucianism and Taosim. Can Hong Kong governmental omission and commission in the housing arena be considered just by the Confucian conception of justice? In a Confucian society, it is just to turn to one's family for assistance in case of need. The social network within a village forms the second tier of help, with governmental assistance serving as the last resort. Though many people in Hong Kong in the post-war years were living in sub-standard housing, they tended to solve their housing problem within the family. For example, they lived in a relative's home after first arriving from China, and the whole family tolerated substandard living conditions rather than pressuring the colonial government to provide housing for them. The Taoists advocate a laissez-faire and minimal government. Both the Confucian and Taoist mentality, on the part of the Hong Kong's people, facilitated the non-interventionist governmental approach to housing during this period. Thus, the government inaction to improve the housing plight of the people was considered just or at least not unjust — according to Chinese conception of justice. Government housing assistance was considered as the last resort and an additional gift, rather than as a right in the eyes of the Chinese. In short, there was a clash between the Western (namely, Marxian and Rawlsian) conceptions of justice and the Chinese conception of justice.

In addition to being Confucian, post-war Hong Kong society was also a refugee society with a "refugee mentality" (Chan 1999). People in Hong Kong in the post-war years would be satisfied since they had a "roof over their head", despite the appalling condition of this roof (ibid.). They could tolerate poor living conditions in tenements and squatter areas, and even felt unreasonably contented. Therefore, they did not exert pressure on the government to improve their plight and the government was not compelled to act in any way to remedy it in order to maintain political legitimacy (Chan 1999, p. 177). People did not expect intervention on the part of the government to give assistance. Thus, the Hong Kong's people did not considered the government inaction as unjust.

A laissez-faire approach characterized Hong Kong's housing policy from its establishment as a British colony until 1954. There had not been a great problem of injustice since Hong Kong's population was small and mobile. However, with the great influx of immigrants from China in the post-war period, especially after the communist takeover in China, the housing problem was exacerbated. The government did not, however, alter its non-intervention housing approach. This governmental inaction led to gross housing injustices according to Marxian conception of justice. Yet the non-intervention policy was facilitated by the interplay of demographic and economic factors, together with the Confucian as well as the Taoist conception of justice (held by the general people). Thus, there was no great pressure for the government to alter its minimal interventionist approach to housing provision in Hong Kong.

Hybrid of Marxian and Chinese Conception of Justice (1954–1972)

This period lasted between 1954 and 1972. On Christmas Eve 1953, there was a great squatter fire in Shek Kip Mei, and 53,000 victims became homeless (Fong 1986, p. 16; Fong and Yeh 1987, p. 19; Chan 1999, p. 177). Had the government not acted to assist fire victims, there was a possibility of riots which would have threatened political and social stability. Thus, the government intervened at last, but for political reasons rather than out of concern for social justice. The government could have intervened by providing assistance in cash rather than in kind. Why did the government choose to rehouse the fire victims? The primary reason was economic. According to the Commissioner for Resettlement, the relief cost for fire victims amounted to about $50,000 per day, while it was estimated that a six storey resettlement block could be built for the equivalent amount spent every fortnight on direct relief subsidies (Drakakis-Smith 1979, p. 44). Therefore, the government decided to provide homes for the fire victims. The colonial government intervened by directly providing housing to the homeless for economically and politically expedient reasons rather than out of any desire to serve justice for its own sake, though the resultant action concurred with the Marxian conception of justice through the satisfaction of needs. The provision of aid and housing to homeless fire victims was also considered just according to the Confucian conception of justice, which emphasizes government assistance as a last resort. As the result of the disaster, an entire family would be left homeless, and thus unable to provide support to its members. In such a desperate situation, the government provided assistance as a last resort. According to the Confucians, a benevolent government should reduce the suffering of its people, especially in times of a disaster. Taoist political philosophy also underscores a regime's responsibility to "fill the bellies" of its people, implying that the government needs to keep the basic needs of the people satisfied. With so many people left homeless after the fire, the imminent housing needs of the fire victims, necessitated a governmental response. The convergence of demands from both Western (Marxian) and Chinese conception of justice necessitated intervention, on the part of the government, to relieve the plight of the fire victims. Thus, the government's first intervention into the housing market concurred *partially* with social justice in the Marxian sense — "to each according to his need" — and the Chinese sense.

The Resettlement Department was established in 1954. Squatters were extensively resettled. Government intervention could have stopped after rehousing the fire victims of the 1953 fire, so why did the colonial authorities continue to resettle squatters who had not lost their homes in the fire? Was it implemented out of a concern for social justice? That is, people living in squatter huts were living in substandard housing, representing an unsatisfied housing need. The government resettled the squatters in permanent housing in order to satisfy their housing needs, thereby indirectly satisfying the Marxian conception of justice as a result. The squatters' plight was serious, representing great housing needs. According to Golger (1972), their temporary structures were built from any materials that they could get with ease, from tin sheeting to wooden boards. There was no sanitation and seldom any organized system of refuse collection. There was no water supply immediately available; often, water was collected from public standpipes, or from polluted streams. Because of the scarcity of land, the huts were often built densely, without fresh air and light. Also, some dwellings were extremely overcrowded. There was a continuous threat of destruction of these squatter huts by natural disasters like typhoons and fires. Re-housing the squatters seemed to be an imminent requirement of justice.

There were many reasons behind squatter resettlement. According to the Department of Resettlement (1954):

> Squatters are not resettled simply because they need, or necessarily because they deserve, hygienic and fireproof homes; they are resettled because the community can no longer afford to carry the fire risk, health risk and threat to public order and public prestige which the squatter areas present, and because the community needs the land on which they are in illegal occupation. And the land is needed urgently. (quoted in Lai, 1994, pp. 190–191)

From this, we may conclude that the squatters were resettled more out of concern of the interest of the community as a whole than that of the squatters for its own sake. According to Hopkins (1969), there were three explicit objectives of the Resettlement programme. Firstly, to free land illegally occupied by squatters. Secondly, to eliminate the risk of squatter fires. Fires led to high costs in welfare relief and risk of political disorder. Thirdly, to eradicate the colony of dilapidated huts which spoilt its image, and led to doubts about the rule of the government (pp. 2–3). No doubt, the concern for social justice in the Marxian sense (satisfying the principle of needs) was in the mind of some government officials.

With so many reasons underlying the squatter resettlement in the 1950s and 1960s, which was/were the prime factor(s)? If the resettlement programme was primarily implemented for the reasons of achieving social justice in the Marxian sense, reducing fire risk or improving the image of the government, then the government should aim at resettling all squatters, regardless of the developmental value of the site they were occupying. All squatters had the same housing needs, faced the same fire risks and gave a negative image to the government; they should all be rehoused if the problems were to be solved. However, only squatters occupying land urgently needed for planned development were resettled. Those occupying hilly slopes and land with little developmental value were left neglected (Dwyer 1970, p. 610; Hopkins 1971, p. 293; Hopkins 1969, p. 8; Chan 1999, p. 178). Thus, this suggests that the resettlement programme was pursued primarily for the economic reason of freeing land for development. According to Bray (1991), a retired Secretary for Home Affairs, "the resettlement programme of the nineteen-fifties was not a housing for the poor. It was a means to clear land for development. You could not apply for a resettlement flat. You were offered one if your hut was about to be pulled down" (quoted in Lau 1997, p. 111).

One may argue that if government intervention rested primarily on the economic reason of acquiring land for redevelopment, then squatter clearance would be enough. There was virtually no need to resettle the squatters in resettlement estates. In fact, there was a political dimension to squatter resettlement. "Squatter resettlement and not just squatter clearance [was] best explained by the limitations upon the state's autonomy by the potential for squatter resistance and the risk of destabilization which might result, given the capacity for intervention of another interested state, the People's Republic of China" (Smart 1989, p. 194). Thus, squatter resettlement was politically expedient. It should be noted that compensating the squatters whose homes have been demolished through resettlement may be considered just in the Nozickian sense (which stresses voluntary transfer) since the resettlement of squatters facilitated the voluntary and peaceful handover of their homes to the government.

Because squatter resettlement was driven primarily by economic reasons, supported by political factors rather than Marxian conception of social justice, the housing needs of only some squatters (namely those occupying land for development) were met. Others, especially those occupying hilly slopes of little developmental value, were not resettled. One may say that as a consequence there was a form of injustice towards those not being re-housed in accordance with Aristotle's formal principle of justice — treating equals equally. Not all squatters were treated fairly in the same way, depending on the developmental value of the site they were occupying. This programme thus represented a kind of horizontal inequity.

When a piece of land was needed for development, all the squatters were resettled on estates without means testing (Dwyer 1971, p. 46; Dwyer 1970, pp. 610, 612; Wong and Liu 1988, p. 2). It should be emphasized, however, that not all squatters were poor, despite the shattered appearance of their dwellings. According to a 1968 survey, 17% of the squatter households had incomes above $700 per month, positioning them approximately on the lower sectors of the middle class (Hopkins 1972, p. 205). Rehousing all squatters occupying land needed for development without a means-test contravened Aristotle's formal rule of justice, in that it treated unequals equally. Those "better-off" squatters ought not to have been offered housing subsidies in the form of subsidized rents on resettlement estates if social justice rather than acquisition of land needed for development had been the primary reason for squatter resettlement. In order to prevent opposition to squatter clearance, the government resettled all squatters, rich and poor without means-test, treating unequals equally, resulting in a form of injustice in the Aristotelian sense.

Did the resettled ex-squatters really have their housing needs satisfied after moving to resettlement estates, thereby genuinely satisfying the requirements of Marxian theory of justice? This appears far from being true. The initial resettlement estates were of extremely low standard. "[T]here is evidence that many rehoused families experience[d] more mental and physical discomfort after relocation than in their original accommodation" (Drakakis-Smith 1979, p. 10) In the resettlement estates, "each adult was allocated 2.2 m^2 of usable floor space, while children under the age of ten were allocated half that area. The resettlement blocks were in the form of six or seven-storey H-shaped blocks with communal washing and toilet facilities. Each unit was essentially a single room of 11 m^2, with units arranged back to back with access from external corridors. There was no provision of kitchen facilities, and cooking was usually done in the external corridor" (Fong 1986, p. 6). Thus, resettling the squatters, in fact, meant moving them from temporary inadequate housing to permanent inadequate housing, itself overcrowded and poorly maintained and managed. It was far from true that the housing needs of the resettled ex-squatters were satisfied. It can be said that resettlement only gave the sham appearance of justice (in the Marxian sense), rather than genuine justice. There was only a superficial satisfaction of the requirements of justice as a result, since justice was not consciously pursued by the policy-makers.

The rent for the resettlement accommodation was fixed at a very low level for all ex-squatters without discrimination, charging $10 per month for a room of 120 ft^2 (about 11 m^2). The rent stayed fixed at this level until 1965. The charging of low rents reflected the government's assumption that the squatters were poor. Cheap rents were an influential tactic used by the government to persuade the squatters to move from their homes, which were often more spacious and convenient for work, without leading to serious disorder (Hopkins 1969, p. 3). Charging uniformly low rent for all ex-squatters violated Aristotle's formal principle of justice ("treating equals equally, treating unequals unequally"); the just requirement that those who are poorer should receive more subsidies from the government and pay lower rent, while those better-off should receive less subsidies by paying higher rent. Charging the same rent for all resettlement estate households meant subsidizing all families equally, and thereby treating unequals equally and causing injustice as a consequence.

Government intervention mainly took the form of squatter resettlement, neglecting those poor people who lived in the slums in private tenement slums (Keung 1981, p. 6), many of whom suffered worse living conditions than those living in squatter areas (Drakakis-Smith 1972, p. 158; Drakakis-Smith 1970, p. 115; Hopkins 1972, p. 204; Golger 1972, p. 33). An official statement in 1963 about the conditions in post-war private buildings highlighted the problem:

> The people in these buildings may well present a more serious health hazard, and bring up their children mentally, socially, and physically more handicapped or stunted than if they had been in controlled or even uncontrolled squatter shacks on the hillsides. (quoted by Goodstadt 1969, p. 281)

The tenement flats were usually overcrowded, containing two or three times as many as the space was designed to shelter. Filth, vermin, lack of light and fresh air were prevalent in most buildings. With rooms being sub-divided into cubicles, many occupants did not have light or ventilation (Goodstadt 1969, p. 281). According to Hopkins' 1968 survey in one of the districts of private tenements done, 22% of households lived in less than 16 ft^2 (1.48 m^2) per person, while 48% were living at below 24 ft^2 (2.22 m^2) per person, and shared toilet facilities with other households

(Hopkins 1972, p. 210). According to Hopkins (1972), while it was true that the most prosperous people lived in private tenements, it was also true that the poorest also lived in such places. In fact, many more poor people lived in private tenements than in squatter areas (p. 205).

Although the poorest people lived in the worst living conditions in private tenements, the government failed to help them. The government, thus, indirectly violated the Marxian conception of justice, with the housing needs of the poorest people left unsatisfied. This also violated the Rawlsian concept of justice: government inaction brought no benefit to the most disadvantaged, namely, to the poorest people living in private tenements. The government concentrated its effort on the squatter problem, while ignoring overcrowding in private tenements, because the squatters' shacks presented a more obvious blight. Focusing only on squatter resettlement gave the façade of justice, giving the superficial impression that the government was satisfying the housing needs of the people. This arose from the fact the primary motivation behind governmental housing intervention in the 1950s was not social justice, but from economic and political concerns. If the prime concern was social justice (in the Marxian sense), the government would have tackled the slum problem as well as the squatter problem alike, since both squatters and private tenants had housing needs which necessitated government assistance.

The government's neglect of the housing plight of those living in squatter areas of little or no developmental value and in private slums through official resettlement policies in this period was facilitated by the Confucian and the Taoist concepts of justice. The Chinese people of Hong Kong, mostly embracing Confucian and Taoist values, had low expectations of the government in providing a solution to their housing plight. Therefore, they did not consider the government's neglect of their housing needs as unjust in the Confucian sense, which emphasizes the family as the prime provider of welfare instead of the government. The Taoist assertion of the *wu-wei* mentality, without any conception of assertion of one's rights by artificial and non-spontaneous action, further enhanced this governmental omission. Those squatters fortunate enough to be resettled by the government in resettlement estates (because the government wanted to clear their home for development) were grateful to the government for resettling them, as they did not expect any government assistance, though their housing plight in the resettlement estates was as serious as before, if not even more serious. Thus, resettlement policy in this period saw a superficial implementation of the Marxian conception of justice (according to need), facilitated by the Chinese conception of justice, demonstrating a hybrid of the two. Hong Kong's majority Chinese population never exerted pressure on the government to better implement the Marxian conception of justice, which would have required the rehousing of all squatters and slum dwellers into adequate housing.

In 1961, the government introduced the Government Low Cost Housing Programme. The government at last provided a public housing service with an explicit objective of serving the poor, satisfying their housing needs. This was in line with the Marxian and Rawlsian conceptions of justice, as the government satisfied the housing needs of the poor and the most disadvantaged. Those households, with monthly income of less than $500, living in substandard or overcrowded conditions were eligible to apply for Government Low Cost Housing (Yu 1997, p. 540). This housing programme was relatively small scale when compared to the resettlement programme. In 1964, the ratio of resettlement housing to Government Low Cost housing available to poor inhabitants of private tenements was 17:1 (Hopkins 1972, p. 204). In reality, the Government Low-Cost Housing did not primarily serve the poor. Instead, a large proportion of applicants came from the upper working class and lower-middle class. Hopkins' 1968 survey indicated that 47% of tenants in Government Low Cost Housing had household incomes above the upper limit (at allocation) of $500 per month and that one-fifth were white-collar workers. According to him (1972), this was possible because of the administrative procedure of counting one-half of dependents' income when calculating the household income of applicants. Thus, there was a social bias towards better-off applicants (p. 211). Therefore, the government was not sincere in providing housing assistance to the poor, with a superficial implementation of social justice in the Marxian sense.

In conclusion, the colonial intervention in the housing market was triggered partially by social justice (in the Marxian and Chinese sense) and sustained primarily by the economic end of clearing land for development. The poor conditions on resettlement estates and the constant neglect of the plight of those poor people living in private slums represented a superficial or sham implementation of Marxian conception of justice, satisfying the housing needs of some half-heartedly. This was facilitated by the Chinese values embraced by the people of Hong Kong. Housing policy in this period may be regarded as a hybrid of Marxian and Chinese conception of justice.

Marxian Conception of Social Justice in Housing as a Means to Political and Economic Ends (1973–1986)

This period started in 1973, when the government launched the Ten-Year Housing Programme, and lasted until mid-1980s. Despite nearly two decades of government intervention in housing, housing problems remained acute. In 1972, about 300,000 people still lived in squatter huts or temporary housing. There was overcrowding on resettlement estates, with no separate wash places and toilet facilities. Another 310,000 people lived in non-self-contained homes in shared private flats and tenements and paid unaffordable rents to private landlords (Hong Kong Government 1972[3]). In short, many people in Hong Kong had great unsatisfied housing needs in 1972.

In 1972, the new Governor, Sir Murray MacLehose, announced the Ten-Year Housing Programme in order to tackle the slum and squatter problem, as well as the overcrowding on resettlement estates. The target was to house 1.8 million people in permanent self-contained units with good facilities and a satisfactory environment as well as living conditions within ten years at a standard area of 3.3 m^2 per person. The Programme planned for the construction of 400,000 public housing units within ten years, with an average of building 40,000 units per year. The Housing Authority was restructured in 1973 under the New Housing Ordinance and was responsible for policy formulation, while the Housing Department would serve as its executive arm, implementing and managing the housing programmes (Fong 1986, p. 12; Fong and Yeh 1987, p. 22).

According to Keung (1981), a significant feature of the Ten-Year Housing Programme was the emphasis on quality. This marked a major divergence from the previous policy of housing as many, as quickly, as cheaply as possible in low quality public housing. In the new programme, emphasis was put on quality, incorporating the refurbishment of all the oldest resettlement estates, and the construction of high quality public housing units for rent or for sale. The programme also called for design improvements and better management. The new public housing units were self-contained, with individual kitchens, toilets and balconies. Facilities such as air-conditioned shopping complexes, gas pipes, and communal antenna were provided (pp. 17, 19).

The Ten-Year Housing Programme required substantial land for the construction of public housing. This called for the development of new towns in the New Territories — Tsuen Wan, Tsing Yi, Kwai Chung,

Sha Tin and Castle Peak (Fong and Yeh 1987, p. 22). In 1976, the Ten-Year Housing Programme was expanded to include the Home-Ownership Scheme which sold public housing units at discount prices to lower-middle and middle income families. The Private Sector Participation Scheme[4] introduced in 1978 also served a similar purpose (Fong and Yeh 1987, p. 22).

In 1980, however, the government announced the failure of the Ten-Year Housing Programme. From 1973–74 to 1980–81, the government only built 119,177 units, housing 713,935 people, achieving less than 40% of the intended target (Chan 1999, p. 179). The decrease in government expenditure as a result of the recession following the oil crisis in 1973–4 delayed the building of public housing. Also, the overheating of the construction industry in 1979 led to a slow down of public housing production. To make the situation even worse, the inflow of immigrants made it necessary to postpone the hopes for a better-housed population (Hong Kong Government 1981[5]; Fong and Yeh 1987, p. 23). "To sum up, the objective of meeting housing needs within the ten-year period of the plan [was] nothing but over-ambitious, highly unrealistic and, at best rhetorical" (Keung 1981, p. 17).

The Ten-Year Plan aimed to house those living in substandard housing in self-contained adequate housing. This scheme was in line with the Marxian conception of justice, distributing public housing according to need. This was also considered just in the Rawlsian sense of the word, with the interest of the least advantaged (the inadequately housed) being addressed. Housing policy in this period largely concurred with Western concepts of justice, namely the Marxian and the Rawlsian. With the government providing public housing on such a large scale to the Hong Kong people, state intervention in the housing sector was considerable. The Home-Ownership Scheme introduced in 1976 had the effect of extending housing subsidies to assist the lower-middle and the middle class in achieving home-ownership. Such extensive governmental housing assistance went beyond the demands made by the Confucian conception of justice, which only necessitates limited governmental provision of welfare as a last resort, as after natural disasters. Such provisions also went beyond the Taoist conception of justice, which requires a small government that merely satisfies the basic needs, rather than the desires, of the people. Home-ownership, as opposed to basic (often rental) accommodation, was obviously a desire, rather a necessity, whose satisfaction went beyond the requirements of the Taoist conception of justice. Thus, housing policy from 1972 onwards was influenced predominantly by Western concepts of justice, with little or no influence from Chinese political philosophy.

However, the resulting social justice (in the Marxian and Rawlsian sense) in housing was not considered by the government as an end by itself, but as a means to further political and economic ends. The riots in 1966 and 1967 gave a strong warning to the government. According to Scott (1989), these riots made the government realize that it could only ensure political legitimacy and social stability either by its representativeness (established through elections) or by improving the material conditions of the populace (Wilding 1996, p. 14). After the riots, the government prioritized public housing development in order to maintain social stability and bolster political legitimacy (Castells, Goh and Kwok 1990, p. 149). According to Yu (1997),

> Public housing services contributed to the maintenance of political stability. In general, there are two ways a ruler can gain legitimacy. This first is to obey some formal principles such as to pass the test of general elections or to obey the constitution. The second is to improve the social and economic conditions of the ruled. The Hong Kong government is a colonial government. As it cannot rely on the first method to gain legitimacy, it largely relies on the second one to increase its political acceptability. One of its main tools is housing services. The Hong Kong Government was confronted with serious riots in 1966 and 1967. Since it felt that its rule had been threatened, it tried to appease the public by improving their economic and social lives (Youngson, 1982). The Governor in his 1973 opening address to the Legislative Council identified education, medical care, housing and social welfare as the four pillars of society. Behind this description lay the Governor's expectation that housing services could help to build a sense of community and greater social integration among Hong Kong's people. (Yu 1997, p. 543)

The political factors at play behind the colonial government's push to achieve housing justice in the early 1970s was further confirmed in Governor MacLehose's 1972 speech to the Legislative Council announcing the Ten-Year Housing Programme. MacLehose concluded, "The inadequacy and scarcity of housing and all that this implies, and the harsh situations that result from it, is one of the major and most constant sources of friction and unhappiness between the government and the population. It offends alike our humanity, our civic pride and our political sense" (Hong Kong Government 1972)[6].

Housing justice (in the Marxian and Rawlsian sense) also served as a means not just to further political ends, but also to further economic ends. According to Chan (1999), in the 1970s, industrialization accelerated in Hong Kong. Besides relying on the large pool of highly-skilled, cheap labour; high quality products; and efficient production methods were needed to increase the colony's competitiveness in international markets. Thus, the economy required a stable, high quality and skilled labour force. To improve the social services such as housing, education, became a priority in the 1970s (Chan 1999, p. 180). The provision of public housing to the working class, the period's most important group for industrialization, enabled a supply of cheap, stable and high-quality labour to drive rapid economic development. Providing public housing to the working class in the 1970s was just in accordance with Aristotelian conception of justice, which calls for the distribution according to merit or desert. The working class made a great contribution to industrialization in the 1970s. Public housing was distributed to them according to merit, namely, their effort towards industrialization.

Public rental housing after 1973 was allocated to two categories of households. The first category was comprised of waiting list applicants, whose income fell below an income limit, and who owned no housing. The second category was those who had lost their homes through fire or other hazards, or through squatter clearance or urban renewal. They were not subjected to any income scrutiny (Yeh 1990, p. 447; Li and Yu 1990, p. 108; Lau 1997, p. 100). According to Lau (1997), between 1974 and 1994, 623,000 public rental housing units were allocated to eligible households and 52% were not required to go through the income means-test at the point of entry. Thus, it was reasonable to expect that some of them were from higher income groups, who might sometimes hold sizeable assets. The remaining 48% were from the waiting list who had undergone means-test scrutiny and proven that they were from the low-income group (Lau 1997, p. 100). Requiring some public housing tenants to go through means-test at allocation, while others were not required to do so violated the Aristotelian formal principle of justice — treating equals equally.

According to the 1990 Census and Statistics Department Study, 62% of households admitted into public rental housing had incomes over the limits fixed for those on the waiting list. A quarter of these households had incomes exceeding two or three times the waiting list income limit (Lau 1997, p. 101). By the Marxian and Rawlsian concepts of justice, these well-off households should not have been allocated public rental housing because they could satisfy their housing need themselves. These well-off households were mainly those rehoused because of government clearance or redevelopment projects. They were allocated public rental housing without going through a means-test so as to facilitate the smooth operation of squatter clearance, thereby freeing for economic development valuable land occupied by squatters (Keung 1985, quoted by Lau 1997). According to Lau (1997), "[p]ublic housing allocation policy [was] regarded as a tool to aid economic development". The allocation of public rental housing in Hong Kong was not purely based on the just motive (in the Marxian and Rawlsian sense) of meeting the need to house the poor.

The allocation of public rental housing to waiting list households was largely based on time spent on the waiting list, that is, on a first-come-first-serve basis. This established a kind of procedural justice, as stressed by Hayek, as opposed to justice in results. Marx and Rawls stressed resultant distribution according to need. In line with their conceptions of justice, there should be a points system measuring the degree of overcrowding, availability of amenities, and general environment, to assess the applicants' degree of housing need. It would be more just to allocate rental units to those with the greatest housing need first, regardless of how long they have been on the waiting list. According to Rawls and Marx, the allocation of public rental units by the government based on the length of waiting time, rather than the degree of housing need, was not very just.

In this period, "once a prospective tenant [was] allocated a public housing flat, lifelong tenure was guaranteed. Even if, later on, the household's income increase[d] and exceed[ed] the income limits, the household [did] not have to fear eviction or pay higher rentals" (Li and Yu 1990, p. 110). This created an unjust housing subsidies for well-off public housing tenants, occupying housing units which could be allocated to those more in need on the waiting list. This led to an unjust situation in which the already well-off were subsidized in public housing rather than the poor and needy living in inadequate private housing. This outcome contravened the just principle of needs in the Marxian and Rawlsian sense. In addition, "the right of tenure [of public rental housing] was hereditary, even though the next generation [could] be many times better off than the present one" (Hong Kong's housing Authority 1984, p. 1; quoted by Li and Yu 1990, p. 110). This hereditary right of tenure of public rental housing prevented the housing units of deceased tenants being allocated to more needy households on the waiting list. This indirectly caused another form of injustice (in accordance with Marx's and Rawls' principle of justice) as housing units were not re-allocated according to the just principle of needs.

In addition to the provision of public rental housing, the government built flats for sale to middle income families through the Home-Ownership Scheme. By paying a discount price and agreeing to the resale limitations, the Home-Ownership Scheme flat-owners gained property rights over their own flat. This transfer of property right was voluntary and by consent, satisfying Hume's and Nozick's requirement of justice. Because demand exceeded supply, Home-Ownership Scheme flats were allocated by ballot. This coincidentally established a form of procedural justice, as stressed by Hayek's concept of justice, which emphasizes justice in the process rather than the result.

The Home-Ownership Scheme flats were sold to public housing tenants (green-form applicants) without means-testing and lower-middle and middle income households living in private housing (white-form applicants) subject to income scrutiny. Moreover, green-form applicants were not prohibited from owning private domestic property. They were also given priority in the unit selection process. The green-form applicants had to return their rental unit upon the purchase of a Home-Ownership Scheme flat. The Home-Ownership Scheme could be regarded as unjust as it was biased in favour of green-form applicants, violating Aristotle's formal principle of justice of treating equals unequally. The white-form applicants were subjected to income scrutiny, while the green-form applicants, no matter how well-off, could continue to accept subsidies from the government. This strategy was pursued to recover more public rental units occupied by green-form applicants upon their purchase of Home-Ownership Scheme flats for re-allocation to waiting list households.

Moreover, the ratio of white-form to green-form applicants was higher than 2:1. However, despite the difference in the number between green-form and white-form applicants, the government usually adopted a 50:50 quota arrangement for the two batches of applicants (Yu 1997, p. 545). Thus, the chance of buying a subsidized flat was greater for green-form applicants than the white-form applicants. This was unjust as it treated equals (Home-Ownership Scheme flat applicants) unequally by being biased towards green-form applicants, violating Aristotle's formal principle of justice. "This shows that the Home Ownership Scheme ... was geared more towards regaining public rental units from the Green Form Applicants than solving the housing problems of White Form Applicants" (Yu 1997, p. 545).

With the launching of the Home-Ownership Scheme, the government introduced an assisted home-ownership programme. The desire for home-ownership represented a tenure preference, rather than a housing need. The government's effort to assist home-ownership in view of the great number of households living in inadequate housing (as represented by the long waiting list and waiting time for public rental housing[7]) indirectly led to some form of injustice (in the Marxian and Rawlsian sense), as the housing needs of many were left unsatisfied. In short, the just principle of need was secondary to the satisfaction of the superfluous desire for home-ownership on the part of the lower-middle and the middle class.

To conclude, there was an attempt to implement social justice (in the Marxian and Rawlsian sense) in public housing schemes from 1973 into the mid-1980s. The influence of the Chinese conception of justice was minimal. However, social justice (in the Marxian and Rawlsian sense) was pursued as a means to further political and economic ends. Because it was not pursued as an end in itself, social justice was often compromised and instances of injustice occurred.

Conflicts Between Marxian Conception of Justice and Home-Ownership Promotion (1987–2002)

The development of justice in Hong Kong's housing policy entered a new phase in 1987 with the promulgation of the Long-Term Housing Strategy. Further, according to Chan (1991), the Private Sector Priority Strategy was adopted. Basically, it mainly relied on private sector housing to satisfy housing demands, with a remarkable decrease in the supply of public rental housing and the belief that sales of Home-Ownership Scheme would prevail over the development of public housing policy (p. 181). The promotion of home-ownership became a clear and overt aim of the government's housing policy.

According to Chan (1999), from the mid-1980s the government adopted a private sector led housing strategy. When it became obvious that British colonial rule over Hong Kong would end in 1997, with sovereignty transferred back to China, the colonial government was disinclined to extend its public services in general, with public housing included. As a result, the government primarily relied on the private sector to satisfy the housing demands of Hong Kong's people from the mid-1980s onwards (p. 182). This was also in line with the trend of privatization.

Chan (1999) points out that meanwhile Hong Kong's economy was restructuring, with factories moving northward to China in the 1980s after the implementation of China's Open Door Policy in China. Hong Kong's economy reverted back to mainly rest on entrepôt trade, and the importance of having a stable, efficient and cheap labour supply diminished. Accordingly, the importance of public rental housing as a stabilizing force for labour supply also dwindled. In addition, in light of the fact that the income of Hong Kong's people increased as the economy continued to develop, expectations on home-ownership also increased (pp. 182–183).

The spirit of the 1987 Long-Term Housing Strategy continued even after the transfer of sovereignty in 1997. The 1998 White Paper on Long-Term Housing may be regarded as a continuation of its predecessor. In his first Policy Address in October 1997, the Chief Executive pledged to build at least 85,000 flats a year in the public and private sector; to achieve a home-ownership rate of 70% by 2007; and to reduce the waiting time for public rental housing to three years by 2005 (Hong Kong SAR government 1997 and 1998[8]).

According to the government, home-ownership would bring about greater family cohesion, deepen commitment to Hong Kong and reinforce individual responsibility (Hong Kong Government 1990[9]). Also, it would foster social stability, a sense of belonging and help families provide for their own future financial security (Hong Kong SAR Government 1998). In addition, there was a lack of retirement protection[10] and welfare benefits in of Hong Kong. Thus, in the absence of state pension funds, Hong Kong's people had to rely on their own plans to achieve financial security. Investments in the housing sector represented the most common "retirement protection scheme" (Chan 2000).

The government provided various encouragement measures to promote home-ownership. There was increased production of Home-Ownership Scheme flats. In 1988, the government introduced the Home Purchase Loan Scheme which allowed eligible applicants and sitting public rental housing tenants interest-free loans for the purchase of private sector flats. In 1993, the government provided $2 billion for the implementation of the Sandwich Class Housing Loan Scheme to assist middle-income households (income ranged between $22,001 to $40,000) to achieve home-ownership through low interest loans. The Sandwich Class Housing Scheme was implemented in 1994 which sold public flats at 20–25% below the market price to middle income households (Wong, Yeung and

Howes 1995, p. 42). The Home Starter Loan Scheme was also launched in 1998, targeting first time home buyers with monthly household incomes below $70,000, providing low-interest loans for mortgage downpayment (Hong Kong Government 1998[11]). In late 1997, the government also started selling public rental units to sitting tenants at 12% of the market price through the Tenant Purchase Scheme. This had the effect of spreading home-ownership to lower-middle income households.

The main housing issue from the mid-1980s up till the Asian Economic Crisis was centred upon the tenant's preference to own, rather than the question of satisfying the basic need of having a basic shelter. In a survey conducted by Lee (1991) in late 1980s, 75.6% of the respondents aspired to self-owned housing, while 13.6% preferred Home-Ownership Scheme flats (p. 69). That is, an overwhelming majority preferred to own their own flats, whether private or public. In view of escalating house prices, the desire for home-ownership was even greater as investment in housing was viewed as the most effective protection against inflation. This further boosted house prices, making home-ownership unaffordable to many. Between 1986 and 1996, the prices of private housing increased nearly eight times (Chan 1999, 186). Various home-ownership assistance schemes were introduced by the government in response to the strong desire for home-ownership (Chan 1999, p. 183). The community was in favour of home-ownership, viewing government assistance towards home-ownership in a positive light and regarding such governmental moves as just. The promotion of home-ownership is thus in line with the communitarian conception of justice.

There was a clash between the Marxian conception of justice and the promotion of home-ownership in this period. It should be noted that the desire for home-ownership does not represent a housing need. If a household cannot afford home-ownership, it does not mean that they will be living in inadequate housing, as they could possibly afford adequate housing in the rental sector. Justice, in the Marxian and Rawlsian sense, emphasizing housing needs, does not require governmental effort to promote home-ownership. However, it does require the government to subsidize poor households who cannot afford decent accommodation. Thus, the promotion of home-ownership by itself is not unjust. However, if the government prioritizes promoting home-ownership above that of providing decent accommodation to the needy or before full satisfaction of the needs of the poor, a form of injustice (in the Marxian and Rawlsian sense) occurs as a result, since this leaves the just principle of needs unsatisfied. This was exactly what the Hong Kong government did in its promotion of home-ownership.

According to Chan (2000), as a strategy to promote home-ownership, the government increased the production of Home-Ownership Scheme flats, while decreasing the production of public rental housing for the poor and needy. Chan pointed out that the production of public housing (rental and home-ownership scheme units) remained at about 35,000 per year; however, as a proportion of new housing production, the public rental housing share fell from 85.9% in 1980–81 to 49.5% in 1995–96. There was a shift of emphasis from public rental housing to assisted home-ownership in the 1990s. The government was more willing to assist middle-class households, earning up to $70,000 per month to achieve home-ownership (through the Home-Starter Loan Scheme) than to assist the poor to have adequate housing. This policy represents a form of injustice in the Marxian and Rawlsian sense, as it leaves the housing need of the poor, the least advantaged, unattended. By 2000, the waiting list for public rental housing remained at 150,000 households and the applicants for public rental units had to wait an average of seven years before being allocated a rental unit (Lee 2000, p. 2). "The middle class is a class possessing human capital, which enables them to earn above average long-term income. To subsidize this class is indefensible except for political reasons" (Lai 1994, p. 207).

On the other hand, the middle class replaced the blue-collar working class in forming the backbone of the economy in the 1980s and 1990s, as Hong Kong changed from an industrial centre to a commercial and financial centre. The middle class contributed greatly to the development of the economy in this period, whereas in the 1970s, the working class was the main driving force of the economy. From the 1980s onwards, the government shifted from primarily subsidizing the working class in the form of public rental housing to assisting the middle-class to achieve home-ownership. Subsidizing home-ownership of the middle-class, while neglecting the housing needs of the poor, on the part of the government, did not represent genuine justice.

In its drive to promote home-ownership, the government commenced selling of public rental flats to sitting tenants through the Tenant Purchase Scheme. Those who could afford to buy public rental flats were tenants that were comparatively better-off than their working-class counterparts. After the purchase of a rental unit, these better-off households were "encouraged" to stay in their existing flat. This scheme prevented mobility in public rental units: those better-off were not encouraged to move out of their units, and therefore never vacated flats which would have been made available to the more needy. The selling of public units created injustices (in accordance with Marx's and Rawls' principle of justice) as the comparatively better-off (those who could afford to buy) received subsidies from the government (in the form of discounted prices) while the poor (those on the waiting list) received none. The poor households on the waiting list had to wait longer than otherwise, since the comparatively better-off public housing tenants were "encouraged" to stay in their flats through the purchase of the unit, instead of moving out of the rental flat once their financial circumstances improved. The needs of the poor were disregarded in view of the drive to achieve a higher home-ownership rate. This was contrary to the Marxian and Rawlsian just principle of needs.

The government had various loan schemes, to assist home-ownership through the purchase of flats in the private market. These included the Home Purchase Loan Scheme, the Sandwich Class Loan Scheme, and the Home Starter Loan Scheme. These initiatives boosted demand for flats in the private market, thereby giving private property developers opportunities to gain more profit than they might have otherwise (Yu 1997, p. 547). This was more unjust in the Rawlsian sense than in-kind provision of housing, as it increased concentration of wealth in the hands of a few property developers, transferring money from the government to private developers. For in-kind provision of housing, money gained through the government's sale of public flats could be re-allocated to the poor. The provision of housing loans created a greater concentration of wealth in the hand of property developers, without enabling assistance to the poor, except in the form of taxation on their profits, which was very low[12] in Hong Kong.

The extension of housing subsidies in the form of different loan schemes to the middle class involved even greater governmental intervention within the housing arena than that of the previous period. Such extensive governmental involvement contravened the Confucian concept of justice, which stressed that housing problems should primarily be solved within the family by pooling family resources, rather than through government assistance. Such an artificial interventionist approach to housing was also against the Taoist *wu-wei* mentality, which emphasizes spontaneous, non-artificial action in accordance with nature, or the Tao. The promotion of home-ownership from 1987 onwards implied putting the political objective of maintaining stability ahead of implementing the Chinese concept of justice.

As well as the strong drive to achieve a high home-ownership rate, there was another aspect of Hong Kong's housing policy after 1987: the rational allocation of public rental housing resources. This plan was in line with Marxian and Rawlsian concepts of justice; public rental housing was to be distributed to the least advantaged, namely, the poor, according to their need. Those better-off tenants, with less housing need, received less or no subsidies from the government by paying higher rent or even market rent. Under the Housing Subsidy Policy, public housing tenants who had been living in public housing for 10 years or more had to declare their household income every 2 years. If it exceeded twice the Waiting list Income Limit, they had to pay double rent. The policy was implemented by stages from 1988 onwards. This policy was fully implemented in 1992. By April 1992, about 11% of all Housing Authority households were paying double rent (Lau 1997). The Housing Subsidy Policy, also unofficially known as the "rich-household policy", was revised in 1993. From 1993 onwards, tenants concerned having household incomes between two and three times the waiting list income limit had to pay 1.5 times net rent. Those having incomes above three times the waiting list income limit were required to pay double rent (Lau 1999).

Many of the well-off public tenants also possessed private property. Two surveys in 1993 and 1995 showed that about 13% of public housing tenants owned private property (Lau 1997, p. 99). In 1997, the government introduced a new policy. Under the new policy, tenants paying double rent had to declare their assets every two years. If their households' assets exceeded 110 times the Waiting List Income Limits, they had to pay a market rent. This policy was revised in 1999 and tenants, having paid market rent for a year, were required to vacate their rental unit (Lau 2002, p. 71).

If well-off tenants had to pay higher rent, are the worst-off public housing tenants entitled to pay less rent? The Rent Assistance Scheme was introduced in 1992 to assist tenants who faced temporary financial hardships. The qualified households are granted a 50% rent reduction. With the exception of elderly households and households with disabled members, recipients of rent assistance are required to move to lower rent flats within the same district if they have been receiving rent assistance for more than 2 years. In such cases, the household concerned may receive Domestic Removal Allowance and a one-month rent-free period. Although rent reduction for poorer public rental households is in line with Marxian and Rawlsian conception of justice, the strict criteria of the scheme make it difficult for households to be eligible for assistance.

Since its introduction in 1992, only 9,280 households have benefited from the scheme. In August 2002, 4,573 households received rent assistance under the scheme, out of which 1,703 were elderly households[13]. Thus, only a few households benefit from rent assistance. Furthermore, the scheme only aims to assist households with temporary financial problems, not to ease the burden of worse-off tenants. It would be more just (in the Marxian and Rawlsian sense) if the government were to charge lower rents for poorer households, regardless of the length of assistance the household concerned had received, provided that they pass the periodical income assessment.

Another means by which the government has made more rational use of public rental housing resources was the introduction in 1998 of both income and asset means-test for *all* public housing applicants (Hong Kong Government 1998, p. 26). Before 1998, there was only an income limit as one of the eligibility criteria for public rental housing applicants. Hitherto, there was no limit on assets, except the restriction on the ownership of private property. Moreover, prior to 1998, households from categories such as clearance, compassionate and emergency rehousing, were allocated rental units without having to undergo any form of means-test. The introduction of both income and asset means-test for *all* prospective public rental housing applicants increased horizontal equity, thereby satisfying the Aristotelian formal principle of justice, treating equals equally. It also indirectly ensured that public rental housing were allocated according to needs, the Marxian conception of justice.

Another policy in line with Marxian and Rawlsian concept of justice was the cancelling in 1998 of the right of the next generation to inherit public housing tenancies from the older generation. Adult members of a family whose principal tenant and the spouse were both deceased had to undergo a means-test, covering income and net assets, before a new tenancy will be granted. Families who fail the means-tests and who still have a temporary need for housing may be allowed to stay in the public rental flat for the limited period of one year. Yet they are required to pay the market rent during their stay (Hong Kong Government 1998, p. 21). This policy ensures that the next generation who are allowed to stay in public rental housing are only those in genuine need. If not, they have to vacate their rental unit which will be re-allocated to those in more need, thereby satisfying the Marxian just principle of need.

In conclusion, there were two main aspects of development of Hong Kong's housing policy between 1987 and 2002. The first was the promotion of home-ownership; the second was the more rational use of public rental housing resources. The former represented a clash with Marxian and Confucian conceptions of justice, while the latter was in line with an implementation of Marxian and Rawlsian conceptions of justice.

Marxian Conception of Justice as a By-product (2002 onwards) — Policy Responses to the Asian Economic Crisis

After the Asian Economic Crisis in late 1997, the property market collapsed. Housing prices decreased by 60% and the problem of negative equity struck Hong Kong. According to the chief executive, the fall in property prices accounted for 60% of the problem of deflation. In response to the situation, the government introduced various short-term remedial measures in an attempt to stabilize the property market. However, the major policy changes occurred in November 2002 when the Secretary for Housing, Planning and Lands, Michael M.Y. Suen, made a speech in the Legislative Council, outlining the major housing policy changes aimed at stabilizing or slightly boosting property prices. These major policy changes were unofficially known as "Suen-Nine Measures". In an interview with Mr. Won[14], the government spokesman of housing policy, in April 2003, he highlighted the major policy changes of "Suen-Nine Measures":

> In the past, the government involvement was comparatively great. We not only granted land, at the same time, we were the greatest land supplier. We were also involved in building flats, for example, and through the Home-ownership Scheme of the Housing Authority, in selling flats to the people. The market situation has changed in recent years. After consideration, we find out that it is not appropriate for the government to continue in such a role. The main part of "Suen-nine measures" is that the government should withdraw from the role of being a developer in the private market, focusing mainly on supplying land, providing sufficient land ... The government will not control the quantity of flats. The target of providing 85,000 flats [per year] does not exist now. Another related target was the achieving 70% home-ownership rate by 2007. In the past years, we worked towards this and now the home-ownership rate is 56%. After consideration, we think that this target should be withdrawn. In public housing, we will focus on the provision of public rental housing, taking care of the low-income group in society. If they cannot afford to rent decent accommodation

> in the private market, we provide housing subsidies to them, allowing them to move into low-rent public housing, improving their living standard. We aim to maintain the average waiting time [for public rental housing] at three years. In fact, we have already achieved this ...

The main spirit of the changes in 2002 is the reduction of governmental intervention in the housing market. The most dramatic change is the abandonment of the target of achieving a higher home-ownership rate. In his speech, the Secretary of Housing, Planning and Lands pointed out, "We realize that in the current circumstances home-ownership should be a matter of personal choice and affordability. It is therefore unnecessary for the government to continue to hang on to the long term target of achieving the 70% home-ownership rate by end of 2007". He also stressed that "the thrust of Government's subsidized housing policy should be to assist low-income families which cannot afford private rental housing". This represents an end to nearly two decades of unjust policy (in the Marxian and Rawlsian sense) of putting priority on promoting home-ownership over the provision of public rental housing to the poor and needy, satisfying the just principle of needs. On the other hand, home-ownership has become less attractive to the Hong Kong community following its experience with negative equity. Investment in housing was and is no longer considered a good safeguard against inflation (as in the early 1990s) since the Asian Economic Crisis. Thus, the government's withdrawal from assisting home-ownership in 2002 was not considered unjust by the Hong Kong's people. The withdrawal of governmental intervention in the housing arena was more in line with the spirit of Chinese conception of justice, though the remaining intervention in the form of provision of public rental housing still fell beyond the demands of Confucianism and Taoism, which stress even less involvement of the government in the economy, with the former emphasizing the role that both family and the social network play in the provision of welfare.

Various measures have been implemented to further the spirit of the new policy. The government stopped all scheduled land auctions. The Application List (of land available for sale) would be suspended until the end of 2003. Thereafter, the supply of new land would only be triggered from the Application List. The production and the sale of Home-Ownership Scheme flats would cease indefinitely from 2003 onwards, except for a small number of unsold and returned flats, which would be sold to Green Form Applicants. The unjust policy (in the Marxian and Rawlsian sense) of selling of public rental housing units under the Tenant

Purchase Scheme was to be halted. The government hoped that these measures would decrease the supply and increase the demand for private property, thereby stabilizing property prices. The conversion of some of the excess Home-Ownership Scheme flats into public rental housing has also decreased the waiting time for public rental housing. The waiting list decreased from 150,000 households in 1997 to around 90,000 household in 2002. The average waiting time for public rental housing in 2002 was just under three years, down from over six years in 1997[15]. The government has pledged to keep the average waiting time for public rental housing at three years. Thus, the housing needs of the poor have been given more priority in light of the abandonment of home-ownership promotion as the housing policy of the government (Chiu, 2002, p. 161). This was in line with the Marxian and Rawlsian conceptions of justice, stressing the needs of the least advantaged. However, this just result was a by-product rather than the main focus of the government policy, which was to stabilize the property market.

Because social justice was not the main aim of the policy changes, the policy package still contained some unjust measures. The Housing Authority would continue to provide loans to help eligible families buy private property through the new Home Assistance Loan Scheme[16]. The government hoped that the housing loans would increase the demand for private property, thereby stabilizing or even boosting property prices. However, compared with a "bricks and mortar" approach, housing loans would eventually transfer money from the public purse to the private property developers, leading to an even more unfair concentration of wealth in hands of a few. This approach was comparatively less just in the Rawlsian sense.

To conclude, the government drastically changed its housing policy in 2002 to save the property market from collapsing. To bring about justice was not the focus of its policy changes. Nevertheless, just results (in the Marxian and Rawlsian sense) occurred as a by-product, with the housing needs of the poor more effectively satisfied (through a shorter waiting list and time for public rental housing), thereby satisfying the just principle of needs.

* * * * * *

We have argued that different concepts of justice have played different roles in Hong Kong's housing policy during different phases. Social justice may be pursued as one of many aims of the housing policy. Or it may be pursued as a means to further other ends. Also, it may result as a by-product. No matter how it comes about, social justice plays, or should play, a significant part in housing policy and indeed in any policy. We will analyze the views of different stakeholders (in housing policy) on justice in Hong Kong's housing policy in the coming chapter so as to throw more light on the issue concerned.

6

Justice Conceived by the Hong Kong Community

We have examined various conceptions of social justice, and the implications of equity in public policy and housing policy. In the last chapter, we also traced the historical development of fairness in the Hong Kong housing arena. We will now examine justice in Hong Kong housing policy, as conceived by different stakeholders to see if they agree or disagree with each other. We will also probe into the question of whether people who have similar stakes in housing policy share similar views on the question of justice. We will first examine the context of the interviews and the profile of the interviewees.

* * * * * *

Context and Profile

Between March and June 2003, twenty-eight interviews were undertaken in Hong Kong to evaluate the views of different stakeholders in Hong Kong housing policy on justice in housing policy. The interviews were undertaken after the collapse of the property market in 1997. Property prices had plummeted and the problem of negative equity adversely affected many property-owners. The interviewees[1] can be divided into five groups according to the stake they held in the Hong Kong housing policy. They include Group 1: four representatives or members of institutions (including two property developers, one government official and one ex-government official); Group 2: six interviewees living in private rental housing; Group 3: six home-owners living in private housing; Group 4: six interviewees living in public rental housing and Group 5: six interviewees in publicly assisted home-ownership. The interviewees were not randomly selected, but were contacted directly (through sending an invitation letter or by telephone) or through referrals by social services organizations. The interviews were conducted in Cantonese (which is the mother tongue of most Hong Kong people), except two which were conducted in English as the interviewees concerned were British nationals residing in Hong Kong.

Group 1: Representatives or Members of Institutions (RMI Group)

This group includes four interviewees. Two were government housing officials (RMI-G). Mr. Won (case 1) represented the Housing, Planning and Lands Bureau and the Housing Department for the interview. The interview was undertaken at a time when the government had stopped intervening in the housing market after introducing the "Suen-Nine Measures" in November 2002[2]. Another interviewee was a retired housing official, Mr. Chung (case 4). He was a government housing official in early to mid-1970s.

Another category of representatives or members of institutions interviewed were property developers (RMI-D). One of the interviewees was Mr. Yeung (case 2) who was Managing Director of a major property development company in Hong Kong. Another interviewee was Mr. Sung (case 3), who managed another major property development company.

Group 2: Interviewees Living in Private Rental Housing (PriRH Group)

Group 2 includes six interviewees. This group can be divided into two categories. The first category includes those renting an adequate self-contained flat in private housing (PriRH-A), while others belong to the second category, renting an inadequate, non-self-contained rooms or board-partitioned rooms in private housing (PriRH-I). Interviewees of the PriRH-A category had skilled, white-collar jobs, while those belonging to PriRH-I category took up manual, unskilled work or are unemployed and dependent on Comprehensive Social Security Assistance (CSSA)[3]. Usually, those renting inadequate housing in the private sector are waiting list households for public rental housing and three of the interviewees belonged to this category. The following is a profile of the interviewees of Group 2:

Mr. Chan (case 5), who belonged to the PriRH-A category, was aged below 40, and worked as a freelance writer for a newspaper. He lived with his wife, who was a newspaper reporter. His household income was around $25,000 per month. He rented a private housing flat for $4,300 per month, which he could afford. He has lived in his present housing for slightly more than a year and he was satisfied with his present housing and did not plan to move. Before living in his present housing, he lived in public housing, both in public rental housing and in a Home-Ownership Scheme flat:

> I have lived in public rental housing and in a Home Ownership Scheme flat. Before I lived here, I lived in a Home Ownership Scheme flat. Before that, I lived in public rental housing. Before [living in public rental housing], I lived in private housing. [In public rental housing], I was not satisfied [with the living environment] because the bathroom and the kitchen were comparatively small. The washroom was outside my flat. It was not convenient. I was satisfied with the Home-Ownership Scheme flat. As for the private housing that I lived in when I was young, I forgot about it. I was very young at that time.

Ms. Lee (case 6), belonged to the PriRH-I category, was below 40, and worked as a cleaner, earning $4,000 per month. She was a new immigrant who came to live in Hong Kong two years ago. She lived alone in Hong Kong, while her husband and children stayed in mainland China. She lived in a board-partitioned room (a common type of inadequate housing in urban Hong Kong), renting it for $1,000 per month, which she found it difficult to afford. She was not very satisfied with her present housing:

> It is quite inconvenient if you rent a place. A few households live in the flat. Sharing a toilet and kitchen is quite difficult and inconvenient. Sometimes the time of using them clashes. The flat-mates are quite easy to get along with. It would be more convenient if I lived in [a self-contained] public rental housing unit. If I am allocated public rental housing, I would like to move. If it is private rental housing, I do not want to move. It is very inconvenient to move. For some places, I cannot afford the rent. I do not have any plan to move.

Mr. Hui (case 7), belonging to PriRH-I category, aged 40–59, was unemployed, depending on CSSA. He was a speed-post messenger before being unemployed. He also has worked as a clerk. He was born in Hong Kong and lived alone at the time of interview, with family members in Singapore. He rented a room in old private housing. Though his housing was non-self-contained, he was quite satisfied with it:

> [My room] is quite O.K. Having a place for my things is O.K. Some of my things have to be put in the corridor. There are 12 households living in the flat. There is a toilet, with hot and cold water. There is air-conditioning in the corridor. We share the toilet and kitchen. Everybody uses the rice-cooker to cook in the room. The toilet and the bathroom are just next to my room. There are few occasions when I want to use [the toilet or bathroom], others also want to use them. Some of [my flat-mates] work at night; some work in the morning. They have different working time. There is little chance to meet. If I had the money, with a stable income, I would like to move to a bigger room. Now, the room is very small. I do not have any plan to move.

Ms. Kwan (case 8), also belongs to PriRH-I category, aged 40–59, was also unemployed, depending on CSSA. She was a new immigrant who came to Hong Kong seven years ago. She was a divorcee, living with her son. She rented a room in private housing:

> I am not satisfied with my present housing. There is no formal kitchen. In the sitting room, there are two toilets. The toilets are very small. The landlord, in order to gain more money, changed the kitchen into a room for renting. On the surface, I am renting two rooms. In fact, I get one room and one store room for putting the refrigerator and my son's computer. One toilet was changed into a kitchen. If I use the kitchen, the chief tenant cannot use it and vice versa. It's inconvenient to share a kitchen. The toilet is not formal; it's of an old-style. The wall of the toilet does not reach the ceiling. If you defecate [in the toilet], the bad smell reaches the sitting room and the kitchen next door. I urinate in the toilet of my home. If I defecate, I like to go to a public toilet. Everything is not formal ... Before [I lived here,] I rented another room. The landlord quarreled with his wife and got a divorce. They sold the flat at a low price. Thus, I had to move. I thought I would be allocated public rental housing very soon. If I rent a formal room, they will require me to sign a two-year contract. I don't know why a two-person household has to wait so long for public rental housing. If I moved before the two-year contract ends, they will not give me back my deposit. My present landlord did not require me to sign a contract, only requiring me to pay one-month rent as deposit and pre-pay one-month's rent. I think that I will stay for half-a-year to one year. So I'm not very choosy!

Before living in her present inadequate housing, she also lived in private housing that was also scanty:

> I also rented a room [in private housing] in the past, a suite. Before this, for four years I rented a board-partitioned room in old private housing which was on the ninth floor for four years. I had pains in my leg. The Queen Elizabeth Hospital said that if I didn't move, my leg would not recover. My pain in the knee was so great that I moved to a suite. The suite was overcrowded. The water and electricity fee were very high. When I rented the old private housing on the ninth floor, my electricity bill was about $100. The water bill was shared by all flat-mates. When I moved to the suite, the water bill was up to more than $100 per month. The electricity bill went up to $300 per month, and even went as high as $400 per month in the summer. It was a great burden. The kitchen and toilet were inside the room. If someone used the toilet, you could not cook in the kitchen. It was overcrowded. When I walked out of the kitchen, there was the bed.

Mr. Ko (case 9), belonging to PriRH-I category, was aged 60 or above, and had retired ten years ago. At the time of interview, he depended on CSSA. In the past, he was a hair-dresser. He was born in China and came to live in Hong Kong forty years ago. He lived alone in Hong Kong, with family members on the Mainland. He lived in inadequate private housing, renting a board-partitioned room. However, he was satisfied with his housing, saying that "there is no problem with my present housing". He once lived in public rental housing, but has moved out of public rental housing to live in private housing.

Ms. Ngai (case 10), also belongs to PriRH-I category, was aged 60 or above, and had retired a few years ago. Before her retirement, she washed dishes in a small restaurant. At the time of the interview, she depended on CSSA. She was born in China and came to live in Hong Kong more than twenty years ago. She lived alone in Hong Kong, as her husband had died and her children were in Mainland China. She rented a room in private housing. She did not want to move to public rental housing, as she did not want to move out of Yamatei (a district in urban Hong Kong with little chance of having new public rental housing being built in future) since she was familiar with the district:

> I am satisfied with my present housing. I would not like to move. If it's far, I would not like to move. I would like to live near this [elderly] centre. I come here every day. I'd like to move within Yau Ma Tei.

On the whole, those living in inadequate private rental housing belonged to the lower stratum, needing imminent housing assistance from the government. However, not all of them would ask for government assistance. Some were satisfied with their private housing and would not like to move. There is also another category of private rental housing dwellers who could afford to rent a flat. They could afford adequate housing and belonged to the middle stratum of society.

Group 3: Home-owners Living in Private Housing (PriHO Group)

Group 3 includes six home-owners living in private housing, having achieved home-ownership without government assistance. This group of interviewees typically had managerial jobs, with a household income of $40,000 or above. Three had finished mortgage repayments, while the other three were still repaying their mortgage. One was suffering from negative equity.

Mr. Cheng (case 11), who was not yet 40 years old, was a home-owner of a private housing flat. A financial analyst, he lived with his wife, who was an accountant. His household income was about $80,000 per month — putting him squarely in the middle-income bracket. He repaid $20,000 for mortgage each month, which he could afford. He has lived in his present housing for five years and was not suffering from negative equity:

> I am satisfied with my present housing. It is convenient, with good transportation. The location is appropriate. I do not want to move. I have no plan to move.

Before living in private housing, Mr. Cheng lived in a Home-Ownership Scheme flat. Before that, he lived in public rental housing (before he got married).

Ms. Wong (case 12), aged 35, lived with her husband, two children and two domestic helpers in a private housing flat. She did administrative work at a university and her husband was involved in business, representing a Belgian group that sold fertilizers in Asia. Their monthly household income was about $90,000 to $100,000 per month. They repaid $35,000 per month for their mortgage, which they could afford. Ms. Wong moved to live in the present housing one and a half years ago and was satisfied with her present housing. Before buying this private flat, Ms. Wong and her family lived in private rental housing. Before she got married, she lived with her parents in purchased housing for government staff.

Mrs. Au (case 13), aged 40–59, was the home-owner of a private housing flat. She was a manager of the administrative department of a stock exchange company. Her husband was the facility manager of a university's campus service unit of a university. They lived with two children and a Filipino domestic helper. Their household income was above $60,000 per month; they were repaying about $10,000 as mortgage, which they could afford. They were not suffering from negative equity. Though Mrs. Au was quite at ease with their present housing, she wanted to improve their living conditions:

> I am quite satisfied with my present housing. I would give about 80 marks to it, though I do hope to have a bigger flat. Now, property prices have fallen and changing to a bigger flat would not be easy. I would like to move to a bigger flat. I had a plan to move. However, because of the economic environment, the plan came to nothing.

In the past, Mrs. Au's family had been moving to improve their housing condition because of changes in family size:

> I lived in private housing in the past, also in Heng Fa Chuen. As our family size grew, we needed a bigger flat. When we were a family of two, we lived in a smaller unit. Now that our family size has increased, we live in a bigger one.

Mrs. Chan (case 14), below 40 years old, was also a home-owner in private housing. She was a housewife, living with her husband and two children. Her husband worked as a bank manager, with a household income of $40,000. They have finished their repaying mortgage. Mrs. Chan was very satisfied with their present housing, in which she had lived for eight years. However, she once had an idea of moving:

> I am absolutely satisfied with my present housing in all aspects. I do not want to move. I planned to move, but my plan was ruled out by my husband. My husband wishes to have a snail shell. He works hard for a snail shell. I live in a 1,000 ft^2 (about 93 m^2) flat. I think that because the economy is not good, we do not need to live in such a big flat. But my husband thinks that there is no problem. He will work hard to support the family. I feel very happy that my husband is so positive. I will support him. If we really face financial problems, a 400 ft^2 (about 37 m^2) or 500 ft^2 (about 46 m^2) flat is enough for a family of four. I only ask for a 700 ft^2 (about 65 m^2) flat. It's ideal for four people to live in. We live in a 1,000 ft^2 (about 93 m^2) flat, but I only occupy half a bed.

Mrs. Chan has a history of moving from smaller to bigger flats:

> I lived in private housing. At first, we lived in a 400 ft^2 (about 37 m^2) flat, then a 800 ft^2 (about 74 m^2) flat. Now, we live in a 1,000 ft^2 (about 93 m^2) flat. Our family owned all our houses.

Mr. Ng (case 15), aged 60 or above, bought a flat in private housing. He had retired, once having owned an import and export firm. He was born in mainland China and came to live in Hong Kong 55 years ago. He lived with his daughter, who worked for the government as a lawyer. His wife was in Canada. He was content with his present housing:

> I am satisfied with my present housing. By Hong Kong standards, I am satisfied. By overseas standards, of course, it's small. My flat is about 3,000 ft^2 (about 278 m^2) . I would not like to move.

Ms. Tsang (case 16), aged 60 or above, was retired, having once been a daytime baby-sitter and a part-time domestic helper. She was born in mainland China and came to Hong Kong when the Communists took over China in 1949. She lived with her husband and two adult children in a private housing flat. She has finished repaying her mortgage. Though she was happy with her housing, she would like to move:

> I am satisfied with my present housing. I bought it because I like it. The flat was old. If I re-decorate, it would be very inconvenient. I would like to move to a new flat. The question is whether I can afford it. I have lived here for more than ten years. The flat needs renovating. Sha Tin One City flats are twenty-one years old. But I do not have any plans to move, since I don't have any money.

Ms. Tsang has a history of moving up the housing ladder:

> Before I lived here, I lived in low-rent housing provided by the Housing Society. Of course, I was not satisfied with it. If I had been satisfied, I would not have bought this flat and moved out. It was too small. I lived there for more than twenty years. When I moved in, the children were only three to four years old. When my children grew up, there was not enough space. Of course, I was not satisfied. So I bought a flat and moved. My children were grown up, how could I live there? Those [Housing Society] flats were very small. It was overcrowded. Especially[in my case], since I have a son and a daughter. They couldn't sleep together.

On the whole, the interviewees who were home-owners in private housing were satisfied with their present living arrangements, though some wanted to move. Most were engaged in managerial work, and belonged to the middle or upper-middle class. Some had moved up the housing ladder, starting from public rental housing before becoming home-owners of private housing, while others had always lived in private housing.

Group 4: Interviewees Living in Public Rental Housing (PuRH Group)

Altogether, there were six interviewees living in public rental housing. They or their family members usually took up unskilled or skilled manual work. Their household income was comparatively lower than those home-owner interviewees living in private housing. Most were satisfied or quite satisfied with their present accommodation.

Mr. Ho (case 17), below 40, was a dim-sum cook in a restaurant. He was born in Mainland China and came to live in Hong Kong twenty-one years ago. He lived with his mother, his wife and two children in a public rental housing flat. His wife had a part-time job in a fast-food shop, collecting plates and utensils. His household income was about $15,000 per month. He was quite contented with his present accommodation, yet he would have liked to move to another public housing flat:

> I am quite satisfied, though I have thought about moving. I live on a low floor. Thus, there are a lot of mosquitoes and the noise is quite serious. I applied to move. After half a year, they replied, giving me a flat on the thirty-sixth floor. I thought that it was too high. Thus, I did not accept it. I still want to move to another public housing unit. For the time being, I do not have any plan to move. I may apply to move again. I live on the first floor. There are too many mosquitoes.

Before Mr. Ho lived in public rental housing, he lived in private housing, renting a village house flat and a room:

> Before I lived in public rental housing, I lived in a flat in a village house for four years. Before this, I lived in a room in private housing with my father and my mother. At that time, I was not married. I was not satisfied with the room that I lived in. The living environment and the neighbours were not very good. There were a lot of people. It was over-crowded. We had to wait to use the kitchen and toilet. It was very

> inconvenient. For the flat in the village house, there was a toilet and a kitchen. It was satisfactory, but the rent was high. The rent was $3,500 in 1993 before I moved to public rental housing. At that time, three of the family members worked. We could afford the rent. Later, my parents retired. We applied for public rental housing. We waited for four years. I got married before I moved here. I lived with my parents after I got married. We applied for public rental housing before my parents retired.

Ms. Chan (case 18), below 40, was a housewife. She came from Mainland China seven years ago. Her husband was an electrical appliance maintenance worker, earning an unstable income of about $7,000 to $8,000 if there was sufficient work. She lived with her mother-in-law, her husband and her daughter in public rental housing. She had mixed feelings about her present housing condition:

> [I am] partially satisfied [with my present accommodation]. When compared to [housing in] the Mainland, this is far worse. [Housing on the] Mainland is bigger. My present housing may be considered quite good. Compared to those who rent [private] housing or who live in squatter huts, this is already quite good. "When compared with the better ones, this is inadequate. When compared to worse ones, this is more than sufficient". When compared to [housing] in Mainland, this is worse. There is more land on the Mainland. I cannot afford to move. If I could afford to, I think I would move. I would like to have a flat of my own, like I did on the Mainland. This is government housing. I have to pay rent. Right now, I do not plan to move.

Because her husband had an unstable income, Ms. Chan's family could barely afford the rent in public rental housing, which amounted to $1,500 per month:

> My rent is $1,500. If my husband intermittently has work, I can afford it. We save some money [when my husband has work] to be used in times when my husband does not have work. We can barely afford the rent when my husband has intermittent work. If my husband does not have work, we cannot do anything. Last year, my husband did not have work for about five months. We depended on the money saved [when my husband had work] to pay rent and other household expenditure. We can barely afford it. We must be very frugal.

Mr. Yam (case 19), aged 40–59, lived alone in a one-person public rental housing flat. He was born in China and came to live in Hong

Kong fifty years ago. He was unemployed and was depending on CSSA. His rent was $690 per month and he paid it with the CSSA monthly allowance he received. He was satisfied with his present housing. However, he would like to move to improve his living standard:

> I am satisfied with my housing. Of course, I want to move. In terms of government welfare, this is very good. I thank [the government]. My present housing is paid by CSSA. The government pays rent for me. If nothing happens, the government would allow me to stay [forever]. It is equivalent to a gift and I do not have to pay management fees. I am very grateful [to the government]. However, as for living standards, I would like to have a better living space. I do not have a sitting room. I also want to improve my living standard ... I do not have any plan to move because I do not have financial resources.

Ms. Chu (case 20), aged 40–59, was a part-time baby-sitter. She lived with her husband and two adult children in a public rental housing unit. All her family members were in paid employment. Her husband was a driver. Her son was a salesman, selling mobile phones. Her daughter was a beautician trainee. Their household income was about $20,000 per month. She was not very satisfied with her present housing and would like to move:

> My present housing is a little bit overcrowded. My son will soon move out[4], then three people will be living here. I also would like to move. My daughter always wants to have a room on her own, but she doesn't have it. She has a bed there. It depends on affordability. If I could afford to, I would want to move. I would like to move also to public rental housing, applying for a bigger rental unit.

Before Ms. Chu moved to public rental housing, she lived in a resettlement estate. She had lived in a stone-built house when she was young.

Mr. Lui (case 21), aged 60 or above, retired, lived with his wife and his children in a public rental housing flat. Before retiring, he was a low-grade civil servant in the housing department. His household income was unstable, about $15,000 to $16,000 because his family members had unstable work:

> I live with my wife and my children. I have three sons and a daughter. All [my family members] work. However, their work is unstable. One

> day, they have work to do; the other day, they don't have work to do. If they are lucky, they have more days of work than days out of it. On average, within a month, they have work for half a month. My wife has an unstable job in a restaurant. My son works in the construction site. Another son is a driver. Another son worked in a factory in mainland China in the past. However, the factory closed down. Now, he is a substitute worker in a bakery. If other workers have holidays, he works for a few days. My daughter is an accounts clerk, quite a stable job.

He has lived in his present housing for twenty-five to twenty-six years and was quite at ease with it:

> I am quite satisfied. In light of our ability to pay, I am quite contented to live in public rental housing. There is no question of not being satisfied. If you are not satisfied, you may go to live in luxurious flats. But can you afford it? There is no need to move. I have no plan to move.

Before Mr. Lui lived in public rental housing, he lived in a resettlement estate in Wong Tai Sin. Before that, he rented a stone house.

Ms. Yuen (case 22), aged 60 or above, was retired, and lived alone in a public rental housing unit. Her husband had died and her children had moved out. Before retirement, she worked in the laundry of a hotel, ironing shirts. She was born in China and came to live in Hong Kong more than sixty years ago. She was financially dependent on her children who gave her $4,000 per month, which was barely enough. She had to pay $1,405 as rent. She had to be frugal in order to pay for the rent. She was satisfied with her present accommodation and had no plan to move. Before she moved to live in public rental housing, she lived in police quarters since her husband was a policeman. Before that, she lived in a board-partitioned room which was inadequate:

> Before living here, I lived in police quarters. My husband was a policeman. Once my husband retired, we had to move out of the police quarters. Before living in police quarters, we lived in a room in old private housing. The police quarters were very good. It was very big in size. In the old private housing, it was merely a small room, very crowded. We shared the toilet and kitchen with others. There were a few rooms and bedspaces in the flat. It was a board-partitioned room. It was very inconvenient. Many people squeezed [into the kitchen] when

> cooking. We had to take turns to take a bath. For those, like me, who stayed at home taking care of children, we bathed early, allowing those who returned from work to bathe at night. We had to be considerate.

On the whole, those interviewees living in public rental housing came from the lower stratum. They were employed as manual labourers. This is the norm, as there are mean-tests for public rental housing. Most of the interviewees had lived in inadequate housing before moving to public rental housing.

Group 5: Interviewees Achieving Government-Assisted Home-ownership (GAHO Group)

There are six interviewees belonging to this group. Most interviewees had achieved home-ownership with government assistance. They had white-collar jobs, and belonged to the middle-income stratum. Some lived in government flats that had been sold (Home-Ownership Scheme flats), while others received loans from the government to buy private flats. Two out of six interviewees suffered from the problem of negative equity.

Mr. Ng (case 23), aged below 40, was engaged in office machine servicing work. He lived with his wife, who was a teacher. His monthly household income was about $50,000. He received a Sandwich Class Housing Loan from the government to buy a private flat, repaying $12,000 per month for a mortgage, which he could afford. He was quite contented with his present accommodation, but would like to move to better housing:

> I am quite satisfied with my present housing ... It is better for a person to have a target. At present, it's O.K. If I could afford [better housing], then it would be better. Things that I am not satisfied and want to improve [are]: [my flat is] on low floor, [there is] no [good] view outside the windows, no balcony and [there is] insufficient space ... ... It depends on affordability. If I could afford it, of course I would like to move. For the time being, since I cannot afford [better housing], I have no plan to move. For the time being, it's O.K. It's quite difficult to say whether it's O.K. or not. All people have a goal and want to pursue higher living standards. This is what human beings should have. I don't talk about all people. At least, this is my ideal.

Mr. Ng suffered from the problem of negative equity. He lost $600,000 to $800,000 on his housing. Before he lived in his present housing, he lived in private housing, which he had also purchased. Before that, he lived in public rental housing.

Ms. Hung (case 24), below 40, was a clerk in the Housing Department. She lived in a Home-Ownership Scheme flat with her husband, her mother-in-law, her son and an Indonesian domestic helper. Her husband was a construction work supervisor. Her household income was about $40,000 per month. She repaid about $4,000 for mortgage per month, an amount which she could afford. She was not suffering from negative equity. Ms. Hung was satisfied with her housing:

> My present housing is O.K. If I had the money, I might move. I do not have any plan to move. If I move, I would like to move to a flat with a bigger sitting room, with a better view. Now, my flat has a garden view.

Mr. Leung (case 25), below 40, was a placard producer. He lived with his wife, his son and a domestic helper in a Home-Ownership Scheme flat. His wife was a secretary. His household income was about $25,000. He repaid $1,100 for mortgage each month. He was very positive about his present accommodation:

> I am very satisfied with my present housing ... As a small employee, I have a little achievement, owning a small flat, without any problem. I have lived here for more than ten years. It's O.K. I am satisfied. For the time being, I don't think of moving. Even if my financial situation improves, I don't think it is necessary to move. I don't think that moving to a bigger flat necessarily brings about happiness in living in a flat. Happiness is communication within the family. For example, someone gives you a flat in the Mid-Levels, of more than 1,000 ft^2 (about 93 m^2). But if you go home, there is no communication within the family, there will be unhappiness. The way of living with the family members is more important than changing a flat. I don't have any plan to move.

Ms. Au (case 26) was a lecturer in her forties. She lived with her husband and her son in a private housing flat. Her husband was a civil servant, working as an engineer. Their household income reached $110,000 per month. Their family received loans for civil servants to make a down payment when buying a flat, which covered 30% of the down payment. Their mortgage repayment was about $40,000 per month, half of which was covered by housing allowance (for civil servants). Ms. Au had a history of living in private housing. She was not satisfied with her housing and would like to move if she could afford:

> I am not satisfied. I think the place is a bit small. I would like to move. However, I have no plan to move because I don't have the money. I cannot afford to repay my mortgage. But if I had enough money, I might want to move.

Ms. Au also faced the problem of negative equity:

> I face the problem of negative equity. I owe the bank about $2.8 million. The value of my flat is about $2.2 million. I bought the flat at $4.3 million. Now, it is worth about $2.2 million. I lost about 50%, even though I didn't buy at the peak level. I bought it in April 1998.

Mr. Leung (case 27), retired, lived alone in a Home-Ownership Scheme flat. Before he retired, he was an interior decoration worker. He now depended on his children financially, with his children giving him $3,000 per month. He had finished repaying his mortgage. He was satisfied with his present housing and did not want to move. Before he lived here, he had lived in public and private rental housing:

> Before moving, I lived in public rental housing in Chai Wan for 20 years. Before that, I rented a room from my friend. I was not satisfied with the public rental housing because it was overcrowded. It was even more overcrowded when I rented a room from my friend. I could not help it, since I did not earn a lot of money at that time. When I first came to Hong Kong, I did not earn enough money.

Ms. Wong (case 28), aged 60 or above, retired, once ran a kindergarten. She lived alone in a Home-Ownership Scheme flat. She received CSSA and got about $3,000 per month from the government. She had finished repaying her mortgage. She has been living in her flat for more than twenty years and was at ease with it:

> I am satisfied. I do not want to move. I am familiar with the environment. If I moved to another place, I would be unfamiliar with the neighbours. Going to this elderly centre is convenient. It's just across the street. I wouldn't want to move somewhere without an elderly centre. I don't have any plan to move.

To sum up, though the interviewees were not randomly selected, they reflected the general characteristics of the housing situation in Hong Kong. For those who were living in private housing at present, they might have received government housing subsidy in the past through living in public housing. They might have moved up the housing ladder. Even though a person might be satisfied with their present housing, they might still want to move to even better housing, reflecting a strong desire to move up the housing ladder and to improve living condition. This phenomenon applied to some of the interviewees.

Justice in Housing Policy

Is the housing policy just to different stakeholders of the Hong Kong housing policy? We will examine the views of different interviewees who held different stakes in the housing policy. It should be pointed out that justice conceived by different stakeholders may differ from justice in the normative sense, as the stakeholders may define justice to their own advantage. First, we will look at the views of Group 1 interviewees (RMI), representatives or members of institutions, including the government officials and property developers.

An Institutional Perspective

In examining justice in Hong Kong policy, the first question that one may raise is: How far does justice play in the formulation of Hong Kong housing policy? In an interview with Mr. Won (case 1: RMI-G), he pointed out that justice was one among many important principles that the government took into consideration when formulating housing policies. But because justice was not the sole principle, compromise with other principles might be made:

> Justice is undoubtedly an important principle [in decision-making]. However, justice is not the sole principle ... Justice is an important consideration. Of course, there are other considerations ... Besides justice, we have to consider other practical matters, for example, simplicity, whether it is easy to implement, and administrative costs. For example, the CSSA considers the needs of each individual household, whereas the public rental housing policy merely considers the need of a general 4-member household, setting the income limit at the general level of $14,600. From this point of view, CSSA policy is more just. However, if the government tried to achieve justice to such a level, the resources involved would definitely have to be much greater ... The great administrative cost of CSSA is well-known, much greater than

> that of our income and asset means-test [of public rental housing]. We have to strike a balance with other considerations, like whether the resources involved are rational; simple; easily comprehensible; and acceptable to society ... The administrative cost is undoubtedly an important consideration ... Efficiency is another consideration, societal views are also important, the level of acceptance of citizens, political reasons are other considerations.

Because justice was only one among many considerations in the formulation of housing policy, injustices might arise from the compromise. According to Mr. Won (case 1: RMI-G),

> We follow the principle of rational allocation of resources. We believe that this is a just principle. However, as far as the process of implementation, it is difficult to say. It is difficult to make everyone agree [that there is justice]. For example, for the "rich household" policy, we conduct means-test after the public housing tenant has lived in the public rental unit for ten years. If a 4-person household's income is two to three times the waitlist income limit, we will charge him one and a half times rent plus rates. If a 4-person household has about $40,000 as income, we charge double rent plus rates. In addition, if they have about $1 million in assets, we then ask them to move out after paying market rent for twelve months. The criterion is quite loose. The waitlist households may criticize that those public rental households are earning twice as much as they are, the government only asks them to pay a few hundred dollars and allows them to continue to stay ... No wonder we have to wait so long ... There should be a balance. Public rental housing, besides solving people's need, should play a social role, acting as a housing pump, hoping to improve the living standard of the lower stratum people ... The policy is loose by providing "carrot and stick", with Home-Ownership Scheme and loans to encourage them to vacate public rental housing to allow those in more need to move in. Those on the waiting list think that there is injustice towards them. [They may say], "those richer than us are occupying public rental housing, while we are suffering from high rents in the private market." From another point of view, we have to consider social stability. If we had a means-test every year, there would be high administrative cost and the public rental households will be disturbed to a great extent. There would be no incentive to work hard to gain money. They do not want to take up one more job because gaining more money will allow the government to take back the rental unit. There would be a lack of incentive to improve living standards. There should be a balance, not

> merely a consideration of justice. We should consider the acceptability, on the part of the people, social stability, social objectives, and political reasons.

Though the official stated that justice was an important principle in the government's formulation of the housing agenda, many people thought that the government housing policy favoured the property developers, leading to injustices. However, this was denied by the property developers. Mr. Yeung (case 2: RMI-D) believed that the government's main focus was to stimulate the economy, while benefiting property developers as a by-product:

> Property development is the main pillar of Hong Kong's economy. For the last six years, from 1997 up till now, the [prices] in the property market have decreased 50–60%. The property prices have devalued by more than half. This affects the economy. Negative equity, unemployment, weak consumption power also centres upon the sharp decrease in property prices. The government takes this problem into account. Thus, in order to revive the Hong Kong economy, one of the measures is to facilitate the healthy development of the property market. This does not imply that the government should boost the property market up to peak levels all at once, leaving most people unable to achieve home-ownership. That would be wrong. [The government] should stabilize the property market, restoring confidence in the property market, boosting their desire to buy flats, making the property market develop stably and healthily. This benefits the Hong Kong economy in the long run. The government works from the property market to revive the Hong Kong economy. This should not provoke disagreements. I do not believe that the Hong Kong government tried to boost the property market to inflate property developers' profits. The government has taken into consideration the interest of Hong Kong as a whole, not only the property market. If you reflect deeply: if property prices stabilize, of course property developers will benefit. When people have confidence in [investment in] properties, [cases of] negative equity will decrease. As consumption desire increases and stimulates consumption, the economy as a whole will benefit, including the retail industry and travel industry. [The government policy] is not to benefit only the property developers, but to benefit the Hong Kong economy as a whole.

Mr. Sung (case 3: RMI-D), however, pointed out that the government had been very socialistic in providing public housing to half of the Hong Kong population, thus, not especially favouring private developers:

Half of Hong Kong's people are housed in subsidized housing by the government. If there were an accusation of government favouring property developers, I would say that the other half of the story is that the government has been very socialistic in its housing policy. About half of Hong Kong is in subsidized housing. So they have been very even — if they have looked after the developers, they have also looked after the man in the street. There is no favouritism. They are trying to deal with both [parties]. The government does not particularly, not specially, favour property developers. Look at the Housing Authority. Look at the work they have done. There are over 2 million people in public housing. That's a lot. It's nearly half of Hong Kong's population. If only half is in private housing, government deals with it even-handedly.

Mr. Won (case 1: RMI-G), the spokesman of the present government, considered the current Hong Kong housing policy as just through the implementation of the principle of rational allocation of housing resources by taking into consideration housing need of the people:

Justice is difficult to define. It may vary from individual to individual. Some people may think that there should be justice in results. In the end, all the resources should be equally distributed. Some people may think that justice is equal opportunity. Some views may be a mixture of the two. In housing, [in relation to justice], we talk about the rational allocation of limited housing resources. This is expressed in different housing policies. For example, for public rental housing, we have a waiting list. We conduct means-tests. There are income and asset limit. If their income or asset is above the limit, we will not allocate public rental housing to them. We set the [income and asset] limit in accordance with the spirit of our policy, that is, if they cannot afford decent accommodation in the private market ... The spirit is that if you have ability to satisfy your housing need, you can afford private rental housing of a standard similar to public rental housing, you do not need government assistance. We defend this baseline.

On the other hand, the rational allocation of public rental housing resources policy is also expressed through our so-called "rich household" policy. If you are allowed to move into public rental housing, there are income and asset means-tests after a period of time, which is now set at ten years. The public rental housing household has to inform the government of their income. If their income is above certain limit, they are required to pay higher rent or are asked to move out. [The provision of] public rental housing is expensive. Public rental housing is run at a loss. We have to ensure that public assets are used appropriately, helping those in need. From this angle, [this policy] is just. Allocation [of public rental housing resources] according to need is the spirit [of our policy].

Mr. Chung (case 4: RMI-G), an ex-government housing official who worked for the government in the housing field in early to mid-1970s, considered the resettlement policy in the 1950s and 1960s as just for taking care of the basic housing need of the people:

> Now, let me answer your question about whether I consider the [resettlement] policy ... as just. The answer is definitely yes on the grounds that what was being done was an attempt to meet a basic human need, the need for shelter, which could not be met in a more satisfactory way, taking into account the vast scale of the clearances and the rehousing operations. Certainly, I have no recollections of any offer of resettlement housing being refused or any general complaint about the policy, except where the only housing available for allocation at the time was considered too remote from the applicants' normal working place. On the contrary, the desire to get into the Resettlement Department's Housing Estates was so great that whenever a fire broke out in a squatter area, hundreds of imposters would appear at the fire site claiming to be fire victims and demanding to be registered for housing.
>
> Given the huge scale of these operations, the system had to be seen to be as fair as possible to all, and by and large, I think it was. One possible complaint of injustice might lie in the fact that people allocated units in resettlement estate were not means-tested. So some of those who were allocated housing got more than they needed or deserved at the tax-payers' expense. But in the circumstances prevailing at the time, means-testing would not have been practicable or cost-effective.

Both property developer interviewees considered that the government housing policy was unjust to property developers in some aspects. Mr. Yeung (case 2: RMI-D) thought that the government competed with the property developers for profit and this was therefore unjust:

> The housing policy in the past was very confused. Policies came from many departments ... The government does not want to be unjust. However, its implementation [of policy] makes people think that it is unjust. For example, what is unjust? As for the Mass Transit Railway and the Kowloon-Canton Railway [Corporation], in order to finance [these two corporations] to build the railway, the government gave land

> to them in a good location. The two railway corporations, after getting land in a good location, built flats: how can the private property developers compete [with the railway corporations]? Their land is on a better location than mine. Their price [of flats] is lower than mine. How can I have the ability to compete? Where can there be justice? The two Railway Corporations are thus also property developers. Though the Housing Society is not a government institution, the government gives land on a good location and sells flats there at market prices, directly competing with me. How can I compete with it? This is, of course, unjust to [property developers]. If the government unites [all its housing departments], only supplying land, then the property developers would be happy. This is not to pacify the property developers, but to put the development of the property market on the right track. There should not be policy coming from many departments and the government competing directly with the property developers.

Mr. Sung (case 3: RMI-D) also thought that the government housing policy was unjust to the property developers, especially those smaller ones without a big land bank:

> At the moment, there have been no land sales at all and there was a lot of pressure for that. I don't think you need the policymakers to be quite so dramatic. The government has got many sites for sale, over a hundred. I think the application system is a perfectly sensible system. Some developers may not have a land bank. Some guys are very lucky; we have a huge land bank. So there are no land sales; that favours us. We can continue developing, but other developers can't. That seems to be wrong if you are looking for a balanced market. I think the application list system should be kept in place. So if the developer needs to replenish its land bank, he can ask the government to put a particular ... If there is a need for particular site of development or a piece of land, that developer can ask the government to put the site up and guarantee to pay a minimum price. He can continue developing. So the total ban on land sales is too dramatic and totally unnecessary. It favours those with a land bank because they can continue to work. We are not the only company with a land bank. But those developers without a land bank, what happens? Are they going to go bankrupt because they've got nothing to do? That doesn't seem right. It's just unnecessary. I don't know [whether this] is a question of justice. I would think from their point of view, they would say it is unjust.

Views of Private Tenants

After examining the views of interviewees in Group 1 (RMI), let us turn our attention to Group 2 (PriRH) which includes interviewees living in private rental housing. Did they consider that the government was just in not providing housing subsidy to them? This group of interviewees can be divided into two categories, namely, those living in adequate private rental housing (PriRH-A) and those living in inadequate accommodation (PriRH-I), such as non-self-contained private housing, board-partitioned rooms.

Mr. Chan (case 5: PriRH-A), living in a self-contained private rental housing flat considered the non-provision of housing subsidy to him as just since he was not in need:

> I haven't thought of this. A ... [The non-provision of housing assistance, on the part of the government] can be considered rather appropriate ... because the government should provide assistance to those in more imminent need. Right now, I do not have an imminent [housing] need. I think it's just for the time being.

The other interviewees belonging to this group lived in inadequate private rental housing. Three out of five in this category considered the government housing policy was unjust to them. Ms. Lee (case 6: PriRH-I), a new immigrant, considered the government's interim housing policy as unjust to her, disregarding her needs:

> The Housing Department sent me a letter, saying that we could apply for interim housing in Tuen Mun and Yuen Long. It is very far. I may not get a job there. Thus, I did not apply. It's quite unjust. There should be a choice of interim housing in districts nearer [to the city centre]. The allocation of interim housing in far away districts, on the part of the government, to new immigrants is quite unfair. The transportation cost is as high as $100. It is a burden. It also wastes time [in travelling].

Ms. Kwan (case 8: PriRH-I), thought the government has been unjust to her by specifically asking her to apply for public rental housing after she has received her divorce papers. Also, she considered the cessation of building 2-person public rental flats as unjust:

> Of course, it's unjust. The Housing Department cheated me. I applied for public rental housing many years ago. I handed in the form. [The officer of the Housing Department] said that if you did not receive a

> letter in three-month's time, you should come and ask. I didn't receive a letter after three months, so I went to the Housing Department to ask. I went to the Homantin headquarters to ask. The officer used the computer to check, saying that my number was not on the list, so maybe my application was not accepted. He said that after I had received my divorce papers, I could then apply [for public rental housing] ... I listened to him. At that time, I didn't know that I could go to Kaifong Association to find a social worker to help. In fact, after the Legal Aid Department gave me a number [for the arrangement of divorce], I can apply for public rental housing, and submit the formal divorce papers later. I listened to the officer of the Housing Department. I waited until I got the formal divorce document before I applied. I first attempted to apply for public rental housing in 1997. The whole divorce process lasted for three to four years. I separated from my husband for two years before the Legal Aid Department accepted my application for a divorce ... I waited for about four years. I officially applied for public rental housing in 2001. My number [for the allocation of public rental housing] is big[5]. It's unjust. Now, they say that there are many people applying for 2-person public rental units, but there are only a few 2-person units. It's difficult to be allocated a two-person unit. I went to Lok Fu [Housing Department] headquarters to ask why I was not allocated a public rental unit. The officer said that the queue for two-person units was long, because there were no new two-person units being built. I am even willing to go to Tin Shui Wai if I am allocated [public rental housing there]. They say that there will not be any new two-person [public rental] units being built. They are only building one-person, three-person, four-person units. It's unjust to those applying for a two-person unit ... We have to wait for old [two-person] rental units [vacated by other tenants]. The chance for the vacating of old rental unit is small. The officer of the Lok Fu [headquarters] said that he could not tell me how long I had to wait. The Housing Department should build all types of units. Why don't they build two-person units? ... I thus have to stay in overcrowded housing. This affects the development of my son.

Mr. Ko (case 9: PriRH-I), now living in a private rental board-partitioned room, once lived in public rental housing. He was "forced" to move out of public rental housing because the government disregarded his specific need, thereby being unjust to him:

> I once lived in public rental housing. Three persons lived in a flat. One of them threatened me. Once I was in the toilet. He rushed in. I went out. He followed me and wanted to beat me. I told the warden, asking

to move to another room [since] I could not live with this person. The warden asked me to go to the Housing Department. I filled in the forms [to apply for transference to another room]. Two weeks later, [the Housing Department] replied, saying that I could not move [to another room]. They asked me to call the police. I thought if I called the police, the man would have beaten me to death. Then, I moved out and rent a room in private housing. Now, there is no problem, but I don't know about the future. Maybe, if they increased the rent in the future to a level I could not afford, then I will be in difficulties. I think the government is unjust. I asked [for transference to another room], and they didn't allow me to. They "forced" me to move to private housing. This is unjust.

Views of Private Home-owners

Group 3 interviewees (PriHO) include those living in self-owned private flats. They achieved home-ownership without government assistance. They tended to think that the government was just, or at least not unjust, in not providing assistance to them in achieving home-ownership because they could afford home-ownership on their own, and there were others in more need of government assistance. Ms. Wong (case 12: PriHO) had a household income of $90,000 to $100,000 per month. She did not think that the government was unjust in not helping her with housing:

It's acceptable [that the government does not give housing assistance to us]. It is because many other people have a greater need [for government assistance]. If we can afford [our housing], it's acceptable. It's O.K. that the government does not help us. In the past, I lived in a private rental housing flat. The government did not assist us. I do not think that it was unjust. The standard of your accommodation is your own choice. If you can afford to live in a more comfortable flat, this is your choice. If you cannot afford to, but you try very hard to live [in a comfortable flat], you may think that the government should support you. I don't think this is necessarily so. I don't think that if the government does not help us is a problem or is unjust.

Mr. Ng (case 15: PriHO) had a similar view as Ms. Wong:

It depends on affordability. One cannot say that the government is unjust. Many people have to depend on government [assistance] before they have their housing. If you can afford, but you still depend on government [assistance], it's unjust. The government should assist those

> who cannot afford to buy a flat. I can afford my housing. The government does not assist me. It's just.

Ms. Tsang (case 16: PriHO), now retired, was once engaged in unskilled work, such as baby-sitting, providing part-time domestic help, and had worked hard to achieve home-ownership with great effort. She thought that it would be good if the government helped her. However, she did not think that the government was unjust in not doing so:

> If the government has the resources, it would be good if it lent me money to buy a flat. We do not satisfy the lending criteria; this means we do not have [housing loans]. The government does not assist all people [to buy a flat]; it helps those who are eligible. It is not the case that I do not need housing assistance. Of course, it would be good if the government assisted me. I cannot say that it's unjust [that the government does not assist me]. The government has criteria for eligibility for housing assistance. I, of course, desire government assistance, but I am not eligible. If the government helped me, I would have less difficulty in repaying my mortgage. I repaid mortgage over 15 years. I've just finished repaying mortgage.

Views of Public Tenants

Group 4 interviewees (PuRH) lived in public rental housing. Generally, they regarded government housing assistance in the form of the provision of public rental housing to them as just mainly because they had housing need that they could not satisfy through their own efforts. Ms. Chan (case 18: PuRH), a housewife, with an unstable household income of $7,000 to $8,000, thought that it was just for the government to subsidize her family by providing them public rental housing since she had housing needs in the sense that they could not afford market rent:

> If I had the ability to work, I would not agree to accept government assistance ... If you need help, [the government] should help. If you do not need help, you should try your best ... It's just ... In Hong Kong, most people live in public rental housing. The rent is below market rates. Only if you can afford market rent, can you live [in private housing]. If you cannot afford [full market rates], how can you rent [a private housing flat]? It's just for the government to help those who cannot pay market rent — like me — because there is need. There is no reason for us not to have a place to live.

Ms. Yuen (case 22: PuRH), retired, thought that it was just for the government to provide housing assistance to her by appealing to her husband's and her contributions to society during their working years:

> I have worked [in Hong Kong] for a long time. My husband has worked for a long time. I made contributions, and thus I deserved government assistance. It's just. My husband was a civil servant [as a policeman], helping to maintain law and order. He made a contribution to society. It's just that the government helps us. There are people in more need, and the government should assist them to a greater extent. As for us, [we are in less need], the government may assist us to a lesser degree.

Views of Government-Assisted Home-Owners

Group 5 interviewees (GAHO) include those with government-assisted home-ownership in the form of loans or subsidized public housing for sale. They tended to regard the government housing assistance as just, since they had non-self-satisfiable need for home-ownership. Ms. Hung (case 24: GAHO) shared this view:

> I deserve government assistance. The price [of Home-Ownership Scheme flats] is not too high. I can afford [to buy a Home-Ownership Scheme flat]. The down payment is not very great. The government is just in doing so. We are not earning a lot of money. We cannot afford to buy private housing. We have the need of home-ownership, but we cannot afford [to buy private housing]. Government assisting us is just.

It should be mentioned that Hong Kong people consider the inability to achieve unassisted home-ownership as a housing need. However, it should be pointed out that if home-ownership is unaffordable, it is usually possible to afford decent private rental accommodation. There is therefore no imminent housing need. However, Hong Kong people have a strong desire for home-ownership and therefore regard the inability to achieve it as a housing need. Mr. Leung (case 27: GAHO), living in a Home-Ownership Scheme flat, thought that his receipt of government subsidy as just since he could not afford home-ownership:

> I deserve government help. Private housing is more expensive than Home-Ownership Scheme flats. The interest rate [for Home-Ownership Scheme flat] is fixed. There is protection against high prices. It is just [for the government to help people like me]. The government helps me.

Of course, the government is just [in doing so]. If the government did not help me, I could not afford to buy a flat. Buying a flat requires a great sum of money. I may [buy a Home-Ownership Scheme flat] by instalments. At that time, I could not afford home-ownership.

Ms. Au (case 26: GAHO), who received government housing assistance for civil servants, disagreed with other interviewees in Group 5, and thought that the government was unjust to her though the government subsidized her, mainly because she was not given a choice to buy or to rent:

The government subsidized us in buying a flat. The government would only subsidize us to for *purchasing* a flat. If we did not buy a flat, we would not get any subsidy. The government would not subsidize us for *renting* a flat. The government subsidy "forced" us to buy a flat. To get the subsidy, we had to buy a flat. The result turned out to be disastrous to us, because of the negative equity problem. Why didn't the government allow us to rent? The policy is problematic. In the past, the government subsidized civil servants in renting. Later, they did not subsidize renting. Maybe, the government wanted to boost the market, and that's why it introduced the policy ... I think this is not just. As for our class of civil servants, [in order to get the subsidy], we could only buy. As for the staff of other government subsidized institutions, [the institution] allows them to buy or rent. Thus, it is quite unjust to our grade of civil servants, [that the subsidy is contingent on purchasing a flat]. Of course, having a subsidy is a good thing ... Look at the staff of universities, they can rent or buy [with their subsidy]. But for us, if we want to have subsidy, we must buy. If we don't buy, we don't get any subsidy ... Why doesn't the government housing subsidy allow us the choice of renting or buying? Of course, I feel unjustly treated. This policy in the end trapped us in the problem of negative equity. [One may say that] you may give up [government housing subsidy if you want to rent] at first. However, there is no reason to give up [government subsidy].

To summarize, it is evident that most stakeholders interviewed considered that they were justly treated by the government housing policy, except for those living in inadequate private rental housing and the property developers. It might the case that the government housing policy is unjust towards the lower strata of society since they complain a lot about their unjust treatment. It should also be pointed out that justice (and injustices) conceived by the stakeholders might differ from justice in the normative sense. This applies to the case of the property developers who are often favoured by governmental housing policies, despite the fact that those developers interviewed believed that they were unjustly treated by the government.

Is Absolute Equality of Results Just?

Do the stakeholders consider an absolute equality of results just? Let us look at Group 1 interviewees (RMI) who represent or are members of institutions. Mr. Sung (case 3: RMI-D), a developer, thought that all households, large or small, rich or poor, living in the same type of housing was problematic. He stressed that there should be choices in selecting one's housing to cater for differences among people:

> No, [everybody living in same type of housing] is not equality, because there is no incentive to improve [your circumstances]. I think if you earn more money, or you do particularly well, and you want to go up the social ladder; you want to have better housing. You should always allow people to improve their standard of their living. You don't want everybody living in public housing. That's not right ... People are very varied. People have different requirements. People have different family sizes. More and more people get married and don't have children. More and more people live together and don't get married. Family size is getting smaller. You need different sizes of accommodation to deal with different requirement. Some people like to live in the city. Some people like to live in the countryside. There are different choices. It's not one size fits everybody. You must have a variety.

If absolute equality of results is problematic, then what kind of inequality of results is considered just? In Hong Kong, some people live in luxurious flats, while some live in inadequate housing such as board-partitioned rooms, and bedspaces. Is this phenomenon considered just by the government? Mr. Won (case 1: RMI-G), the government official representing the government, gave the following response:

> From the government's point of view, we follow capitalism in our society. We trust the free economy. We respect private property. The basic principle is that everyone, if he depends on normal means — hard work — gains private property, regardless of one's achievements and the amount of money gained, the government allows the private market

to work freely. Every person has an equal opportunity to compete. The baseline of the government is to ensure everyone reaches the minimum level, that is, everyone has shelter and no one is homeless. Of course, there are still street-sleepers. However, the government has done a lot in this aspect. Half of the population live in government housing. Before the return of sovereignty [to China], the average waiting time [for public rental housing] was about six to seven years, with 150,000 to 160,000 waitlist households. Now, it has been reduced to about 90,000, with the waiting time reduced to within three years. That is a great improvement within five years. There were 270,000 households moving into public rental housing within five years. There is another index — inadequately housed households ... including those living in bedspaces and board-partitioned rooms. Before 1997, there were 180,000 [inadequately housed households]. Now, it has been reduced to 100,000 households.

Mr. Sung (case 3: RMI-D), the property developer, thought that it was not unjust for some people to live in luxury housing, while the government should help those inadequately housed. He pointed out that the governmental emphasis on building housing for sale while neglecting those in need represented a kind of injustice:

[Some people living in luxurious flats while some live in board-partitioned rooms or bedspace] is a reflection of society, not a question of justice. If those people have earned the money or inherited money, what's wrong with them living in nice houses? I don't see that's unjust ... [Concerning those living in inadequate housing], this is why the government should not be building housing for sale. It should be building accommodation for the people who need it. The bedspace apartment should be eliminated because that is obviously substandard housing ... The government should help those who need help, or can't help themselves, whether they are unemployed, unemployable, or elderly, for example, or if they have disabilities, then the government has a role to play ... ... When it went too deep into HOS[6], PSPS[7], the government took its eyes off the ball. It was helping the wrong sector of the community. It resulted in injustices, because resources were not being spent in the right way. The government should now re-focus. I think it is because it's now withdrawing from PSPS, withdrawing from HOS. It can focus more on the welfare side of housing. The government does not have to do all of that. It can use the Housing Society. There are NGOs[8] that can help them. There are specialists, say, in housing for the elderly.

Mr. Won (case 1: RMI-G), the government official, thought that it was just for people of different incomes to live in different types of housing:

> If we merely look at the result ... some live in better housing; some live in more basic housing, it is difficult to say that it is unjust.

Mr. Yeung (case 2: RMI-D), a property developer, also shared similar views:

> I agree [that it is just for people of different incomes to live in different types of housing]. Of course it's just. This is a capitalist society ... Under a just society, with fair competition, some people are rich while some are poor; this is just. Under unfair competition, some get rich while some are poor; this is unjust. Under fair competition, there results in some rich people and some poor people, I think this is just.

Group 2 interviewees (living in private rental housing) tended to think that it was unjust for all households to live in the same type of housing, since some people deserved to live in better housing. Ms. Ngai (case 10: PriRH-I), depending on CSSA, renting a room in the private sector, had the following view, which was similar to that of other Group 2 interviewees (PriRH):

> If all people, the industrious or the lazy, lived in the same type of housing, of course it would not be just. If I work hard and become rich, I should live in better housing. If I am lazy, and accumulate less money, I should live in worse housing. It's just. If all people live in the same type of housing, all people will be lazy.

Mr. Chan (case 5: PriRH-A), who rented a private flat, did agree with other Group 2 interviewees that it was unjust for all households to live in the same type of housing. He rested his views, however, on a different reason — whether choice played a part in the outcome:

> [All households living in same type of housing] is unjust. If the income [is high] and there is desire to improve living standards, they could choose housing units in accordance with their preference and affordability. Compulsory measures are unjust, even for a poor person. [All people living] in the same type of housing is unjust. Allowing people to choose freely, depending on their needs and preference, is just. Everyone should have the free choice to decide.

All six interviewees in Group 2 agreed or strongly agreed that it was just for people of different income levels to live in different types of housing. Ms. Kwan (case 8: PriRH-I), who rented a room in private housing, articulated the views of other interviewees in Group 2:

> I strongly agree. If I am rich, I live in a luxurious flat. The money is earned by hard work, not by robbing. The lower strata live in worse housing. There should be no complaint.

All interviewees in Group 2 (PriRH) thought that it was just for some people to live in luxurious flats or detached houses because they deserved it. Ms. Lee (case 6: PriRH-I), who lived in inadequate private rental housing, did not feel jealous of those living in luxurious flats, nor did she think that injustices were involved:

> Different people have different levels of income. Some have higher incomes. Some have lower incomes. It depends on affordability. If a person has the ability, gains money and lives in better housing, this is just. One improves step by step. Others came to Hong Kong a long time ago and worked very hard. New immigrants, like me, are just starting out. There is no possibility of coming here for just one or two years, but being able to afford private housing, except for those who do business or have a large sum of money at hand. The fact that some people are living in luxurious flats is not unjust. They have worked hard.

Mr. Chan (case 5: PriRH-A), renting a self-contained flat in private housing, thought that the government should help those living in inadequate housing. As for those living in luxurious flats, he did not think that this was a form of injustice, so long as they had worked hard for it. Mr. Chan emphasized that justice involved equal opportunities which the government should promote:

> I sometimes feel ... [that] a person who lives in a board-partitioned room may have suffered because of bad luck, or because of innate limitations, like a complicated family background, low educational standards, or a disability. I think the government should provide public rental housing for those who, because of innate limitations, live in housing like board-partitioned rooms ... The definition of justice is that if the one who lives in luxurious flat depends on hard work and legally gains a large sum of money, I think this is just, as he has worked hard

> ... All government policies should be just by giving all people the opportunity for upward mobility, allowing them to move up. The government should help those who, because of initial limitations, cannot use their talents and thus live in the lower strata. The government should create equal opportunities for them to move upwards justly.

All, except one, Group 3 interviewees (PriHO: Private Home-owners) believed that absolute equality of result was unjust. Mrs. Au (case 13: PriHO) thought that it was unjust for all households to live in same type of housing, as some deserved better type of housing which was agreed upon by most interviewees in Group 3:

> [All households living in same type of housing] is unjust. If I can afford to, if I want to have a better environment, I go out to strive to achieve all I can achieve ... If a person has the ability to achieve better [environment], there is no reason to "force" him to be like others ... If all people are having the same, that would be communism, not a capitalist society. Capitalism is just, since "if you work more, you gain more".

Mr. Cheng (case 11: PriHO) differed from all other home-owners in this group. He believed it was just to have absolute equality of results. However, this might bring about other problems. Thus, it should not be implemented:

> [All households living in same type of housing] is against the principle of capitalist society. This arrangement is just, but might lead to many problems in society. If we look into history, socialist societies did not work. When we're born, life at the beginning is the same. If everybody's rights at the beginning are the same, suppose they will get things which are the same. If they live in the same type of housing, equalizing all resources in society, this is good and right. But such an arrangement would lead to other problems in society, which would lead to other injustices. If we equalize all the resources each individual gets in society and if one has the opportunity to get extra benefits, he will bring about injustices. This is difficult for the government to prevent. For example, in the judiciary, how can we ensure the judge makes just judgements? If we do not give extra benefit to the judge so that he makes judgements carefully, the judge may make unjust judgements, leading to injustices. If a society cannot prevent this, then it should not use equalizing all benefits each one gets to run the society.

Most interviewees in Group 3 (PriHO) thought that it was just or natural (in a capitalist society) for some people to live in luxurious flats, while others lives in inadequate housing. Ms. Tsang (case 16: PriHO) shared this majority's view:

> [Some people living in luxurious flats, while some living in board-partitioned rooms and bedspace apartments] is just. Some people are rich; of course they live in better housing. Some people do not have money; they do not have any other option but to live in board-partitioned rooms. Everybody wants to live in good housing. The poor only desire, but cannot fulfil their wish ... In this world, there must be some people living in good housing while others live in worse housing. It's not possible for everybody to live in the same housing. It's like we have ten fingers; some are long, while some are short.

Ms. Wong (case 12: PriHO), a non-government assisted home-owner, disagreed and thought that it would be unjust for all those who gained "quick and easy money" to live in luxurious flats. In fact, she suggested that gaining money in Hong Kong did not necessarily imply having worked hard. She believed that it was unjust for the people to live in inadequate housing and the government should help them:

> Of course, it's unjust. Everybody has his own working ability. If one can earn a certain level of money, he can choose to live in housing of certain standard. In Hong Kong society, people can earn money in a quick way. People can use different ways to earn a lot of money, to speculate. They gain money and they can afford a comfortable life. Not all people have such opportunities. This is also not an ideal way to gain money, if injustice is involved. If people speculate and gain a lot of money, living in a luxurious flat, this is unjust. If people work very hard, gain money and live in a luxurious flat, this is fair enough. Of course, [those speculators] have to bear the consequences. Many of them face the problem of negative equity or even go bankrupt after 1997. It's unjust for people to live in board-partitioned rooms and bedspaces. The government should do more. They suffer from initial inadequacies, for example, they may be uneducated, of [old] age or having other barriers. They thus cannot hold down a stable job, and have low living standards. If the government can, it should help them.

All interviewees, except one, in Group 3 (PriHO) agreed or strongly agreed that it was just for all people of different incomes to live in different types of housing usually by appealing to the fact that they deserved it. Ms. Wong (case 12: PriHO) shared this view:

> I agree. Different people have different working ability, enjoying different result of their hard work. They live in different housing is acceptable.

Group 4 (PuRH) includes interviewees living in public rental housing. Two out of six of them thought that it was, in principle, just for all households to live in same type of housing. Ms. Chan (case 18: PuRH) rested her views on the equality of all human beings:

> It would be just for[all household to live in same type of housing]. Every person is equal ... Based on humane grounds, this may be considered just. However, in reality, this is impossible ... Everybody is equal. You are a human being. I am also a human being. But just because you have money does not indicate that I'll ask you to give me some.

The other four interviewees in Group 4 (PuRH) believed that it was unjust to have absolute equality of results in housing since some deserved to live in better housing. They indicated that people who put more effort at work should gain more i.e. living in better housing. Mr. Ho (case 17: PuRH) held this view:

> [All households living in same type of housing] is not just. If you work hard, you live in public rental housing, and if you are lazy, you also live in public rental housing. This is not just. If I work hard and gain more money, why can't I live in a Home-ownership Scheme flat? The standard of Home-ownership Scheme flats and public rental flats are different — the quality and the management standard are different. If you work hard, gain more money, you should live more comfortably, live in better housing. If you are lazy or with lower ability, you should live in worse housing. If you contribute more, you should gain more.

Ms. Chan (case 18: PuRH), living in public rental housing, believed that people who lived in luxury flats have worked hard for it, thereby being just. As for those living in board-partitioned rooms and bedspaces, the government should help them:

> It depends on the person. Each person's luck, living conditions, education levels are different. Why do some people live in luxurious flats? Maybe, his father leaves him [money]. Or maybe, he fights for it.

For example, he is well-educated, thus gains a lot of money. Therefore, he can enjoy [luxury]. It depends on in-born or after birth [qualities]. For those who receive good education, work hard to gain money so that they live in a luxurious flat, [I think] this is just because they have put in the effort. For those who live in board-partitioned rooms, they may still work hard. However, some people do not have any luck ... For those who live in board-partitioned rooms, most of them do not have [family] support or are elderly. There is no reason for those in their twenties to live in board-partitioned rooms. The government should give some help to those people. The discrepancy between the rich and the poor in Hong Kong is very great, very great. The government should help those living in board-partitioned rooms and bedspaces. This is just. Everyone should have a stable home. All people are equal. Why do I live in board-partitioned room, while you live in a luxurious flat? It depends on individual luck, and on nature and nurture. There are many factors involved.

Other interviewees in Group 4 (PuRH) shared similar views with Ms. Chan (case 18: PuRH), except Mr. Ho (case 17: PuRH) who pointed out the great discrepancy in housing condition in Hong Kong could not be regarded as just:

If one can afford or runs a business, he may live in ideal housing. For people like us, living in public rental housing is very satisfactory. [Some people live in luxurious flats, while some live in board-partitioned rooms] cannot be said to be just. There is no reason to explain the great discrepancy between their living environment. If one has a high income, one may live in a good environment. If one cannot afford [an alternative], one lives in public rental housing. However, if one may not be eligible to apply for public rental housing, he is forced to rent private housing. There is a great discrepancy between the rich and the poor. All people work hard, [not just the rich]. But because the economy is bad, wages have fallen, [adversely affecting the poor].

All interviewees in Group 4 (PuRH) agreed with the view that it was just for people with different incomes to live in different types of housing. Ms. Chan (case 18: PuRH) gave the following response:

I agree [that it is just for people of different income to live in different type of housing]. If you have a low income, the government provides you with public rental housing. If you have a high income, you buy private housing. This is just.

Group 5 includes interviewees (GAHO) who achieved home-ownership with government assistance. All Group 5 interviewees agreed that it was unjust for all households to live in the same type of housing. Mr. Ng (case 23: GAHO), received Sandwich Class Housing Loan, related this issue to the lack of incentive for people to work hard, in addition to the view that it was unjust:

> [All households living in same type of housing] would not be normal. It's not just. It is like communism. The society will lack motivation to move forward. "If you work, you get thirty-six [dollars]. If you do not work, you also get thirty-six [dollars]." Then, nobody would work and will depend on government support. The society will not move forward. People will not work hard. In the past in China, "if you worked, you got thirty-six [dollars]; if you did not work, you also got thirty-six [dollars]". This explains why China deteriorated to such a great extent. If you work hard, you earn a more comfortable living environment. It depends on individual choice. There is freedom. The fact that through hard work, you can get a better living environment, is just.

All interviewees in Group 5 (GAHO) agreed or strongly agreed that it was just for people of different incomes to live in different types of housing. All Group 5 interviewees (GAHO) thought that the fact that some people lived in luxury flats was just in light of the fact that they deserved it, while the government should help those living in inadequate housing. Ms. Au (case 26: GAHO) represented the general views of interviewees in this Group:

> You must look at what a person contributes and what he receives. Those who are unwilling to contribute and who live in board-partitioned rooms deserve it. For those who are not unwilling to contribute but in the end live in board-partitioned rooms, like those disadvantaged or the mentally disabled, then there may be some injustices. However, the Hong Kong welfare system has already given them protection to a certain extent, for example, it gives them subsidized housing in the form of public rental housing. As for the rich, if they work very hard and thus live comfortably, I think there are no injustices. If because of inheritance, they are rich and live comfortably, I think that there is no reason to protest ... Because of their hard work or hard work of their [extended] family's in the past, they deserve the reward. If you are poor because of unwillingness to work hard, you deserve to be poor. If someone works hard and cannot get ahead, the Hong Kong social security system has already protected them ... Of course, the Hong Kong social security

has loopholes. In the past, you had to wait seven years [for public rental housing]. Now, it is shortened to three years, but you still have to wait. The government has not done enough. But if someone can move to public rental housing, it's already quite just.

On the whole, most interviewees, regardless of the stake they held in Hong Kong housing policy, considered absolute equality of result in housing condition (in the sense that all households, regardless of their income and family size, lived in same type of housing), as unjust since some people deserved to live in better housing. The phenomenon that those people work hard to gain money, thereby could afford to live in luxury flats, was regarded as just, because those people were enjoying the results of their effort. The interviewees tended to believe that it was just for people of different incomes to live in different housing. However, there were a few interviewees who disagreed with these views. These minorities did not share a particular stake. Thus, one cannot conclude that people, holding a certain stake, have a specific view on the question of absolute equality of results in housing condition.

Rational Allocation of Resources in Public Rental Housing

The official view of justice in housing policy is reflected in the principle of rational allocation of resources in public rental housing and the "rich-household policy", charging double-rent and market rents for well-off public housing tenants. All interviewees, no matter what stake they held in housing policy, considered it just for the government to provide public rental housing to low-income households.

Let us examine the views among the group representing institutions (Group 1: RMI). Mr. Won (case 1: RMI-G), appealed to the housing need of the people:

The baseline is that everybody has shelter and there are no homeless people. In regard to whether the government is just when implementing public rental housing policy, there definitely will be different views. The aim of the government is to assist those in need, helping them to improve their living standards ... The rent of public rental housing on average is 40% of the market rent ... We have done surveys. People agree that the government should provide public rental housing to those in need. Basically, there is no disagreement ... Justice and rational allocation of resources is undoubtedly one of our targets. Our priorities — by what

> means, allocating how many resources should be reviewed constantly, and the public should express opinions on these.

Mr. Yeung (case 2: RMI-D), a property developer, justified the provision of public rental housing on the part of the government, by appealing to the housing needs of low-income people. However, Mr. Yeung did not think that the government should build public rental housing itself. He suggested that the government could buy flats from property developers and rent them to low-income households as public rental housing:

> I think the government should [provide public rental housing to low-income people]. Clothing, food, housing, transport are four most important necessities of a person ... Everybody should have shelter. Some people's income levels are not sufficient to rent a flat at market price. If the government does not help them, is it true that you ask them to live in the street? The whole society would break down. If the government does not subsidize their housing, it should also use other means, such as CSSA, so that they can afford to rent private housing. I think the government does not need to build flats. The government can buy flats from private developers and rent them to public rental housing households ... The government can also subsidize [low-income] households to rent from private developers.

Let us examine the views of public tenants. One would expect that public rental housing households will definitely think that it is just to provide public rental housing to low-income families. All interviewees in Group 4 (PuRH: living in public rental housing) agreed to the provision of public rental housing, on the part of the government, to low-income families. Ms. Chan (case 18: PuRH), belonging to Group 4, rested her views on the housing needs of low-income households:

> [The provision of public rental housing to low-income households, on the part of the government] is acceptable. It is just. For example, my monthly income is a few thousand dollars. It is already difficult to pay for family expenditures. I cannot afford to pay a large sum of money to rent housing. Many families cannot afford it, either. In Hong Kong, many family problems result from this. The government should help. This is just.

All interviewees living in private rental housing (Group 2: PriRH) shared similar views to public tenants, thinking it was just for the government to provide public rental housing to the poor. Mr. Hui (case 7: PriRH-I), rented a room in private housing and had applied for public rental housing, also rested his views on the housing needs of poor households:

> [The provision of public rental housing to low-income households] is just. [Living in public rental housing] saves money. It's of lower rent. One has a self-contained flat [if one is in public rental housing]. One does not need to "squeeze" into a room [in private housing], eating and conducting all the activities in a room. It's terrible for a family to stay in a room. These people have housing needs. The government should help them by giving them public rental housing. Thus, they don't have to "squeeze" into a room, being overcrowding.

All interviewees in Group 3 (PriHO: Private Home-owners) considered it just that the government provide public rental housing to low-income households. They did not think that the housing welfare provision to the poor might increase their burden as tax-payers, thereby being unjust. Mr. Cheng (case 11: PriHO), a private home-owner who had once lived in public rental housing, believed that the government had a responsibility to satisfy the housing needs of the low-income households. It might serve as a means to social stability:

> As for living in public rental housing in the past, it was just and there was a need. For long time in Hong Kong society, there has been high land price policy, making many lower-middle class people unable to afford decent accommodation. The government has a responsibility to keep society stable, necessitating the solving of livelihood problems, such as clothing, food, housing and transport. Housing is one of the problems that needs to be tackled. The government has the responsibility to solve livelihood problems. Thus, of course it is just [to provide public rental housing]. For people similar to me [in the past], if we do not live in public rental housing estates, our living environment may be worse, leading to more societal problems.

Among the Public Home Ownership Group (Group 5: GAHO), all agreed that it was just to provide public rental housing to low-income households. Ms. Au (case 26: GAHO), in receipt of civil servant housing loan, also rested her views on the housing need of the poor:

> The definition of justice is that if you work hard, you get more. If you work less hard, you get less. If you have worked, you should live in

> housing of a certain standard ... If you work hard, but still cannot afford a minimum standard of private housing, it would be just that the government provides the minimum standard of housing in form of public rental housing.

As has been mentioned, one strategy for implementing rational allocation of public rental housing resources is the "rich household policy", charging double-rent or market rent for well-off public rental households.

The most direct stake-holders being affected by the "rich household policy" are the public rental households. One might expect public rental households to oppose such a policy, saying that it is unjust, since their interest may be adversely affected. However, most (Group 4: PuRH) thought that the double-rent or market-rent policy was just. Ms. Chan (case 18: PuRH), with an unstable household income of $7,000 to $8,000 per month, was barely able to afford the living expense of a family of four, thought that the "rich-household policy" was just:

> [Charging well-off public rental housing household double rent or market rent] is just. And if you can afford it, why don't you move out [of public rental housing]? Means-testing is just. Suppose five to six people [in a household] are working and each person's income is about $20,000 to $30,000. [The total household income] is more than $100,000, but there is no reason not to move out [of public rental housing]. Some households have only one person working. For example, my husband earns a few thousand dollars if there is work, and out of that he has to support four people ... Meanwhile consider a household of five, all of them are working. Their financial situation is better. They should pay market rent because they can afford to.

She also thought that it was just for public rental housing to be rented on contract basis and the contract would only be renewed if the tenant could pass income and asset means-tests. If not, they should vacate their rental flats which were to be allocated to people in more need:

> [Renting public housing on contract basis] is quite rational. [The government] rents [a public housing flat] to you for three years. If you can afford to repay mortgages, you should move out. I think it's quite just. Some people cannot afford to repay mortgages. Each month, you have to repay a few thousand dollars or even $10,000 for mortgages. If your monthly income is only a few thousand dollars, how can you

afford to repay mortgages? For those who live in public rental housing, if they have affordability, [they should move out]. For example, a household of five; all are working and have stable income. They can afford to live in private housing. I think they should [move out] ... Suppose you have a large sum of money, why don't you buy a flat? The government's policy is to take care of the needy. The needy are the low-income people or those whose financial position is not very good. They live in public rental housing for three years [on a contract basis]. If they can afford [to live in private housing], they should move out [of public rental housing]. This is what should be.

Most of the interviewees in this group agreed with Ms. Chan. They belonged to the category of low or unstable income. The comparatively well-off public rental housing tenants disagreed, and thought that the "rich-household policy" was unjust. They also thought that to rent public housing on contract basis, with the contract subjected to renewal only after being able to pass a means-test, was unjust. Ms. Chu (case 20: PuRH), with all her family members in paid employment, was comparatively well-off. She held the following view:

[The "rich-household" policy] is unjust. To calculate the household income, the government includes all the income of the children. In reality, the children will not contribute all of their income to the family. They only give a little bit to the family. Very often, the household expenditure is born by the father. The children will give a little bit [to the family]. They will not give the whole of their income. To calculate the household income for the means-test, they include the whole of the income of the children. This is unjust ... The government calculates household income in this way. If they only include contribution of each child to the family, the family income becomes lower and will not be above the income limit of the means-test.

Ms. Chu thought that renting public housing on contract basis, with the renewal of contract only if the tenant passed the means-test was unjust:

This is not quite just. Those people live in public rental housing, thereby saving some money. You cannot say that they are well-off households. Those living in luxurious flats are well-off households. Those living in public rental housing have a little bit of savings, then you classify them as well-off households. For example, like us, [our income] is not above the income limit [of the means-test]. Some [public rental housing households] gain a little bit more, $1,000 to $2,000. The government

> then classifies them as well-off households and asks them to move. This is not appropriate. I think that one should stay in public rental housing on a long-term basis. Those living in public rental housing gain a little bit more; they are still poor. They still have to be frugal.

To sum up, those public rental housing households with comparatively low or unstable income tend to consider the "rich-household policy" and the policy of renting public housing on a contract basis, renewing the contract only if the tenant passes the means-test, as just since there is comparatively low probability of their interest being adversely affected. However, those comparatively better-off public rental households, with the high probability of being classified as a "rich household" in the near future, tend to think that such policies are unjust, since they may be adversely affected.

Another group of stakeholders indirectly affected by "double-rent or market-rent policy" and the policy of renting housing on contract basis are those living in inadequate private rental housing, waiting for public rental housing. Ms. Kwan (case 8: PriRH-I), a waitlist household, thought that charging well-off public rental household double-rent and market-rent was problematic. She thought that the government should be more drastic by asking such families to move out of public rental housing, thereby increasing her chance of being allocated public rental housing sooner:

> [Charging double-rent and market rent for well-off public housing tenant] is unjust. The well-off public housing tenant should be asked to move out of public rental housing. The government has stopped building public rental housing. If the government doesn't ask the well-off tenants to move out [of public rental housing], those on the waiting list cannot move into [public rental housing].

Except Ms. Kwan, all others in Group 2 (PriRH: living in private rental housing) thought that it was just to charge well-off public rental households higher rent. Mr. Hui (case 7: PriRH-I), living in a private rental room, shared this majority view:

> Why do the well-off households still want to stay in public rental housing? If he considers it is a place that brings him luck so that he becomes prosperous, then the government should charge him higher rent ... You charge him double rent. If he thinks that he has no benefit in staying, he will move [out of public rental housing]. Charging him

> higher rent is just. If he still wants to stay even though he's paying double rent, the government can allow him to stay. Charging higher rent indirectly "forces" him to move out.

All interviewees in Group 2 (PriRH), except Ms. Lee (case 6: PriRH-I), thought that it was just to rent public rental housing on a contract basis, with the contract subject to renewal if the tenant passed through the means-test, basing on housing needs. Mr. Chan (case 5: PriRH-A) rented a flat in private housing. He thought that renting public rental housing on contract basis was just:

> In principle, this is just. The public rental housing policy is to help low-income people. If the household is above this stratum, they should vacate their flats, which could be allocated to people more in need. The allocation of public rental housing should be according to need. This is just.

Ms. Lee (case 6: PriRH-I) thought that the government should not force the public rental households out of public rental housing by not renewing the rental contract even though they are well-off:

> Suppose I live in public rental housing, if I can afford, I, of course, would like to buy a flat of my own. Without affordability, nothing can be done. Those with affordability should be given a choice to buy a flat or to stay in public rental housing. The government should not "force" them to move out [of public rental housing].

Mr. Sung (case 3: RMI-D) belongs to Group 1 (representatives or members of institutions), a property developer, echoed Ms. Lee and thought that it was unjust to rent public rental housing on contract basis, with the contract renewed only if the tenant could pass through means-test:

> No, I think it's very unjust. You should never take the position of forcing somebody out ... This is the only area that the government deals with as regards transitional housing. I felt, if you went right back to the beginning of the Home Ownership Scheme ... The original principle of the Home Ownership [Scheme] was to my mind quite sound. The government builds properties for sale. But the only people who could buy the Home-Ownership flats are existing tenants. They are the only people who are eligible. They offer subsidized home-ownership, but in

> return somebody must vacate a flat that could be given to somebody on the waiting list. That to me is sensible ... The whole idea of having a stable society is to give people the confidence that they will never be forced out of their homes. They may be very wealthy. Their wealth may have increased. They may be quite happy to live in public rental housing. Why not let them choose? Why force them? That's a communist attitude, not a humanitarian or a just attitude. So I think the only area of ownership that the government should assist is Home-Ownership [Scheme], but the only applicants are existing tenants of public rental housing who when they buy subsidized housing vacate a rental unit that can be used by somebody on the waiting list. That to me is logical.

Mr. Sung (case 3: RMI-D) thought that forcing the well-off public housing tenants to move out was unjust. However, he thought that charging them market rent was just:

> Yes, probably [it is just to charge well-off public housing tenants market rent]. I think that's the deal. If after say ten years, they choose to stay in rental housing and not move, they should be allowed to do that, but the deal is you have to pay a higher rent; you pay the market rent because you can now afford it. You don't need the additional subsidy. All I am asking you to do is to pay the market value. There's nothing wrong with that. The only time you give a subsidy is when somebody can't afford what they need. If their salary has now increased, or they've got children bringing in extra income, into the house, why should they get a subsidy? That's not fair.

All interviewees in Group 3 (PriHO: those achieving home-ownership without government assistance) thought that it was just to charge well-off public rental housing tenants market rent or double rent. Mr. Ng (case 15: PriHO), a home-owner in private housing, had the following views, which were representative of those in Group 3:

> [Charging well-off public housing tenant double rent or market rent] is just. If you are rich, the government should charge market rent. If you are rich, but still receive benefits from the government, it means that those people on the waiting list cannot move into public rental housing. This is unjust.

All interviewees in Group 3 considered that it was just to rent public housing on a contract basis, with the contract subjected to renewal only after the tenant passed through means-test. Mr. Cheng (case 11: PriHO), who belonged to Group 3, rested his views on housing needs:

> The process of conducting means-test is just. Government resources are intended to help those with genuine needs to live in public rental housing. After many years [of living in public rental housing], those who once could not afford to rent private housing, may have improved their lot to the point of being able to afford private rent. If the government takes back their public rental unit, and asks them to move to private housing, paying private rent, this is absolutely just. The government, no doubt, should do so. This would be a rational use of resources.

All interviewees in Group 5 (GAHO: those achieving home-ownership with government assistance) thought that it was just to charge wealthier public tenants higher rents, except Mr. Leung (case 25: GAHO) who thought this policy was useless:

> [Charging double-rent and market rent] is useless. If your income is above the income limit, you have to move out [of public rental housing]. The government may give you one year to find another flat, but you have to pay market rents. In Hong Kong, there is no possibility of not finding a place to move if you have the means; three to six months would already be enough. The government should not charge the well-off households higher rent, but rather should make the tenants give back their public rental unit. Some people may think that the public rental unit brings them good luck. Even if the government charges them rent four times higher, they will still pay the higher rent even though they live in the Mid-Level at present.

All interviewees in Group 5 (GAHO) believed that a means-tested contract system was just. Mr. Leung's (case 25: GAHO) views might represent his Group:

> This is good and just. However, the time limit of the contract should be longer, not only two or three years. If I apply for a public rental unit, I have to wait for about four years. It's too short if the contract lasts only two to three years. Maybe, for the first five years, there should be a guarantee that you may stay in the public rental unit. If your income reaches a certain level, you have to inform the government. If the income is high, you have to move ... If suddenly one of the family members is unemployed, you have to inform the government. Based on discretion,

> the government can renew the contract, but maybe you have to move to a different district after five years. The public rental unit is not something given to you. For the time being, you live in a public rental unit for five years. After five years, you may have to move to another public rental unit if you are still poor or move out of public rental housing totally if you are rich.

In sum, most interviewees considered that the renting of public housing on a contract basis, (with the renewal of the contract only if the tenants could pass the means-test), as just since they regarded the target of public rental housing was improving the living standards of Hong Kong's low-income residents. Those comparatively well-off should move out to allow those in more need to move in.

The Inheritance of Public Rental Housing

Concerning the inheritance of public rental housing, Mr. Won (case 1: RMI-G), an official representing government's view, gave the following response:

> In public rental housing, if the tenant ... would like to pass the tenancy to a spouse, we do not have any limitations. If he wants to pass it to the children after death, we do not allow automatic transfer. We have comprehensive income and asset means-test ... This is in line with the rational allocation of resources. In short, it is [to distribute] according to need. For those with need, we will allow them to have or continue to have housing subsidy. Those who do not have need, we would reduce the subsidy, or ask them to give the rental unit back [to the government]. This is rational allocation of societal resources.

Mr. Yeung (case 2: RMI-D), a property developer belonging to Group 1, agreed with the governmental policy regarding the inheritance of public rental housing:

> For public rental housing, there should not be inheritance right. Those without the means live in public rental housing. If you have the means, you should go out to rent private housing. After parents die, there should be means-test. If the children are rich, they should move out. This is in line with "rich household" policy. If the son is rich, there is no reason for him to stay in [public rental housing].

All interviewees living in public rental housing (Group 4: PuRH) agreed that it was just for a child to undergo means-testing if s/he was to inherit public rental housing, in line with the government policy. Ms. Yuen (case 22: PuRH), a public housing tenant, had the following view:

> For public housing, it depends on the children's income. If their income is insufficient to pay for other types of housing, they should be able to stay in [the public rental housing unit after their parents die]. There should be a means-test. If they are rich, they should move out. It's just.

All interviewees achieving government-assisted home-ownership (Group 5: GAHO) agreed that means-testing for the surviving child should be conducted if s/he was to inherit the right to continue to stay in public rental housing after the death of his/her parents. Mr. Leung (case 25: GAHO), however, had a more drastic view:

> For public rental housing, there should not be inheritance. This has been changed after so many years. It's too bad ... If the son is poor, he should apply for public rental housing himself.

Similarly, Ms. Tsang (case 16), belonging to Group 3 (PriHO: home-owners in private housing), shared the following view with Mr. Leung (case 25: GAHO):

> For public rental housing, after the parents die, the rental unit should be given back to the government. If the son is poor, he can apply for a public rental unit himself. If inheritance of public rental housing were allowed, there would be no chance for new applicants to be allocated public rental housing. If the tenant dies and returns the rental unit [to the government], then there would be a greater chance for others to apply and be allocated [public rental housing].

All other interviewees in Group 3 (PriHO) agreed with the official policy concerning inheritance of public rental housing. Mr. Cheng's (case 11: PriHO) views are typical:

> For public rental housing, inheritance is unjust. The rental contract is between the government and the parents. The ownership of the flat belongs to the government. There is no contract between the children and the government. How can one transfer the contract to the children? This is against the spirit of making a contract. Have the children

> undergone means-testing? Does the government need to use its limited resources to help the children? If [the means-test] is not carried out, this would be unjust ... If the children can pass the means-test and they have lived in the rental unit for a long time, then based on humanitarian reasons, the government should allow them to stay, and make a new contract with the children. If the children are rich, the government should terminate the contract. There is no reason for the children to hold onto the flat if they are millionaires.

Most interviewees living in private rental housing (Group 2: PriRH) agreed that it was just to conduct means-testing for a child if s/he was to inherit public rental housing. Ms. Lee (case 6: PriRH-I), renting a board-partitioned room, thought that unconditional inheritance of public rental housing was unjust, and argued that there should be means-testing for the child:

> According to government policy, inheritance of public rental housing is unjust. The government allocates public rental housing to the parents. If it is passed to the next generation and the next, then those eligible will struggle to get public rental housing. It depends on discretion. If the son is poor, faces difficulty and needs help, the government should not "force" him to move out [of public rental housing]. There should be a means-test for the son. If the son has genuine need, he may be allowed to stay.

All interviewees, regardless of their personal interest in government housing policy, agreed or strongly agreed that it was just for all those who receive government housing assistance to undergo income and asset means-tests. Mr. Leung (case 25: GAHO) strongly agreed with this scheme and thought that the mechanism for conducting the means-test should be improved:

> I strongly agree. The way of conducting a means-test should be improved. For example, a taxi-driver's income is difficult to check. If you don't inform the government of your income, or you give false information, this should be considered as the equivalent of committing a criminal offence. It should carry a jail sentence, require repayment of the subsidy, and [the offender's] family members be barred from getting government housing assistance for the rest of their lives. This should be clearly and strongly stated.

To conclude, most interviewees agreed with the official policy of requiring the next generation to undergo a means-test before allowing them to inherit public rental housing from their parents. A few argued against the transfer of public rental housing by inheritance, and suggested that the child should have to queue up in the waiting list himself/herself, if s/he was poor. Such measures, though stringent, would allow more people in need to benefit from public rental housing policy. All interviewees agreed that all those who received housing assistance from the government should undergo a means-test.

Assistance towards Home-ownership

In response to the question of whether or not it was just to help middle-income households to achieve home-ownership, Mr. Won (case 1: RMI-G) gave the following answer:

> Whether one should achieve home-ownership is an individual's own choice. Our home-ownership plan is to help those who want to achieve home-ownership, but cannot afford to do so without assistance. The question of whether this is just will differ from person to person. Some people think that the programme is unjust, because the government's responsibility of solving the basic needs of the people is already enough. The government provides public rental housing to the poorest people ... People will not die because they can't buy a flat. In other countries, the homeownership rate is about 20–30%. Renting a flat for life is happy and unproblematic. Why do people worry about not being able to afford to buy a flat? Some people may think that they do not want to live in public rental housing, but cannot afford to buy private housing. They want to improve their living standards and own long-term assets. They would like the government to help ... The government stance is that for the time being, the government will still maintain this housing loan plan. We will review the policy to see whether it is still appropriate within two years.

Mr. Yeung (case 2: RMI-D), a property developer, thought that there should be no disagreements over assistance towards home-ownership. He suggested that, instead of building Home-Ownership Scheme flats for sale at discount prices, the government could subsidize the Home-Ownership Scheme applicants to buy private housing:

> This policy has been implemented for many years. The government implements this policy so that most people can achieve home-ownership. There should be no debate about the question. The effect of giving loans for people to buy flats is not very great. This scheme won't spur people into [very actively] buying flats. The government builds HOS[9] flats, or cooperates with developers to build HOS flats, before selling them to HOS applicants at rates 30–40% below market prices. This means the government is subsidizing HOS applicants. Why can't the government subsidize HOS applicants in cash to buy private housing flats?

Let us look at the views of government-assisted home-owners. Most interviewees in Group 5 (GAHO) thought that it was just for the government to assist the middle-class to achieve home-ownership. Mr. Ng (case 23: GAHO), himself the beneficiary of the Sandwich Class Housing Loan, rested his views on desert of the middle-class, since they paid tax:

> The fact that the government helps the middle-class, instead of only helping low-income people living in board-partitioned rooms, may not be very just. On the other hand, in terms of taxation, the low-income people have not helped the government, because they do not pay tax. The middle-class pay tax; that the government helps them is appropriate ... If everyone paid tax, if even the low-income people pay tax, then the government should help the low-income people also ... In other countries, if you work, you have to pay tax. In welfare states, the government shoulders the responsibility. For example, when you are unemployed, you have problems, and the government will help you, not lavishly, but it will help you to a certain extent. You have some responsibility towards the government, it will then help you. If one has rights, then one has responsibilities. If this weren't the case, it would be disastrous.

Ms. Au (case 26: GAHO), receiving civil servant loans to buy a flat, disagreed, arguing that it was unjust for the government to help middle-class households to achieve home-ownership. Instead the government should concentrate on helping the poor:

> [Helping middle-income households to achieve home-ownership] is unjust. If a flat is bought, it is owned. It is personal property. That the government provides adequate housing to people in need is just. However, for the government to subsidize a household to own a personal asset is not just. How big an asset you own should depend on

how much money you earn, regardless of the size of the flat ... In principle, this policy is inappropriate. There are people who are queuing for public rental housing. They need minimum housing. Why does the government subsidize people [already able] to buy flats while ignoring those most in need? ... If a person for whatever reason has no safety net, the government should help him ... The government should help people if they have inadequacies, rather than help people to own a property. Owning a property is an investment ... The government should help people to solve housing problem, instead of helping people to own an asset ... Why does the government help some people to own an asset and not help others to own an asset? Why doesn't the government help the very rich and the poor to own assets? If there is to be justice, the government would have to help everybody to own an asset.

Those living in inadequate housing in the private rental sector (Group 2: PriRH-I) envied the great amount of assistance the government gave to the middle-class to achieve home-ownership. They thought that the government should instead use the money involved to help poor people, like them, first. Ms. Lee (case 6: PriRH-I), renting a board-partitioned room, thought that home-ownership assistance for middle-income people was unjust:

[That the government assists middle-income households to achieve home-ownership] is unjust. Why doesn't the government subsidize low-income people, like us, rather than subsidizing those with middle-income? There should be priority in helping those with difficulty first, before helping the middle-income people. The middle-income people have their own means; they can take care of their housing needs on their own. The government should help the low-income people by giving them public rental housing before helping the middle-income people. The middle-income people have their own means; but they still complain. They can afford to rent a flat. New immigrants, like us, have low incomes and little savings; we live with difficulty. If we don't rent a room, we have no place to stay. For those who buy HOS flats, the government subsidy amounts to $100,000 to $200,000. However, the government does not subsidize us. This seems unjust.

Ms. Kwan (case 8: PriRH-I) agreed with Ms. Lee:

[Helping middle-income households achieve home-ownership] is unjust. Those having more receive more. Those middle-income people can afford to rent a flat. The government does not build public rental

> housing, "forcing" people to buy flats. How can those low-income people afford to buy one? It's terrible for low-income people ... Like us, we wait for so long to be allocated public rental housing. We live in poor housing. It affects the development of a child.

Group 3 interviewees (PriHO: home-owners in private sector) disagreed with one another over whether it was just for the government to assist the middle-income households to achieve home-ownership. Ms. Tsang (case 16: PriHO) agreed with those living in inadequate housing in the private rental sector:

> [The provision of home-ownership assistance to middle-income households] is unjust. The middle-income people have money. Why does the government need to help them? There are many poor people waiting for government assistance. The middle class people earn much money before they can be classified as "Sandwich Class [People]." If these people have a certain level of income, they should buy a flat on their own. There is no need for the government to help them. I think the government should use the resources [for helping the middle-income people to buy a flat] to help the poor. There are a lot of poor people who have no place to live. Helping the middle-income people is unjust.

Mr. Ng (case 15: PriHO) thought that government assistance was just if there was a need for home-ownership. If a household already lived in good housing, subsidizing it to move to better housing was unjust:

> The government should conduct a means-test. If the person is in need, the government will then subsidize him. If the person already lives in good housing, but wants to live in bigger housing, subsidizing him to live in a luxurious flat is not very good. If the government subsidizes a person with a need for home-ownership, then it's fair. If the government subsidizes a person to move to bigger housing, then it's unjust.

Most interviewees living in public rental housing (Group 4: PuRH) believed that it was just for the government to assist the middle-income household to achieve home-ownership by appealing to home-ownership need on the part of the middle-class. Ms. Chan (case 18: PuRH) shared this view:

> I also think that [helping the middle-income households to achieve home-ownership, on the part of the government] is just. Although the middle

> class' income is high, they should bear some expenditure. All people are equal. Why do you help some [people] and not help others? If the [middle-class] have need, [the government] should help. The middle class's working ability reaches a certain level, though their income reaches the middle-class [income level], some of them cannot afford [home-ownership], [the government] should help. There is no reason to say that my income is high, the government does not have to help.

Group 2 interviewees (PriRH: living in private rental housing) were divided over whether it was just for the government to only provide housing assistance to the very poor. Half agreed with the statement "It is just for the government to only provide housing assistance to the very poor", while half of them disagreed, saying that other classes, in addition to the very poor, also needed government assistance.

Most interviewees in Group 3 (PriHO: home-owners in private sector) tended to agree that it was just for the government to only provide housing assistance to the very poor. All interviewees in Group 4 (PuRH: living in public rental housing) disagreed that it was just for the government to provide housing assistance only to the very poor. Ms. Chan (case 18: PuRH), living in public rental housing, gave the following response:

> I disagree [that it is just for the government to only provide housing assistance to the very poor]. Not only the very poor need housing assistance. Some not so poor also need housing assistance. Helping the very poor is what the government should do. There is no reason to help only them, and not others. [The government] should also help the middle-class, Sandwich Class. All of us are human beings. There is no reason that if you are very poor, the government should help you in all aspects ... If you are very poor and are healthy, you may find a job. Then you will not be so poor. There are some people who bought a few million dollars flat and are suffering from negative equity, living in the flat instead of speculating. [The government] should help them. Speculators are another matter.

Interviewees in Group 5 (GAHO: achieving government assisted home-ownership) were also divided over whether it was just for the government to only assist the very poor in the housing arena. Mr. Leung (case 25: GAHO), living in a Home-Ownership flat, strongly disagreed with the statement, "It is just to only provide housing assistance to the very poor":

> I strongly disagree. The very poor need a lot of assistance. Those less poor need less assistance. This is irrational and illogical.

All interviewees, no matter what stake they held in Hong Kong housing policy, thought that it was just for the children to inherit private housing from their parents.

The official view was represented by Mr. Won (case 1: RMI-G):

> In private housing, there is private property right. It is the individual decision of the parents. How to handle their property is their individual decision.

On the whole, home-owners in private sector (Group 3: PriHO) supported inheritance of private property by children. Mr. Cheng (case 11: PriHO) appealed to property rights as the justification:

> As for the private housing, there is absolutely no room for disagreements. As for private flats, the ownership rights belong to the parents. If the parents die, the private flat is part of their property. They have the right to give it to anybody after they die, according to their legal will.

Those achieving government-assisted home-ownership (Group 5) also considered the inheritance of private housing as just. Mr. Ng (case 23: GAHO), recipient of a Sandwich Class Housing Loan, shared this view also by appealing to property rights:

> [The next generation inheriting private housing from their parents] is just. The flat belongs to you. You can give it to anybody. If you do not want to give it to your son, you can give it to somebody else. It is a property right. I am talking about private housing, not public rental housing.

Renters, public (Group 4: PuRH) and private (Group 2: PriRH) also agreed with the home-owners, though they did not own private housing. Ms. Chu (case20: PuRH), a public housing tenant, gave the following response:

> For private housing, the flat is bought by the parent. If they die, of course, it should be passed to the children ... There are blood ties between my son and me. I have the right to give it to my son.

Mr. Chan (case 5: PriRH), a renter of private housing, also shared similar views:

> [The next generation inheriting housing form their parents] is just. If I buy a property, the property right belongs to me. I have freedom to give it to anyone, not just the next generation. I can even give it to a stranger. It is because the property right belongs to the owner.

From these responses, we may conclude that Hong Kong people think it is likely to be just to respect private property rights and their transfer by consent.

Concerning whether it was just to impose inheritance tax, Mr. Sung (case 3: RMI-D), a property developer, thought that inheritance tax was unjust if it was too high:

> For private housing, inheritance is the law. It's written down in my will — my children inherit my property. It's a matter of fact. It's not a question of justice. The justice is dealt with by estate tax. You've to pay death duty or estate duty. It's certainly the case in England, not necessarily in Hong Kong. It's a difficult question. It's quite a political hot potato. I don't believe in pure socialism. If you are a pure socialist, you say, "Why should you inherit that wealth if you haven't earned that wealth?" I don't totally subscribe to that. If your parents have worked hard, I am a parent myself, I want my children to inherit my property when I die and I don't think there is anything fundamentally wrong with that. They have to pay a tax. It's treated as unearned income; therefore the government taxes it. It's taxed in England. I have reservation about that ... I believe in the coherence of society and family. What happen if the tax is so high that the children have to sell the house to pay the tax? Is that just? I don't think so. There are certain cases in England when the children are forced to sell the house to pay the death duty. To me, it's wrong. That's fundamentally wrong. It means the death duty is too high. If it's low, it's O.K.

One may expect home-owners to oppose the institution of inheritance tax as their descendents will be adversely affected. Ms. Tsang (case 16: PriHO), belonging to Group 3 (home-owners in private housing), who had made a great effort to buy a flat, thought that inheritance tax was unjust:

> Inheritance tax is unjust. It's very difficult for the flat-owner to buy a flat. Why should the government levy inheritance tax? Like us, we work

> very hard to repay mortgage in order to buy a flat. After I die, why should inheritance tax be levied? This is unjust. If one is rich, paying inheritance tax is O.K. Those rich may not earn money with difficulty. However, the poor earn money by working very hard.

However, not all home-owners agree with Ms. Tsang. Mr. Cheng (case 11: PriHO), achieving home-ownership without government assistance, thought that inheritance tax was just:

> Inheritance tax is a part of the government's strategy to re-allocate resources, maintaining justice and stability in society. I tend to regard it as just. However, how much inheritance tax the government should levy should be considered carefully. In principle, I agree that it is just.

Those achieving government-assisted home-ownership (Group 5: GAHO) tended to regard inheritance tax as just. Mr. Leung (case 27: GAHO), living in a Home-Ownership Scheme flat, regarded inheritance tax as a way of re-allocating resources:

> Inheritance tax is just ... The money is left by the past generation, not gained by yourself. Part of it should be given to the government to help the needy.

Mr. Leung's view is echoed by Ms. Yuen (case 22: PuRH), a public housing tenant (Group 4), whose views on inheritance tax were mostly shared by other interviewees in her Group:

> Inheritance tax is just. The children gain money [from inheritance], paying tax is just. The money was not earned by the children. It is left behind by the parents. It is something extra. The government should levy tax.

Those interviewees living in private rental housing (Group 2: PriRH) tended to regard inheritance tax as just, since it generated revenue for the government to help the needy. Mr. Chan (case 5: PriRH-A), who rented a private housing flat, shared this view:

> I agree that the government should levy inheritance tax. It is a kind of revenue stream for the government. It is more rational [that the inheritance tax is levied] if the [value of] the property exceeds a certain level. This applies not only to housing, but to all kinds of property.

Similarly, Mr. Hui (case 7: PriRH-I), depending on CSSA, renting a room in old private housing, also had the following opinion:

> If the [value of the] property is above a certain limit, levying inheritance tax is just. If the value of the property is great, paying inheritance tax will not hurt. It's the law of the government. The government needs revenue.

Generally, the interviewees were divided over whether it was just for the government to assist the middle-class towards home-ownership, to provide housing assistance only to the very poor, and to levy inheritance tax on the transfer of housing. However, they all agreed that it was just for the next generation to inherit private housing from their parents by mostly appealing to private property rights.

* * * * * *

In this chapter, we have examined the views of different stakeholders of Hong Kong housing policy on various housing policies. Most did not feel unjustly treated by the government, though a few of them did feel so. In the next chapter, we will discuss the philosophical implications of the stakeholders' views on justice in Hong Kong housing policy on the general conception of fairness in public policy.

7

Justice, Public Policy and Housing

In the previous chapter, we examined how justice was conceived by various stakeholders of Hong Kong's housing policy. In this chapter, we will discuss the philosophical implications of the stakeholders' views on fairness. We will examine what should be the role of equity in public policy. Lessons learnt from the discussion of justice and housing as experienced in Hong Kong will be discussed in this chapter.

* * * * * *

Philosophical Implications

Most philosophers, such as Marx, Hume, consider justice as single-principled. They mainly focus on a single principle, whether of needs, rights or deserts. However, the interviewees conceived justice as multi-faceted, just like Miller (Miller 1976); yet even he considered justice as having merely three strands (the principles of needs, rights and deserts). Nevertheless, in assessing the justness of various housing policies, the interviewees' understanding of justice was more complex . On the whole, nine principles of justice can be identified from their responses.

The first principle of justice in housing policy that the interviewees identified was the communitarian principle of justice. Mr. Won (case 1: RMI-G), the government spokesman, said that the government resorted to popular consensus on the definition of justice when formulating housing policy, so that programmes could be smoothly implemented with the support of the general public:

> The definition of justice varies from individual to individual. The government cannot say that "this is just" and not listen to the people, imposing [unpopular policies] on the people. This would be impossible. If we all agree to pursue justice, there are still different means for pursuing justice and different degrees of justice. There should be a discussion. We use democratic ways in an open society, hoping to find a consensus and then implement it. The policy can then be accepted and supported by the people. This should lead to the intended result.

The second principle that the interviewees appealed to in assessing the fairness of Hong Kong's housing policy is the Aristotelian formal principle of justice "to treat equals equally; unequals unequally". Ms. Kwan (case 8: PriRH-I), a waitlist household, pointed out that the discrimination against 2-person waitlist households, on the part of the government, in not building new 2-person public rental units, was unjust, since 2-person waitlist households were "forced" to wait for old 2-person units vacated by other public tenants, and thus had to wait longer than other applicants. Ms. Kwan believed that the government should treat all public rental housing applicants equally, by building public rental housing units of various sizes for households of different sizes, thereby putting all waitlist households on an equal footing. Ms. Au (case 26: GAHO) thought that she was unjustly treated by the government, since the government did not allow a specific group of civil servants, including her husband, to choose whether to buy or to rent when they received the civil servant housing allowance; other civil servants, however, had this choice. In short, Ms. Au considered that the government was not treating all civil servants equally in providing them with housing assistance.

Another principle of justice that the interviewees rested their views on was the principle of needs. Many interviewees, including government officials, suggested public rental housing was to be allocated according to needs. Ms. Hung (case 24: GAHO), living in a Home-Ownership flat, believed that it was just for the government to subsidize her in buying a flat, since she had a need for home-ownership. Ms. Tsang (case 16:PriHO) thought that the government's provision of home-ownership assistance to the middle-class, was unjust and that the government should divert the resources used for helping the middle-class to help the poor, who has imminent housing needs. Ms. Tsang's views were in line with the Rawlsian concept of justice, which stresses the greatest benefit to the least advantaged (who have the greatest need).

The principle of rights was another principle that the interviewees relied on to justify their views on justice. All interviewees agreed that it was fair for the next generation to inherit private housing from their parents. Most based their judgement on the private property rights that the parents had in their ownership of private housing, and the just transfer of such rights by consent. This view is in line with the Humean and Nozickian conception of justice, which emphasize private property rights and their just transfer by consent.

Another principle of justness that the interviewees drew on to legitimize their conception of fairness was the principle of deserts. Most interviewees, regardless of the stake they held in Hong Kong's housing market, considered it just for some to live in luxurious flats, since they have worked hard to gain money and therefore deserved to live comfortably. Some interviewees justified levying an inheritance tax on housing by appealing to the fact that inherited properties amounted to unearned income. Thus, part of inheritance should revert to the government as tax so that, on the whole, people would enjoy the fruits of their own hard work and therefore live by their own deserts, rather than those of a past generation.

Some interviewees appealed to the principle of choice in assessing the justness of certain housing policies, in line with Le Grand's theory of justice. For example, Ms. Au (case 26: GAHO), who received government housing assistance for civil servants, thought that she was unjustly treated by the government because her husband (a civil servant), in receiving government housing assistance, was "forced" to buy their flat, instead of given the choice to buy or to rent, which in the end trapped them in the problem of negative equity. Another interviewee, Mr. Chan (case 5: PriRH-A) believed that all households living in the same type of housing would be unjust. He indicated that compulsory measures were unjust and allowing people to choose freely, according to their needs and preferences, was just. Thus, the principle of choice was one of the principles of justice that some interviewees held in evaluating housing policies.

The principle of equal opportunities and fair competition is another measuring rod that some interviewees used. Mr. Chan (case 5: PriRH-A) suggested that justice should involve the government providing equal opportunities to those with initial limitations so they might move up the social and housing ladder. Mr. Yeung (case 2: RMI-D) indicated that under fair competition (involving equal opportunities), some people became rich while some people were poor would be just, while inequalities arising from unfair competition would be unjust.

One of the interviewees, Mr. Leung (case 27: GAHO) mentioned that justice involved fair transactions between two consenting parties. This argument would be in line with Hayek's conception of justice, which emphasizes the process of transacting in a market economy rather than the consequences of transactions. This marks the contrast with utilitarianism. Mr. Leung gave the following response when he was asked whether it was just for the government to provide public rental housing to low-income households:

> It's just. The government is willing to help. If you are willing to rent, then you rent from the government. It's like transactions. If you are willing to sell, I am willing to buy, then it's just. If you sell at $1,000 and I like your goods, I still buy even your goods cost $1,000. I don't rob from you or steal from you. It's a fair transaction. The government provides units for renting, you are willing to rent one, then it's fair. If both sides agree to transact, then it's just. If you forcefully rob from others, then it's unjust.

Most of the interviewees were Chinese. Did they hold views on justice which were Confucian in nature? Some interviewees held views which had a Confucian colour. For example, Ms. Chu (case 20: PuRH) stressed the blood ties between her and her son, saying that she had a right to pass a private housing flat to him when she died; her views underscored the intimate relations within a Confucian family. Ms. Au (case 26: GAHO) considered that if one had worked hard, or one's extended family had worked hard, and one was rich and lived comfortably, one deserved the reward and there was nothing unjust about that. Ms. Au's views on justice — a person enjoying the fruits of the hard work of the extended family — emphasized the autonomy of family (in making provisions for a child) in a Confucian society, as opposed to the stress on equal opportunities given to a person (regardless of one's family background) in a Western society.

The above are the nine principles of justice that some of the interviewees appealed to when asked to evaluate justice in Hong Kong housing policies. On the whole, the interviewees did not hold onto one single principle of equity when assessing justice of all housing policies. Usually, an interviewee appealed to different principles of fairness when evaluating different housing situations. Among all the principles of justice used by the interviewees, the most common ones were the principle of needs, rights and deserts, which were the same as the ones suggested by Miller in his three-principled conception of justice.

From the interviews, one might notice that the just principle for the distribution of a particular good is not randomly selected. For example, according to the interviewees, the distribution of public rental housing should be based upon the just principle of needs, rather than the principle of rights; while luxurious flats were to be distributed in accordance with the principle of deserts, rather than needs. The just principle for the distribution of a particular type of housing rests upon its social meaning. For example, according to the interviewees, luxurious flats should be treated as a reward to one's hard work. Thus, they were to be distributed according to deserts. They should not be distributed for the satisfaction of housing needs, for example, distributed to those living in inadequate housing as a form of assistance. This is in line with Walzer's conception of justice.

It should be underscored that justice conceived by the people may differ from justice in the normative sense. Some interviewees might define justice in their favour or stressed a version of justice in a biased way. For example, Mr. Yeung (case 2: RMI-D), a property developer, asserted that the government was unjust in competing with property developers for profit and suggested that the government should buy flats from property developers and rented them out as public rental housing, instead of building them. Similarly, he proposed that the government should subsidize the Home-Ownership Scheme applicants in cash to buy private flats from developers, rather than building flats for sale. These suggestions, no doubt, will increase the profit-making chances, on the part of the developers. That is, Mr. Yeung was defining justice in his favour. In a similar way, the government-assisted home-owners defined justice in a self-interested way, by stressing their need for home-ownership even though they could afford private rental housing, (but not unassisted-home-ownership), thereby having no imminent housing need. Ms. Hung (case 24: GAHO) and Mr. Leung (case 27: GAHO) may represent those having such kind of biased views. Interviewees from the lower stratum, such as Ms. Lee (case 6: PriRH-I) and Ms. Kwan (case 8: PriRH-I), tended to hold views consistent with the Rawlsian conception of justice, indicating that it was unjust when the government assisted the middle-class in achieving home-ownership, while neglecting the housing plight of the most desperate. Such views are concordant with Rawls' conception of justice, which focuses on bringing the greatest benefit to the least advantaged, rather than those from society's middle or upper strata. In this way, those from the lower stratum also define justice in a way that favours their own needs, embracing the Rawlsian conception of justice.

After reading the interviews, one might conclude that Hong Kong's people adopt principles of justice that are more Western than Confucian in nature. The interviewees envisaged great intervention on the government's part in the housing arena. Assistance from the government was not sought as a last resort. In a Confucian society, family forms the first tier of support, followed by the social network, with government aid serving as the last resort. Hong Kong was and is a place of immigrants from China. Many Hong Kong people have their family or the extended family in China. (Many of the interviewees are examples of this.) Thus, the family and the extended family may fail to provide an effective tier of support to Hong Kong's residents in satisfying their housing needs. Therefore they turn to the government for assistance. The Hong Kong government was and is mainly Western in style, originating from the British rule.

Some interviewees were inconsistent in their responses to different housing situations. For example, Mr. Ko (case 9: PriRH-I) believed that the government should assist the middle-class to achieve home-ownership on the basis of their home-ownership needs:

> The middle income people cannot afford home-ownership. The government should help them. The government will check; if you need assistance, the government will help you. The middle-income people have needs for home-ownership, the government should help them.

Though Mr. Ko indicated that the government should help the middle-class, he agreed with the statement, "It is just for the government to only provide housing assistance to the very poor", representing an example of incompatible views. It may be hypothesized that Mr. Ko believed the primary responsibility of a just government was to help the very poor and if the middle-income people had home-ownership needs, the government should also help. Ms. Chan (case 18: PuRH) also held views that contradicted each other. She mentioned that it was just for all households, large or small, rich or poor, to live in the same type of housing; she buttressed her argument by claiming that every person was equal as a human being. Yet she agreed with the statement, "It is just for people of different income to live in different types of housing". Ms. Chan indicated that though it was just for all households to live in the same type of housing, it was an impossible ideal to realize. It is possible that Ms. Chan believed that, to be more realistic, a less than perfect situation had to be accepted: that is, people of different income lived in different types of housing. Mr. Ng (case 23: GAHO) also had inconsistent opinions on housing policy justice. On one hand, he suggested it was just for the government to provide home-ownership assistance to the middle-class since they paid taxes, depending on the idea that rights rested on responsibilities. On the other hand, he gave the following reply, when asked whether he agreed to the statement, "It is just for the government to only provide housing assistance to the very poor":

> It's just. I agree. In the past, the government used housing and land to gain money. There was speculation over control of the land supply, leading to insufficient land. This was not normal. This meant many people could not afford to buy a flat, even if they wanted to. There was no chance [of buying a flat]. The situation became more and more serious. This was not normal. The government should have been stabilizing the supply of housing, not helping [the middle-class] buy flats. Everywhere, clothing, food, housing and transport are necessities. Why do you use one of these as a tool to gain money, a tool to gain a lot of money? People engage in speculation [on housing]. This is not a normal phenomenon. In normal circumstances, the government does not need to help [people to buy a flat]. Those who are very poor, maybe because of background or family problems — the government should help them. They may have contributed in the past, maybe because of bad luck, and now cannot afford [decent accommodation]. The government should of course help them.

Perhaps Mr. Ng thought that, in abnormal situations when home-ownership became unaffordable to the middle-class in light of the government's failure to stabilize the property market, it would be just for the government to assist the middle-class in buying their own homes, since they paid tax. The fact that some interviewees gave contrasting responses to various questions on justice could indicate that they usually do not give serious thoughts to the concept of fairness in their everyday lives. When asked, they thus gave their immediate casual responses to the questions on equity. If they made deep deliberations on the matter, they might have returned more consistent replies.

To conclude, though the interviewees might not have read the philosophical texts on the concept of justice, they held views similar to those of the philosophers. This is not surprising, since philosophical theories that are totally at odds with commonsense beliefs will not stand. The idea of justice being held by the Hong Kong people does not differ much from the conclusions of earlier philosophical discussion. On the whole, the interviewees held views on justice that were more Western than Chinese in nature, since Hong Kong people are exposed to Western form of education and style of government.

Justice in Public and Housing Policy

From the discussion of the historical development of justice in Hong Kong's housing policy in Chapter 5, it seems that there were and are signs of injustice in different phases. This was agreed upon by the interviewees, who suggested instances of injustices in various aspects of Hong Kong's housing policy, which were highlighted in Chapter 6. One may wonder whether a genuinely just housing system exists or ever existed. Housing systems that involve massive state intervention into the housing sector (such as China's socialist housing policy immediately after the Communist takeover in 1949, or the Singaporean and Swedish housing system) may be criticized as unjust, because of the non-selectivity and non-targeting of housing subsidies, treating unequals (those able to and those unable to satisfy their own housing needs themselves) equally by providing housing subsidy to almost all, thereby violating the Aristotelian formal principle of "treating unequals unequally". Housing arrangements that comprise minimal governmental involvement usually in the form of small residual public housing sector, for example, housing systems in the United States, Japan and Australia, may be condemned as inequitable for neglecting the housing plight of the poor (by not providing them with housing subsidy in kind or in cash). They are unjust in the Marxian and Rawlsian sense, which stress distribution according to needs, especially that of the least advantaged. What about housing systems which allow moderate state intervention? Do they stand a better chance of being more just, with a sizable but not a (almost) total public rental sector? The British housing system may be classified as one with moderate state intervention. However, it is still not completely just. The British government puts emphasis on home-ownership encouragement, even in view of the problem of homelessness, infringing upon the Rawlsian conception of justice (which emphasizes assistance to the least advantaged) since such housing policies benefit the comparatively well-off home-owners rather than the poor and the least advantaged.

All housing systems are unjust in some sense: purely just housing policy did not, and does not, exist. This may not be surprising, given that justice is not the sole consideration in policy-making, but only one among many factors that count in decision-making. Thus, a purely just housing policy may be sacrificed for the pursuit of other ends. It should be noted that a public policy is inadequate if it does not take justice into consideration; so is a public policy which rests solely on justice. One should distinguish between a just public policy and a sensible public policy that is administratively, economically and politically sustainable. One example will suffice. A just housing policy will involve asking those public housing tenants to move out of public housing once their income increases to a level that they can afford private housing rent, so that their rental unit can be re-allocated to people in more need from the waiting list. This is just according to the Marxian and Rawlsian conception of justice. However, if this policy is taken to extremes, there will be social instability, resulting from many public housing tenants' constant fear of forced eviction from their home. There will also be a lack of social mix in public rental housing, leading to stigmatization due to the formation of ghettos or "sink estates". There will also be a lack of incentive for public housing tenants to work hard to gain money (maybe through taking up an additional part-time job) since increased income may immediately lead to the government withdrawing housing welfare. This adversely affects upward social mobility in society. Also, frequent means-tests for the tenants are troublesome and administratively expensive. Thus, a policy solely that rests on justice may have many negative side-effects. Therefore, a sensible public policy should balance justice with other policy considerations. A sensible public policy is not merely a just one, representing a balance struck between justice and other policy considerations. In short, justice is one among many indispensable policy considerations, not the sole consideration in public policy-making. A policy that is not just cannot be a sensible policy, yet so is a policy that only takes justice alone into consideration.

Let us define what a just and sensible housing policy is: one both just and sensible. If a government hopes to implement a just and sensible housing policy, it should put priority on the pursuit of justice in the Marxian and Rawlsian sense, establishing it as the primary good or end of the housing policy. If justice is not pursued as a primary good or end, it will often be neglected in view of the pursuit of other goals, resulting in injustices. For example, the Marxian conception of justice has never been pursued as a primary aim or end by itself in Hong Kong. The Marxian conception of justice played different role in the development of Hong Kong housing policy as discussed in Chapter 5. The Resettlement Policy in the 1950s and 1960s was carried out primarily to regain land occupied by squatters for economic development, with the Marxian conception of justice (that is, the satisfaction of needs of the inadequately housed) playing an incidental role. Since the Marxian conception of justice was not a primary end, those needy individuals living in private tenements were neglected. Also, the resettled squatters in resettlement estates could be regarded as inadequately housed, that is, with their housing needs unsatisfied because of the sub-standard conditions in the resettlement estates. In the 1970s, the Marxian conception of justice in housing was pursued as a means to further the political end of maintaining stability and the economic end of facilitating the economic development of Hong Kong. Because the Marxian conception of justice was not an end, it was sacrificed in face of the drive to promote home-ownership in the form of the shift in emphasis on the production of public rental housing to Home-Ownership Scheme flats in the 1980s and 1990s, leaving the needs of those on the waiting list of public rental housing unsatisfied, leading to injustices in the Marxian and Rawlsian sense. From 2002 onwards, the Marxian conception of justice occurred as a by-product of housing policies aiming at stabilizing the property market. Although the government denied its negligence of justice as an end as expressed by the government spokesman Mr. Won (case 1: RMI-G), in a 2003 interview, saying that justice was one of a few important considerations in the decision-making process of Hong Kong's housing policy, its acts deviated from its words. At best, Marxian conception of justice could only be considered as a secondary or a by-product of economic pursuits in 2003. As a result, instances of injustices in the Marxian sense occurred in Hong Kong's housing policy since justice was compromised or even disregarded in the pursuit of other goals, such as political and economic ends.

There are so many conceptions of justice, one may question why the Marxian conception of justice should be given priority through establishing it as an end in housing policy if a government is to pursue a more just housing policy. What is the reason of not establishing Hume's conception of justice, basing on property rights as the primary end of Hong Kong housing policy? Or the Aristotelian conception of justice, based on distribution according to merit or deserts? It was established in Chapter 2 that in case of conflict between different principles of justice, the need principle should take priority, the principle of rights should be given second priority, followed by the principle of deserts. Thus, if the just principle of deserts is in conflict with the Marxian conception of justice, which stresses that a government should distribute according to needs, genuine justice requires that the Marxian just principle of needs should take priority. Thus, if the government is to pursue a genuinely just and sensible housing policy, it should establish the Marxian and the Rawlsian conceptions of justice which emphasize the needs of the least advantaged as the primary end in housing policy since other conceptions of justice may be "compromised" in case of a conflict with the former. In light of the implementation of the Marxian conception of justice as a primary end, the government should rehouse all those living in inadequate housing by providing public rental housing or providing other forms of housing subsidies, thereby completely eliminating the problem of substandard housing in society.

In light of the just principle of rights, there should be a free and fair private property market, in which people can buy and sell properties, freely transferring property rights by consent at agreed equilibrium price. This is in line with Hume's and Nozick's conceptions of justice which stress property rights and their transfer.

The government should also ensure that people will have choice in finding their own housing that suits their needs and affordability. For example, in the context of Hong Kong, the government should supply different variety of land in different areas in the Application List of land sales for property developers to apply to purchase. For example, low density sites in well-situated districts for the building of luxurious flats, high density sites in outlying districts for middle to low priced basic housing. This is to maintain a balanced supply of different types of housing, allowing people to choose the appropriate type of housing that suits their affordability, specific requirements and desire. Allowing choice in the selection of one's accommodation is in line with Le Grand's theory of justice, which emphasizes that justice involves choice. The provision of different varieties of housing also allows people to enjoy the results of their different degrees of hard work. For example, those who work very hard and save more, may choose to live in luxurious flats. This is in line with the Aristotelian conception of justice, which stresses distribution in accordance with merit or deserts.

Governments in various countries have been promoting home-ownership through different measures. It should be noted that the desire for home-ownership represents a tenure preference, rather than a housing need. If a household cannot afford home-ownership, it may still able to afford decent accommodation in the rental sector. The provision of assistance towards home-ownership should not take priority over the provision of assistance to the needy through the provision of public rental housing, according to the Marxian and Rawlsian conceptions of justice. Only after the government has successfully rehoused all those inadequately housed should the government provide home-ownership assistance.

In the long run, the government should ensure that home-ownership is affordable to the middle-class, rather than directly subsidizing home-ownership which often brings about injustices. For example, in Hong Kong, the government should stabilize prices in the property market through its control over the supply of land. If property prices rise to unaffordable levels, the government should increase the supply of land. If the property prices decrease, the government should decrease the supply of residential land. If the government can control the supply of land skillfully, thereby stabilizing property prices, home-ownership will not be unaffordable to middle-income households. Thus, there will not be a "need" to assist middle-income households to achieve home-ownership, both in the form of "bricks and mortar" and housing loans. The most important thing is to stabilize prices in the private property market, making home-ownership affordable rather than subsidizing home-ownership. In this way, the Home-Ownership Scheme, Tenant Purchase Scheme and different housing loan schemes are made unnecessary, and the government can concentrate its effort and resources in providing welfare housing to the needy in the form of public rental housing, thus satisfying the Marxian and Rawlsian conceptions of justice.

In conclusion, there are various means at the government's disposal to ensure the implementation of a just and sensible housing policy. However, the government may have many goals, with justice as one of them. Therefore, justice may be compromised as a goal. However, justice cannot be neglected totally, or put in a secondary role, if the government is to solve the housing problem of the people.

* * * * * *

To summarize, social justice is multi-principled, involving the principle of needs, rights, deserts and equal opportunity. Justice in public policy involves the economic policy of integrating capitalist and socialist principles, providing minimum income to those who fail to satisfy their needs in the labour market by the just principle of needs. The provision of minimum income is financed by taxation and a just tax system is progressive in nature. The just principle of equal opportunity involves the provision of free and compulsory education for children from poor families. A just housing policy involves the provision of housing subsidies for the needy according to the principle of needs. Different governments use different measures to encourage home-ownership. However, this drive towards increased home-ownership, on the part of the governments, is not justified by the requirement of justice in the Rawlsian and Marxian sense. Injustices in the Marxian and Rawlsian sense may occur, if the government prioritizes the subsidizing of home-ownership at the expense of providing housing subsidies for those needy who live in inadequate housing.

Justice has played different roles during the different periods in the evolution of Hong Kong's housing policy. Governmental intervention in the housing arena in 1954 was initiated by social justice in the Marxian and Confucian sense, when the colonial government sought to rehouse the Shek Kip Mei fire victims. Social justice in the Marxian and Rawlsian sense was pursued as a means to further political and economic ends in the 1970s to mid-1980s, leading to frequent compromises and instances of injustices. Starting in 1987, the promotion of home-ownership caused a clash between the Marxian and Confucian conception of justice, while the more rational use of public rental housing resources was an implementation of Marxian and Rawlsian conception of justice. Since 2002, just results in the Marxian and Rawlsian sense occurred as a by-product of the government's desire to stabilize the property market, with the housing needs of the least advantaged more effectively satisfied through reduced waiting list and time for public rental housing, an outcome that satisfied the just principle of needs. Roughly speaking, the stakeholders interviewed did not feel unjustly treated by the government housing policy, except for those who were renting inadequate housing in the private sector, and the property developers. All interviewees, regardless of the stake they held, considered it just for the government to provide public rental housing to low-income households. Their views differed on the harshness of policy towards public housing tenants who became better-off after living in public housing for a period of time. On the whole, the stake one held affected one's views on governmental home-ownership assistance. In order to make housing policy more just, the government should establish the principle of needs as a primary goal and end by itself, rehousing all those inadequately sheltered in public rental housing, or providing housing subsidies in another form e.g. rent allowance. In the private housing sector, the government should make home-ownership affordable by stabilizing the property market through the SAR government's control of land supply, instead of directly assisting home-ownership.

In conclusion, this research is largely an application of social philosophy to housing studies. It is hoped that light has been thrown on housing studies, introducing new perspectives. Housing studies are not the only arena where philosophy may be applied in order to gain fresh insights. Philosophy may be applied to other disciplines to examine issues of prime importance, for example in examining justice in a country's health policy; moral philosophy can be applied to investigate education, and there may be applications of political philosophy to contrast the political systems of different countries. Though there is enormous potential of doing research on applications of philosophy to other fields, not much has been done. It is hoped that there will be more joint-faculty research efforts in future, with philosophers working with experts in other disciplines, bringing fresh insights into empirical research, thereby reaping fruitful results and contributing to both disciplines.

Notes

1. Philosophy, Justice and Hong Kong Housing Policy

1 This information was provided by the Census and Statistics Department of the Hong Kong government.
2 "He" is used here since all governors of Hong Kong were male.
3 This document was obtained from the website www.cityu.edu.hk/hkhousing/.
4 Information in this section was provided in a speech made by the Secretary for Housing, Planning and Lands to the Legislative Council on 13 November, 2002.

2. Social Justice — An Intricate Concept

1 'He' instead of 's/he' is used here, following Hume's original text.
2 The equality principle here is a part of the just principle of rights as defined in Miller's earlier book: the citizens enjoy equal rights as an equal member of the society.
3 Freedom to select a particular life may be regarded as the opportunity to live a particular life.
4 The four principles of justice are: to each according to his/her needs, rights and deserts and equal opportunity to all.

3. Social Justice in Public Policy

1 One should take note that to date there has not been 'true' or 'pure' form of socialism implemented, though not from the point of view of the so-called "socialist" government.
2 These are meant only to be rough guidelines. One should take note that there may be difficulties in assessing what a minimum income should actually cover in the implementation of the policy in reality.
3 A regressive tax system taxes those with lower income at higher rate than those with higher income.

4 A progressive tax system taxes those with higher income at higher rates than those with lower income.
5 Translated by Roger T. Ames and Henry Rosemont; quoted by Joseph Chan (2003), p. 237.

5. Justice in Hong Kong's housing Policy — A Historical Perspective

1 The style of government remains very much the same after the transfer of sovereignty to China under "One Country, Two Systems" as stipulated in the Basic Law, which has been the Constitution of Hong Kong since 1997.
2 When the situation in China worsened, people moved into Hong Kong. When the situation in China "normalized", people returned to China.
3 This document was obtained from the website www.cityu.edu.hk/hkhousing/.
4 Under the Private Sector Participation Scheme, sites were sold to developers on the condition that the flats developed on these sites had to be sold to buyers nominated by the Housing Authority. The income limit for Home Ownership Scheme and Private Sector Participation Scheme were the same.
5 This document was obtained from the website www.cityu.edu.hk/hkhousing/.
6 This speech can be found on the website www.cityu.edu.hk/hkhousing/.
7 In 1981, the waiting list for public rental housing consisted of 160,000 households, with a waiting time of about seven years.
8 These documents were obtained from the website www.cityu.hk/hkhousing/.
9 This was obtained from the website www.cityu.hk/hkhousing/.
10 Only until 2000 was the Mandatory Provident Fund (a compulsory individual saving scheme for retirement, with 5% [of income] contribution from the employee and 5% contribution from the employer) established. However, it is still not very effective in solving the retirement problem of the general public.
11 This was obtained from the website www.cityu.hk/hkhousing/.
12 The corporate income tax rate in Hong Kong was about 15%–16.5%.
13 This information was provided by the Housing Authority in October, 2002.
14 The name of this government official was deliberately changed to protect his anonymity. The interview was conducted in Cantonese.
15 This information was provided in the speech of the Secretary for Housing, Planning and Lands to the Legislative Council on 13 November 2002.
16 The Home Assistance Loan Scheme was abandoned in 2004 to relieve the budget deficit.

6. Justice Conceived by the Hong Kong Community

1 The names of the interviewees in this book were deliberately changed to protect their anonymity.

2 Please refer to the section "Marxian Conception of Justice as a By-product (2002 onwards) — Policy Responses to the Asian Economic Crisis" of Chapter 5.

3 Comprehensive Social Security Assistance is a social security safety net in Hong Kong.

4 Another son has moved and lived in a Home-Ownership Scheme flat.

5 A bigger number means there are more people before you on the waiting list.

6 HOS stands for Home-Ownership Scheme.

7 PSPS stands for Private Sector Participation Scheme.

8 NGO stands for non-government organization.

9 HOS stands for Home-Ownership Scheme.

Bibliography

Aaron, Henry J. 1972. *Shelter and Subsidies.* Washington: Brookings Institution.

Agassi, J. 1969. Housing the Needy. In *Hong Kong: A Society in Transition*, ed. I. C. Jarvie, 247–256. London: Routledge & Kegan Paul.

Alejandro, R. 1998. *The Limits of Rawlsian Justice.* Baltimore: John Hopkins University Press.

Angel, Shlomo. 2000 *Housing Policy Matters: A Global Analysis.* New York: Oxford University Press.

Aristotle. 1998 *The Nicomachean Ethics, Book V*, translated by David Ross, Oxford: Oxford University Press.

Arneson, Richard J. 2000 Welfare Should Be the Currency of Justice. *Canadian Journal of Philosophy,* 30.4: 497–524.

Ashford, Nigel. 1993. The Ideas of the New Right. In *Public Policy and the Impact of the New Right*, ed. Grant Gordon & Nigel Ashford. 19–45. London: Pinter.

Atkinson, A. B. 1983. *Social Justice and Public Policy.* Sussex: Harvester Press.

Baker, John. 1992. An Egalitarian Case for Basic Income. In *Arguing for Basic Income*, ed. Philippe Van Parijs, 101–127. London: Verso.

Balchin, Paul, 1996. Introduction to Owner-Occupation. In *Housing Policy in Europe*, ed. Paul Balchin, 149–162. London: Routledge.

Balchin, Paul. 1996. Introduction to Private Rental Housing. In *Housing Policy in Europe*, ed. Paul Balchin, 25–35. London: Routledge.

Balchin, Paul. 1996. Introduction to Social Housing. In *Housing Policy in Europe*, ed. Paul Balchin, 69–83. London: Routledge.

Barry, Brian. 1988. Equal Opportunity and Moral Arbitrariness. In *Equal Opportunity*, ed. Norman E. Bowie, 23–44. Boulder: Westview Press.

Barry, Brian. 1989. *Theories of Justice.* California: University of California Press.

Beer, Andrew. 1993. A Dream Won, A Crisis Born? Home-Ownership and the Housing Market. In *Housing Australia*, ed. Chris Paris, 147–172. Melbourne: Macmillan.

Bell, Daniel. 1993. *Communitarianism and its Critics.* Oxford University Press: Oxford.

Bell, Daniel A. 2003. Confucian Constraints on Property Rights. In *Confucianism for the Modern World*, ed. Daniel A. Bell and Hahm Chaibong, 218–235. Cambridge: Cambridge University Press.

Bellamy, R. and Hollis, M. 1995. Liberal Justice: Political and Metaphysical. *The Philosophical Quarterly*, 45:178, 1–19.

Bentham, Jeremy. 1987. *An Introduction to the Principles of Morals and Legislation*. London: Penguin.

Berg, Bruce L. 2004. *Qualitative Research Methods for the Social Science*. Boston: Pearson.

Berger, F. R. 1997. John Stuart Mill on Justice and Fairness. In *Mill' s Utilitarianism*, ed. David Lyons, 45–65. Maryland: Rowman & Littlefield Publishers.

Bishop, P. 1971. Some Aspects of the Hong Kong Resettlement Programme. In *Asian Urbanization: A Hong Kong Casebook*, ed. D. J. Dwyer, 111–122. Hong Kong: Hong Kong University Press.

Boatright, John R. 1993 Justice and the Market System. In *Ethics and the Conduct of Business*, 91–125. New Jersey: Prentice-Hall.

Boatright, John R. 2000. Justice and the Market System. In *Ethics and the Conduct of Business,* 73–103. New Jersey: Prentice Hall.

Bosanquel, Nick. 1984. Is Privatization Inevitable? In *Privatization and the Welfare State*, ed. Julian Le Grand and Ray Robinson, 58–69. London: George Allen & Unwin.

Boulding, Kenneth E. and Pfaff, Martin. 1972. Distributive Effects of the Grants Economy: An Introduction. In *Redistribution to the Rich and the Poor,* ed. Kenneth E. Boulding and Martin Pfaff, 1–11. California: Wadsworth.

Bowie, Norman E. 1988. Introduction. In *Equal Opportunity,* 1–12. Boulder: Westview Press.

Boyne, George. 1993. Local Government: from Monopoly to Competition. In *Public Policy and the Impact of the New Right,* ed. Grand Jordan & Nigel Ashford, 165–92. London: Pinter.

Bradshaw, Jonathan. 1999. The Nature of Poverty. In *Introduction to Social Security*, ed. John Ditch, 11–33. London: Routledge.

Brock, Gillian. 1998. Introduction. In *Necessary Goods*, ed. in Gillian Brock, 1–18. Maryland: Rowman & Littlefield.

Buchanan, A. E. 1982. *Marx and Justice: The Radical Critique of Liberalism.* London: Methuen.

Burke, Gill. 1981. *Housing and Social Justice.* Essex: Longman.

Burton, Elizabeth. 2003. Housing for an Urban Renaissance: Implications for Social Equity. In *Housing Studies,* 18.4: 537–562.

Caputo, R. K. 2002 Social Justice, the Ethics of Care, and Market Economies. *Families in Society: The Journal of Contemporary Human Services*, 83.4: 355–364.

Castells, M. 1986. *The Shek Kip Mei Syndrome: Public Housing and Economic Development in Hong Kong*. Hong Kong: Centre of Urban Studies and Urban Planning, University of Hong Kong Press.

Castells, M., Goh, L., Kwok, R. Y.-W. 1990. *The Shek Kip Mei Syndrome*. London: Pion.

Chan, K. W. 1997. *Social Construction of Gender Inequality in Housing System.* Aldershot: Ashgate.

Chan, K. W. 2000. Prosperity or Inequality: Deconstructing the Myth of Home Ownership in Hong Kong. *Housing Studies*, 15.1: 29–45.

Chan, Kwok Leung. 1989. The Demographic Setting of Hong Kong: Development and Implications. In *Hong Kong Society*, ed. Alex Y. H. Kwan, 13–46. Hong Kong: Writers & Publishers' Cooperative.

Chan, Alex. 2001. *A New Direction for Public Housing in Hong Kong*. Hong Kong: Citizens Party.

Chan, Joseph. 2003. Giving Priority to the Worst Off: A Confucian Perspective on Social Welfare. In *Confucianism for the Modern World*, ed. Daniel A Bell and Hahm Chaibong, 236–253. Cambridge: Cambridge University Press.

Chandler, Ralph Clark. 1988. The Commercial Republic Re-examined: A Critique of the Economization Model of Public Policy Making. In *Market-Based Public Policy*, Richard C. Hulu, 181–203. Hamsphire: Macmillan.

Chau, K. W. 1995. *Market Concentration and Competition in Hong Kong's Residential Market: Some Empirical Evidence.* Hong Kong: University of Hong Kong Press.

Chau, Leung Chuen. 1993. *Hong Kong: A Unique Case of Development.* Washington: The World Bank Press.

Chiu, Chi-Yue. 1985. *The Notion of Justice and Pattern of Justice Behaviour in Chinese Culture* (Unpublished M. Phil. thesis). University of Hong Kong.

Chiu, R. L. H. 1993. *Privatization of Public Housing in Hong Kong: Planning and Policy Issues.* Hong Kong: Centre of Urban Planning and Environmental Management. Hong Kong: University of Hong Kong Press.

Chiu, R. L. H. 1997. The Promotion of Home-Ownership in Hong Kong: Planning and Policy Issues. *Asian Journal of Business & Information Systems,* 2.1: 89–110.

Chiu, R. L. H. 1998. Home Ownership Drive of HKSAR. *Planning and Development, Journal of Hong Kong Institute of Planners*, 14.1: 12–20.

Chiu, R. L. H. 2002. Social Equity in Housing in Hong Kong Special Administrative Region: A Social Sustainability Perspective. *Sustainable Development*, 10.1: 155–162.

Chou, W. L. and Shih, Y. C. 1995. Hong Kong Housing Market: Overview, Tenure Choice and Housing Demand. *Journal of Real Estate Finance and Economics*, 10.1: 7–21.

Christiano, Thomas. 2003. Is Democracy Merely a Means to Social Justice? In *Real Libertarianism Assessed,* ed. A. Reeve and A. Williams, 172–2000. New York: Palgrave Macmillan.

Chua, Beng-Huat. 2003. Housing Provision and Management of Aspirations. In *Housing and Social Change*, ed. Ray Forrest and James Lee, 69–86. London: Routledge.

Chua, Beng-Huat. 1995. Not Depoliticised but Ideologically Successful: The Public Housing Programme. In *Communitarian Ideology and Democracy in Singapore,* 124–146. London: Routledge.

Chua, Beng-Huat. 1997 *Political Legitimacy and Housing*. London: Routledge.

Clapham, David *et al.* 1994. Making Housing Work: Social Justice & Housing Policy. *Housing and Social Justice*, ed. Robinn Goodlad and Kenneth Gibb, 1–26. London: Institute for Public Policy Research.

Clapham, David, Kemp, Peter and Smith, Susan J. 1990. *Housing and Social Policy* London: Macmillan.

Clarke, J. J. 2000. *The Tao of the West*. London: Routledge.

Clinton, David, Yates, Michael and Kang, Dharminder. 1994. *Integrating Taxes and Benefits*. London: Institute for Public Policy Research.

Cohen, G. A. 1991. Robert Nozick and Wilt Chamberlain: How Patterns Preserve Liberty. In *Justice and Economic Distribution*, ed. J. Arthur and W. H. Shaw. New Jersey: Prentice Hall.

Cohen, G. A. 1999. Socialism and Equality of Opportunity. In *Political Thought*, ed. M. Rosen and J. Wolff, 354–58. Oxford: Oxford University Press.

Confucius. 1979 *The Analects*. Translated by D.C. Lau. Hong Kong: The Chinese University Press.

Consumer Council. 1996. *How Competitive is the Private Residential Property Market?* Hong Kong: Consumer Council.

Conway, Jean. 2000. *Housing Policy*. Sussex: Gildredge Press.

Coote, Anna and Hunter, David J. 1998. Better Health for All. In *Social Policy and Social Justice*, ed. Jane Franklin, 262–279. Cambridge: Polity Press.

Copp, David. 1998. Equality, Justice and the Basic Needs. In *Necessary Goods*, ed. Gillian Brock, 113–133. Maryland: Rowman & Littlefield.

Corden, Anne. 1999. Claiming Entitlements: Take-up of Benefits. In *Introduction to Social Security*, ed. John Ditch, 134–155. London: Routledge.

Corry, Dan. 1998 The Role of the Public Sector and Public Expenditure. In *Social Policy and Social Justice*, ed. Jane Franklin, 73–101. Cambridge: Polity Press.

Cowan, David and McDermont, Morag. 2006. *Regulating Social Housing: Governing Decline*. Oxford: Routledge.

Cragg, A. W. 1983. Hayek, Justice and the Market. *Canadian Journal of Philosophy*, 13.4: 563–574.

Cullingworth, J. B. 1979. *Essays on Housing Policy*. London: George Allen & Unwin.

Cunningham, F. 1997. On Relating Justice and Democracy: A Strategy and a Hypothesis. In *Justice and Democracy: Cross-Cultural Perspectives*, ed. R. Bontekoe and M. Stepaniants, 77–91. Honolulu: University of Hawaii Press.

Dasgupta Partha. 1982. Utilitarianism, Information and Rights. In *Utilitarianism and Beyond*, ed. Amartya Sen and Bernard Williams, 199–218. Cambridge: Cambridge University Press.

David, Martin and Leuthold, Jane. 1972. Formulas for Income Maintenance:

Their Distributional Impact. In *Redistribution to the Rich and the Poor*, ed. in Kenneth E Boulding and Martin Pfaff, 312–341. California: Wadsworth.

Davis, L. 1981. Nozick' s Entitlement Theory. In *Reading Nozick*, ed. J. Paul, 344–354. Oxford: Blackwell.

Dawson, Raymond. 1981. *Confucius*. Oxford: Oxford University Press.

De Gregori, T. R. 1978. Market Morality: Robert Nozick and the Question of Economic Justice. *American Journal of Economics and Sociology*, 38.1: 17–30.

Dey, Ian. 1993. Qualitative Data Analysis: A User-Friendly Guide for Social Scientists. London: Routledge.

Doling, John. 1997 Comparative Housing Policy: Government and Housing in Advanced Industrialized Countries. London: Macmillan.

Donnison, David. 1984. The Progressive Potential of Privatization. In *Privatization and the Welfare State*, Julian Le Grand and Ray Robinson, 45–57. London: Allen & Unwin.

Doyal, Len. 1998. A Theory of Human Need. In *Necessary Goods*, ed. Gillian Brock, 157–72. Maryland: Rowman & Littlefield.

Drakakis-Smith, D. 1971. Housing Needs and Planning Policies for the Asian City: The Lesson from Hong Kong. *International Journal of Environment of Environmental Studies*, 1.2: 115–128.

Drakakis-Smith, D. 1971. *Housing Standards and Housing Policy in Hong Kong: Implications for Asian Cities*. Hong Kong: Centre of Asian Studies, University of Hong Kong Press.

Drakakis-Smith, D. 1972. 'Tenement Slum Renewal' *Pacific Viewpoint* 13.2: 155–168.

Drakakis-Smith, D. 1973. *Housing Provision in Metropolitan Hong Kong* Hong Kong: Centre of Asian Studies, University of Hong Kong Press.

Drakakis-Smith, D. 1979. *High Society: Housing Provision Metropolitan Hong Kong 1954–1979*. Hong Kong: Centre of Asian Studies, University of Hong Kong Press.

Drakakis-Smith, D. 1981. *Urbanization, Housing and the Development Process*. London: Croom Helm.

Drakakis-Smith, D. and Yeung Y. M. 1977. *Public Housing in the City-States of Hong Kong and Singapore*. Canberra: Development Studies Centre, Australian National University Press.

Drake, Robert F. 2001. *The Principles of Social Policy*. New York: Palgrave.

Dulebohn J. and Martocchio J. J. 1998. Employee's Perceptions of the Distributive Justice of Pay Raise Decisions: A Policy Capturing Approach. *Journal of Business and Psychology*, 13.1: 41–64.

Dworkin, R. 1975. The Original Position. In *Reading Rawls*, ed. N. Daniels, 16–53. Oxford: Blackwell.

Dwyer, D. J. 1970. Urban Squatters: the Relevance of the Hong Kong Experience. *Asian Survey*, 10: 607–613.

Dwyer, D. J. 1971. Housing Provision in Hong Kong. In *Asian Urbanization: A Hong Kong Casebook*, ed. D. J. Dwyer, 33–47. Hong Kong: Hong Kong University Press.

Dwyer, D. J. 1971. Introduction. In *Asian Urbanization: A Hong Kong Casebook*, ed. D. J. Dwyer, 1–10. Hong Kong: Hong Kong University Press.

Ebreo, A. Linn, N. and Vining, J. 1996. The Impact of Procedural Justice on Opinions of Public Policy: Solid Waste Management as an Example. *Journal of Applied Social Psychology*, 26.14: 1259–1285.

Fan, Rui Ping. 1997. Confucian and Rawlsian Views of Justice: A Comparison. *Journal of Chinese Philosophy*, 24.4: 427–456.

Fan, Rui Ping. 2003. Social Justice: Rawlsian or Confucian. In *Comparative Approaches to Chinese Philosophy*, in Bo Mou, 144–168. Hants: Ashgate.

Fishkin, James S. 1983. *Justice, Equal Opportunity and the Family*. New Haven: Yale University Press.

Fishkin, James S. 1988. Do We Need a Systematic Thoery of Equal Opportunity? In *Equal Opportunity*, ed. Norman E Bowie, 15–21. Boulder: Westview Press.

Fitzgerald, Michael R., Lyons, William and Cory, Floydette. 1988. From Administration to Oversight: Privatization and its Aftermath in a Southern City. In *Market-Based Public Policy*, ed. Richard C. Hula, 69–83. Hamsphire: Macmillan.

Flick, Uwe, von Kardorff, Ernest and Steinke, Ines. 2004. What is Qualitative Research? An Introduction to the Field. In *A Companion to Qualitative Research*, ed. Uwe Flick, Ernest von Kardorff and Ines Steinke, 3–11. London: Sage.

Flood, J. and Yates, J. 1989. Housing Subsidies and Income Distribution. *Housing Studies*, 4.3: 193–210.

Fong, Peter K. W. and Yeh, Anthony G. O. 1984. Public Housing Programme in Hong Kong, 1973–1983. *Raroph Journal*, 1: 1–10.

Fong, Peter K. W. 1986. *Housing Problems and Public Housing Program in Hong Kong: A Case Study of Housing Provision in a Densely Populated Metropolitan Area*. Michigan: UMI.

Fong, Peter K. W. 1980. *Housing Policy and the Public Housing Programme in Hong Kong*. Hong Kong: Centre of Urban Studies & Urban Planning, University of Hong Kong Press.

Fong, Peter K. W. 1989. *A Comparative Study of Hong Kong Housing Policies in Hong Kong and Singapore*. Hong Kong: Centre of Urban Studies & Urban Planning, University of Hong Kong Press.

Fong, Peter K. W. and Yeh, Anthony G. O. 1987. Hong Kong. In *Housing Policy and Practice in Asia*, ed. Seong-Kyn Ha Kent, 12–47. London: Croom Helm.

Forrest, Ray and Murie, Alan. 1995. Accumulating Evidence: Housing and Family Wealth in Britain. In *Housing and Family Wealth*, ed. Forrest, Ray and Murie, Alan, 58–85. London: Routledge.

Forrest, Ray; Murie, Alan; and Williams, Peter. 1990. *Home Ownership: Differentiation and Fragmentation*. London: Unwin Hyman.

Forrester, Duncan B. 1997. *Christian Justice and Public Policy*. Cambridge: Cambridge University Press.

Frankena, William. 1962. The Concept of Social Justice. In *Social Justice*, ed. Brandt, Richard B. Englewood Cliffs: Prentice Hall.

Frankfurt, Harry G. 1998. Necessity and Desire. In *Necessary Goods,* Brock, Gillian, 19–31. Maryland: Rowman & Littlefield.

Fraser, Nancy. 1997. *Justice Interruptus*. London: Routledge.

Freser, Edward. 1997. Hayek on Social Justice: Reply to Lukes and Johnston. *Critical Review*, 11.4: 581–606.

Freser, Edward. 1998. Hayek, Social Justice and the Market: Reply to Johnston. *Critical Review*, 12.3: 269–281.

Fried, Barbara. 1995. Wilt Chamberlain Revisited: Nozick's "Justice in Transfer" and the Problem of Market-Based Distribution. *Philosophy & Public Affairs*, 24:3, 226–245.

Fu, Charles Wei-hsun. 1997. Daoism in Chinese Philosophy. In *Companion Encyclopedia of Asian Philosophy*, ed. Brian Carr and Indira Mahalingam, 553–574. London: Routledge.

Fu, Y. M. 1995. Housing Market and Housing Policies. In *The Other Hong Kong Report 1995*, ed. S. Y. L. Cheung and S. M. H. Sze, 261–285. Hong Kong: Chinese University Press.

Fung, K. K. and Forrest, R. 2002. Institutional Mediation, The Hong Kong Residential Housing Market and the Asian Financial Crisis. *Housing Studies*, 17.2: 189–207.

Galster, George C. 1988. *Federal Fair Housing Policy in the 1980s: The Great Misapprehension*. Massachusetts: MIT Center for Real Estate Development Press.

Geras, N. 1985. The Controversy about Marx and Justice. *New Left Review,* 150: 47–85.

Geras, N. 1992. Bringing Marx to Justice: An Addendum and Rejoinder. *New Left Review*, 195: 37–69.

Gerson, Kathleen and Horowitz, Ruth. 2002. Observation and Interviewing. In *Qualitative Research in Action*, ed. Tim May, 199–224. London: Sage.

Gewirtz, S. and Cribb, A. 2002. Plural Conceptions of Social Justice: Implications for Policy Sociology. *Journal of Education Policy*, 17.5: 499–509.

Gilbert, Neil. 1995. *Welfare Justice: Restoring Social Equity*. New Haven: Yale University Press.

Giloth, R. P.; Moe, K. J.; and McGary, H. M. Social Justice and Public Policy. In *Social Justice and Local Development Policy*, ed. Robert Mier et al., 20–31. Newbury Park: Sage.

Golger, O. J. 1972. *Squatters and Resettlement*. Hamburg: Institute of Asian Affairs.

Goodstadt, L. F. 1969. Urban Housing in Hong Kong 1945–63. In *Hong Kong: A Society in Transition*, ed. I. C. Jarvie, 257–298. London: Routledge.

Gough, Ian. 1998. What are Human Needs? In *Social Policy and Social Justice*, ed. Jane Franklin, 50–56. Cambridge: Polity Press.

Gould, C. C. 1995. Social Justice and the Limitation of Democracy. *Morality and Social Justice: Point/Counterpoint*. Maryland: Rowman & Littlefield.

Graham, Paul. 2007. *Rawls*, Ch.1. Oxford: Oneworld.

Hadland, B. J. 1978. Land Policies in Hong Kong. In *Housing in Hong Kong*, Luke S. K. Wong, 72–90. Hong Kong: Heinemann.

Hammersley, Martyn. 1996. The Relationship between Qualitative and Quantitative Research: Paradigm Loyalty versus Methodological Eclecticism. In *Handbook of Qualitative Research Methods for Psychology and the Social Sciences*, ed. John T. E. Richardson, 159–174. Leicester: The British Psychology Society.

Han, Daniel W. T. 1978. Social Background of Housing in Hong Kong. In *Housing in Hong Kong*, ed. Luke S. K. Wong, 1–19. Hong Kong: Heinemann.

Hare, R. M. 1975. Rawls' Theory of Justice. In *Reading Rawls*, N. Daniels, 81–107. Oxford: Basil Blackwell.

Harloe, Michael. 1999. *Risk, Uncertainty and Housing Market in Europe: Lessons for Housing Privatization in Hong Kong*. Hong Kong: Centre for Comparative Public Management and Social Policy, City University of Hong Kong.

Harrison, J. 1981. *Hume' s Theory of Justice*. Oxford: Clarendon Press.

Harsanyi, J. C. 1985. Rule Utilitarianism, Equality and Justice. *Social Philosophy & Policy,* 2.2: 115–127.

Harvey, David. 1973. *Social Justice and the City*. London: Edward Arnold.

Hayek, F. A. 1976. *Law, Legislation and Liberty Vol.2: The Mirage of Social Justice*. London: Routledge.

Headey, Bruce. 1978. *Housing Policy in the Developed Economy*. London: Croom Helm.

Henley, Andrew. 1998. Residential Mobility, Housing Equity and the Labour Market. *The Economic Journal* 108, 447: 414–427

Henwood, Karen L. 1996. Qualitative Inquiry: Perspectives, Methods and Psychology. In *Handbook of Qualitative Research Methods for Psychology and the Social Sciences*, ed. John T. E. Richardson, 25–40. Leicester: The British Psychological Society.

Hill, Bette S., Blaser, C. Jean and Balmer, Pamela W. 1988. Practical Issues in Developing Competitive Contracting for Home Care Services. In *Market-Based Public Policy*, ed. Richard C. Hula, 84–95. Hampshire: Macmillan.

Ho, L. S. 1992. Rent Control: Its Rationale and Effects. *Urban Studies*, 29.7: 1183–1190.

Ho, Lok Sang. 1989. The Hong Kong Economy: a 1985 Review. In *Hong Kong Society*, ed. Alex Y. H. Kwan, 47–71. Hong Kong: Writers & Publishers' Cooperative.

Ho, Lok Sang. 1996. *Institutional Foundations for a Just Society*. Hong Kong: Lingnan College.

Ho, Shuet Ying. 1986. Public Housing. In *Hong Kong in Transition*, ed. Joseph

Y. S. Cheng, 331–47. Hong Kong: Oxford University Press.

Hochschild, J. L. 1981. *What's Fair? American Beliefs about Distributive Justice.* Cambridge: Harvard University Press.

Hochschild, Jennifer. 1988. Race, Class, Power and Equal Opportunity. In *Equal Opportunity*, ed. Norman E. Bowie, 75–111. Boulder: Westview Press.

Hong Kong Government. 1964. *Review of Policies for Squatter Control, Resettlement and Government Low-Cost Housing.* Hong Kong: Government Press.

Hong Kong Government. 1987. *Long Term Housing Strategy: A policy Statement.* Hong Kong: Hong Kong Government.

Hong Kong Government. 1998. *Homes for Hong Kong People into the 21st Century.* Hong Kong: Hong Kong Government Press.

Hong Kong Government. 2002. *Review of the Institutional Framework for Public Housing: The Report.* Hong Kong: Hong Kong Government Press.

Hong Kong Housing Authority. 1992. *Report on the Review of Schemes to Promote Home Ownership.* Hong Kong: Hong Kong Housing Authority.

Hopkins, Keith. 1969. *Public Housing Policy in Hong Kong.* Hong Kong: Centre of Asian Studies, University of Hong Kong Press.

Hopkins, Keith. 1971. Housing the Poor. In *Hong Kong: The Industrial Colony,* ed. Keith Hopkins, 271–335. Hong Kong: Oxford University Press.

Hopkins, Keith. 1972. Public and Private housing in Hong Kong. In *The City as a Centre of Change in Asia*, ed. D. J. Dwyer, 200–212. Hong Kong: Hong Kong University Press.

Hsu, Leonard Shih lien. 1975. *The Political Philosophy of Confucianism.* London: Curzon Press.

Hugo-Brunt, M. 1967. Hong Kong Housing. In *Taming Megalopolis,* volume 1, ed. H. W. Eldredge, 477–493. London: Frederick A Praeger.

Hui, C. M., Ho, M. F. and Tam, S. H. 1998. Review of Public Housing Rent Policy in Hong Kong. *Journal of Financial Management of Property and Construction*, 3.2: 75–88.

Hui, E. C. M. 1999. Willingness to Pay for Better Housing in Hong Kong: Theory and Evidence (Of Dwelling Space). *Urban Studies* 36.2: 289–304.

Hui, E. C. M., Ho, C. M. F. and Ta, S. H. 1998. Affordability of Public Housing Tenants in Hong Kong: A Critique. *Australian Land Economics Review,* 4.2: 36–43.

Hui, E. C. M. 1999. Public Housing Rents in Hong Kong: Policy and Structure. *Journal of Urban Planning and Development*, 125.1: 36–53.

Hui, E. C. M. 2001. Measuring Affordability in Public Housing From Economic Principles: Case Study of Hong Kong. *Journal of Urban Planning and Development*, 127.1: 34–49.

Hui, E. C. M., Ho, C. M. F., How H. H. H., and Tam S. H. 1999. *The Relationship between Public Sector and Market Rents.* Hong Kong: Department of Building and Real Estate, The Hong Kong Polytechnic University Press.

Hume, David. 1739. *A Treatise of Human Nature*, ed. Ernest C. Mosner. London: Penguin.

Hume, David. 1998. *An Enquiry concerning the Principle of Morals*, ed. Tom L. Beauchamp. Oxford: Oxford University Press.

Huque, A. S., and Tao, L. P. W. J. and Wilding, P. 1997. Understanding Hong Kong. In *Social Policy in Hong Kong*, ed. P. Wilding, A. S. Huque and L. P. W. J. Tao, 1–21. Cheltenham: Edward Elgar.

Ip, Ka-ho. 1999. *The Impact of Housing Development on Public Order in Hong Kong from the 1960s to the Present.* Unpublished M.A. Thesis School of Professional and Continuing Education, University of Hong Kong.

Jencks, Christopher. 1988. What Must be Equal for Opportunity to be Equal? In *Equal Opportunity*, ed. Norman E. Bowie, 47–74. Boulder: Westview Press.

Johnston, David. 1997. Hayek's attack on Social Justice. *Critical Review*, 11.1: 81–100.

Johnston, David. 1997. Is the Idea of Social Justice Meaningful *Critical Review*, 11.4: 607–614.

Jordan, Grant. 1993. The New Right and Public Policy: A Preliminary Overview. In *Public Policy and the Impact of the New Right*, ed. Grant Jordan and Nigel Ashford, 1–18. London: Pinter.

Jordon, Bill. 1998. *The New Politics of Welfare: Social Justice in a Global Context.* London: Sage

Juppenlatz, Morris. 1970. *Cities in Transformation: The Urban Squatter Problem of the Developing World.* St. Lucia: University of Lusensland Press.

Kangas, Olli. 2000. Distributive Justice and Social Policy: Some Reflections on Rawls and Income Distribution. *Social Policy & Administration*, 34.5: 510–528.

Karn, Valerie and Wolman, Harold. 1992. *Comparing Housing Systems: Housing Performance and Housing Policy in the United States and Britain.* Oxford: Oxford University Press.

Kelly, P. J. 1990. *Utilitarianism and Distributive Justice.* Oxford: Clarendon Press.

Keung, J. K. 1985. Government Intervention and Housing Policy in Hong Kong. *Third World Planning Review*, 7.1: 23–44.

Keung, John. 1981. *Government Intervention and Housing Policy in Hong Kong: A Structural Analysis.* Wales: Department of Town Planning, University of Wales Institute of Science and Technology.

King, Estelle. 1996. The Use of the Self in Qualitative Research. In *Handbook of Qualitative Research Methods for Psychology and the Social Sciences*, ed. John T. E. Richardson, 175–88. Leicester: The British Psychology Society.

King, Peter. 1996. *The Limits of Housing Policy: A Philosophical Investigation.* London: Middlesex University.

King, Peter. 1998. *Housing, Individuals and the State.* London: Routledge.

King, Peter. 2000. Can We Use Rights to Justify Housing Provision? *Housing, Theory and Society*, 17.1, 27–34.

King, Peter. 2001. Was Conservative Housing Policy Really Conservative? *Housing, Theory and Society*, 18.3–4: 98–107.

King, Peter. 2003. *A Social Philosophy of Housing*. Hampshire: Ashgate.

Kirkby, Richard. 1990. China. In *Housing Policy in the Socialist Third World*, ed. Kosta Mathey, 289–313. London: Mansell.

Kirzner, I. M. 1981. Entrepreneurship, Entitlement, and Economic Justice. In *Reading Nozick*, ed. J. Paul, 383–407. Oxford: Basil Blackwell.

Kolotolkin, B. 1991. Housing Rent: Cost Accounting and Social Justice. *Problems of Economics*, 34.2: 83–95.

Krishna, D. 1997. Democracy and Justice: Presuppositions and Implications. In *Justice and Democracy: Cross-Cultural Perspectives,* ed. R. Bontekoe and M. Stepaniants, 217–229. Honolulu: University of Hawaii Press.

Kwang-tze. 1968. The Writings of Kwang-tse, trans. James Legge. *The Sacred Books of China: The Text of Taoism* vol. 39–40. Delhi: Motilal.

Kwitko, L. 1986. *Public Housing and Urban Development in Hong Kong: Prolegomenon to an Investigation from a World-Systems Perspective.* Hawaii: Department of Sociology, University of Hawaii.

Kwitko, L. 1988. *Public Housing and Urban Development in Hong Kong*. Hong Kong: Centre of Urban Studies and Urban Planning.

Kwok, R. Y. W. 1983. Land Price Escalation and Public Housing in Hong Kong. In *Land for Housing the Poor*, ed. S. Angel, R. W. Archer, S. Tanphiphat and E. A. Wegelin, 328–345. Singapore: Select Books.

Kwok, R. Y. W. 1983. *Land Sales and Government Housing in Hong Kong 1976–81*. Hong Kong: Centre of Urban Studies and Urban Planning, University of Hong Kong Press.

Kwong, Chun Wah. 2002. *The Public Role of Religion in Post-Colonial Hong Kong*. New York: Peter Lang.

La Grange, A. and Lee, J. 1999. Housing Policy and the New Hong Kong SAR Government: A Preliminary Investigation of Trends and Implications. *Public Administration and Policy*, 8.1: 39–59.

La Grange, A. 1997. Catching the Tiger by the Tail: Implementing the Hong Kong Government's 1987 Long Term Housing Strategy. *Hong Kong Public Administration*, 6.2: 97–118.

La Grange, A. 1998. Privatising Public Housing in Hong Kong: Its Impact on Equity. *Housing Studies*, 13.4: 507–525.

La Grange, A. 1999. Privatizing Public Housing in the Welfare Regime of a Tiger Economy: a Case Study of Hong Kong. *Housing, Theory and Society* 16.1: 17–30.

La Grange, A. and Pretorius, F. 2000. Ontology, Policy and the Market: Trends to Home-ownership in Hong Kong. *Urban Studies*, 37.9: 1561–1582.

La Grange, A. and Pretorius, F. 2002. Private Rental Housing in Hong Kong. *Housing Studies*, 17.5: 721–740.

La Grange and Pretorius F. 1999. *An Innate Desire For Home Ownership or*

Markets At Work: A Case Study of Hong Kong. Hong Kong: Department of Public and Social Administration, City University of Hong Kong.

Lai, L. W. C. 1985. The Formation of Squatters and Slums in Hong Kong: From Slump Market to Boom Market. *Ekistics*, 312: 213–238.

Lai, L. W. C. 1995. *Some Aspects of Land and Housing Supply in Recent Property Price Debate*. Hong Kong: Department of Surveying, University of Hong Kong Press.

Lai, L. W. C. 1994. The Property Price Crisis. In *The Other Hong Kong Report 1994*, ed. Donald H McMillen and Si-wai Man, 187–208. Hong Kong: Chinese University Press.

Lai, L. W. C. 1990. Public Housing Density in Hong Kong: A Theoretical and Empirical Review. *Ekistics*, 57.342–43: 160–171.

Lane, R. E. 1986. Market Justice, Political Justice. *American Political Science Review*, 80.2, 383–402.

Lansley, Stewart. 1979. *Housing and Public Policy*. London: Croom Helm.

Lao Tzu. 2001. *Tao Te Ching*, trans. D. C. Lau. Hong Kong: Chinese University Press.

Lau, K. Y. 1991. 'Housing' in Y W Sung and M K Lee (eds) *The Other Hong Kong Report 1991* Hong Kong: Chinese University Press, pp 343–387.

Lau, K. Y. 1994. Public Housing. In *The Other Hong Kong Report 1994*, ed. D. H. McMillen and S. W. Man, 265–96. Hong Kong: Chinese University Press.

Lau, K. Y. 2002. Hong Kong. In *Housing Policy Systems in South and East Asia*, ed. Agus, M. R., Doling, J. and Lee, D. S. Hampshire: Palgrave MacMillan.

Lau, K. Y. 2002. Safeguarding the Rational Allocation of Public Housing Resources. *Asia Pacific Journal of Social Work*, 7.2: 97–129.

Le Grand, Julian. 1982. *The Strategy of Equality: Redistribution and the Social Services*. London: Unwin Hyman

Le Grand, Julian. 1991. *Equity and Choice*. London: Harper Collins.

Le Grand, Julian, and Robinson, Ray. 1984. Privatization and the Welfare State: An Introduction. In *Privatization and the Welfare State*, ed. Julian Le Grand and Ray Robinson, 1–14. London: Allen & Unwin.

Lee, J. 1991. Housing and Social Welfare. In *Indicators of Social Development: Hong Kong 1998*, ed. S. K. Lau, M. K. Lee, P. S. Wan, and S. L. Wong, 67–82. Hong Kong: Chinese University Press.

Lee, J. 1992. Housing and Social Welfare. In *Indicators of Social Development: Hong Kong 1998*, ed. S. K. Lau, M. K. Lee, P. S. Wan, and S. L. Wong, 53–78. Hong Kong: Chinese University Press.

Lee, J. 1994. Affordability, Home Ownership and the Middle Class Housing Crisis in Hong Kong. *Policy & Politics*, 22.3: 179–189.

Lee, J. 1995. Home-Ownership, Consumption and Social Divisions in Hong Kong. In *New Frontiers of Social Indicators Research in Chinese Societies*, ed.

S. K. Lau, M. K. Lee, P. S. Wan, and S. L. Wong, 235–262. Hong Kong: Chinese University Press.

Lee, J. 1996. *Housing, Home Ownership and Social Change in Hong Kong*. Aldershot: Ashgate.

Lee, J. 2001. Stakeholder Housing, Social Development and Social Policy: Reflections on Role of Public Housing in Hong Kong and Singapore. In *Repositioning of Countries: The Experience and Challenge of Social Policy in Asia-Pacific Region*, ed. Hong Kong Polytechnic University Social Policy Research Centre, 171–95. Hong Kong: Joint Publishing.

Lee, James, Forrest, Ray and Tam, Wai Keung. 2003. Home-ownership in East and South East Asia. In *Housing and Social Change*, ed. Ray Forrest and James Lee, 20–45. London: Routledge.

Lee, J. K. C. and Yip, N. M. 2001. Home-ownership under Economic Uncertainty. *Third World Planning Review*, 23.1: 61–77.

Lee, Thomas H. C. 1995. The idea of Social Justice in Ancient China. In *Social Justice in the Ancient World*, ed. Morris Silver, 126–46. Westport: Greenwood.

Leeds, P. F. 1966. Housing in Hong Kong: Post-War Problems. *Journal of Administration Overseas*, 5; 184–193.

Lenaghan, Jo. 1998. Rationing and Rights in Health Care. In *Social Policy and Social Justice*, ed. Jane Franklin, 280–303. Cambridge: Polity Press.

Leung, W. T. 1993. Housing. In *The Other Hong Kong Report 1993*, ed. P. K. Choi and L. S. Ho, 265–297. Hong Kong: Chinese University Press.

Levi, Isaac. 1982. Liberty and Welfare. In *Utilitarianism and Beyond*, ed. Amartya Sen and Bernard Williams, 239–249. Cambridge: Cambridge University Press.

Li, Chen Yang. *The Tao Encounters the West: Explorations in Comparative Philosophy*. Albany: State University of New York Press.

Li, S. M. and Yu, F. L. 1990. The Redistributive Effects of Hong Kong's Public Housing Programme 1976–86. *Urban Studies*, 27.1: 105–118.

Loizou, Andros. 1997. Social Justice and Social Policy. In *Social Policy: A Conceptual and Theoretical Introduction*, ed. Michael Lavalette and Alan Pratt, 164–81. London: Sage.

Lui, F. T. Hong Kong's Residential Housing Market and Housing Policies. In *The Other Hong Kong Report 1997*, ed. J. Y. S. Cheng, 357–375. Hong Kong: Chinese University Press.

Lyons, David. 1997. Human Rights and the General Welfare. In *Mill's Utilitarianism*, David Lyons, 29–43. Maryland: Rowman & Littlefield.

MacIntyre, Alasdair. 1998 *Whose Justice? Which Rationality* London: Duckworth.

Maclennan, Duncan. Stephens, Mark and Kemp, Peter. 1996. *Housing Policy in the EU Member States*. Luxembourg: European Parliament.

Macleod, A. M. 1983. Hayek on Justice and the Market: A Rejoinder to Cragg and Mack. *Canadian Journal of Philosophy*, 13.1: 575–584.

Macleod, A. M. 1983. Justice and the Market. *Canadian Journal of Philosophy*, 13.4: 551–561.

Malpass, Peter. 1986. Conclusion. In *The Housing Crisis*, ed. Peter Malpass, 232–240. London: Croom Helm.

Malpass, Peter. 1986. From Complacency to Crisis. In *The Housing Crisis*, ed. Peter Malpass, 1–23. Kent: Croom Helm.

Malpass, Peter. 1986. Housing Policy and Young People. In *The Housing Crisis*, ed. Peter Malpass, 215–231. Kent: Croom Helm.

Malpass, Peter, and Murie, Alan. 1999. *Housing Policy and Practice*. London: Macmillan.

Margolis, J. 1977. Political Equality and Political Justice. *Social Research*, 44.2: 308–329.

Marx, K. 1959. *Critique of the Gotha Programme and A Contribution to the Critique of the Social Democratic Draft Programme of 1891*. Moscow: Foreign Languages Publishing House.

Mason, Andrew. 2001. Equality of Opportunity, Old and New. *Ethics*, 3.4: 760–781.

Mason, Jennifer. 2002. Qualitative Interviewing: Asking, Listening and Interpreting. In *Qualitative Research in Action*, ed. Tim May, 225–241. London: Sage.

Maunder, W. F. 1969. *Hong Kong Urban Rents and Housing*. Hong Kong: Hong Kong University Press.

McConnachie, Margaret *et al.* 1994. Making Housing Pay: Social Justice & Housing Finance. In *Housing and Social Justice,* ed. Robina Goodlad and Kenneth Gibb, 27–61. London: Institute for Public Policy Research.

Meek, Colin. 1998. Privatization Doesn't Necessarily Equal Competition. In *Who Benefits from Privatization*, ed. Moazzen Hossain and Justin Malbon, 100–18. London: Routledge.

Mencius. 1979. *Mencius*. Trans. D.C. Lau. Hong Kong: Chinese University Press.

Michel, R. and Ricoem, P. 1994. Justice and the Market. In *Why Market Socialism?* ed._Frank Roosevelt and David Belkin, 109–120. New York: M.E. Sharpe.

Miles, M. B. and Hubermann, A. M. 1984. *Qualitative Data Analysis: A Sourcebook of New Methods*. California: Sage Press.

Mill J. S. 1987. *Utilitarianism*, ed. Alan Ryan. London: Penguin.

Miller, David. 1976 *Social Justice*. Oxford: Clarendon Press.

Miller, David. 1978. Democracy and Social Justice. *British Journal of Political Science,* 8: 1–19.

Miller, David. 1999. *Principles of Social Justice*. Cambridge: Harvard University Press.

Miners, Norman. 1991. *The Government and Politics of Hong Kong*. Hong Kong: Oxford University Press.

Mithaug, Dennis E. 1996. *Equal Opportunity Theory*. Thousand Oaks: Sage Publications.

Morris, Jenny and Winn, Martin. 1990. *Housing and Social Inequality*. London: Hilary Shipman.

Murie, Alan. 1983. *Housing Inequality and Deprivation*. London: Heinemann.

Nagel, T. 1975. Rawls on Justice. In *Reading Rawls,* ed. N Daniels, 1–16. Oxford: Basil Blackwell.

Nathanson, S. 1998. *Economic Justice.* New Jersey: Prentice-Hall.

Neilsen, Kai. 1980. Capitalism, Socialism and Justice: Reflections on Rawls's Theory of Justice. *Social Praxis*, 7.3–4: 253–277.

Neilsen, Kai. 1982. Capitalism, Socialism and Justice. In *And Justice for All*, ed. T. Ragan and D. Van DeVeer, 264–86. New Jersey: Rowman and Littlefield.

Ngan, Raymond M. H. 1989. The Overall Governmental Structure in Hong Kong. In *Hong Kong Society*, ed. Alex Y. H. Kwan. Hong Kong: Writers.

Norman, Richard. 1992. Equality, Needs and Basic Income. In *Arguing for Basic Income*, ed. Philippe Van Parijs, 141–52. London: Verso.

Nozick, R. 1974. *Anarchy, State and Utopia.* Oxford: Blackwell.

Nussbaum, Martha C. 1999. *Sex & Social Justice.* New York: Oxford University Press.

O'Day, Ken. 1994. Hume's Distinction Between the Natural and Artificial Virtues. *Hume Studies*, XX.1: 121–141.

O'Neill, Onora. 1998. Rights, Obligations and Needs. In *Necessary Goods,* ed. Gillian Brock, 95–112. Maryland: Rowman & Littlefield.

Okin, Susan Moller. 1989. *Justice, Gender and the Family.* New York: Basic Books.

Okner, Benjamin A. 1972. 'Alternatives for Transferring Income to the Poor: The Family Assistance Plan and Universal Income Supplements. In *Redistribution to the Rich and the Poor*, ed. Kenneth E. Boulding and Martin Pfaff, 348–57. California: Wadsworth.

Palmer, Martin. 1991. *The Elements of Taoism.* Dorset: Element Press.

Paris, Chris. 1993. *Housing Australia.* Melbourne: Macmillan.

Parkin, Frank. 1992. *Durkheim.* Oxford: Oxford University Press.

Partington, Martin. 1993. Citizenship and Housing. In *Rights of Citizenship,* ed. Robert Blackburn, 124–38. London: Mansell.

Pasquariello, Ronald D. 1985. *Tax Justice.* Lanham: University Press of America.

Patton, Michael Quinn. 1990. *Qualitative Evaluation and Research Methods.* London: Sage Press.

Peacock, Alan. 1991. Welfare Philosophies and Welfare Finance. In *State and Social Welfare*, ed. Thomas and Dorothy Wilson, 37–54. New York: Longman.

Peacock, Alan. 1954. Introduction. In *Income Redistribution and Social Policy*, ed. Alan T. Peacock, 7–15. Oxford: Alden Press.

Pechman, Joseph A. 1974. Taxes and Inequality. In *Social Problems and Public Policy: Inequality and Justice*, ed. Lee Rainwater, 201–214. Chicago: Aldine.

Peerboom, R. P. 1990. Confucian Justice: Achieving a Human Society. *International Philosophical Quarterly*, 30.1: 17–32.

Plant, Raymond. 1991. Welfare and the Enterprise Society. In *State and Social Welfare*, ed. Thomas and Dorothy Wilson, 73–88. New York: Longman.

Plant, Raymond. 1998. Citizenship, Rights, Welfare. In *Social policy and Social Justice*, ed. Jane Franklin, 57–72. Cambridge: Polity Press.

Plant, Raymond. 1994. Hayek on Social Justice. In *Hayek, Co-ordination and Evolution*, ed. Jack Birner and Ruby ven Zijp, 164–77. London: Routledge.

Pojman, Louis P. 2006. *Justice*. New Jersey: Pearson Prentice Hall.

Porcano, T. M. 1984. Distributive Justice and Tax Policy. *The Accounting Review*, 59.4: 619–636.

Pryor, E. G. 1983. *Housing in Hong Kong*. Hong Kong: Oxford University Press.

Pugh, Cedric. 1980. *Housing in Capitalist Societies*. Hants: Gower.

Rawls, J. 1999. *A Theory of Justice*. Oxford: Oxford University Press.

Rawls, J. 1982. Social Unity and Primary Goods. In *Utilitarianism and Beyond*, ed. Amartya Sen and Bernard Williams, 159–85. Cambridge: Cambridge University Press.

Reidy, Angela. 1984. Social Justice and Social Policy. *Social Policy & Administration*, 18.1: 27–40.

Richards, Janet R. 1998. Equality of Opportunity. In *Ideals of Equality*, ed. Andrew Mason, 52–78. Oxford: Blackwell.

Ritchie, Jane and Spencer, Liz. 1994. Qualitative Data Analysis for Applied Policy Research. In *Analyzing Qualitative Data*, ed. Alan Bryman and Robert G. Burgess, 173–94. London: Routledge.

Roemer, John E. 1998. *Equality of Opportunity*. Cambridge: Harvard University Press.

Roetz, Heiner. 1993. *Confucian Ethics of the Axial Age*. Albany: State University of New York Press.

Sainsbury, Diane. 1996. *Gender, Equality and Welfare States*. Cambridge: Cambridge University Press.

Savulescu, J. 1998. Consequentialism, Reasons, Value and Justice. *Bioethics*, 12.3: 212–235.

Schiffer, J. R. 1983. *Anatomy of a Laissez-faire Government: The Hong Kong Growth Model Reconsidered*. Hong Kong: Centre of Urban Studies and Urban Planning, University of Hong Kong Press.

Seidman, Irving. 1998. *Interviewing as Qualitative Research*. New York: Teachers College Press.

Sen, Amartya. 1990. Justice: Means versus Freedom. *Philosophy & Public Affairs*, 19:2: 111–121.

Sen, Amartya. 1993. Capability and Well-being. In *The Quality of Life*, ed. Martha Nussbaum and Amartya Sen, 30–53. Oxford: Clarendon Press.

Sher, George. 1988. Qualifications, Fairness and Desert. In *Equal Opportunity*, ed. Norman E. Bowie, 113–27. Boulder: Westview Press.

Shower, Dennis J. 1996. What is the Domain of the Welfare State? In *Equity, Efficiency and Growth: The Future of the Welfare State*, ed. Mario Baldassarri and Luigi Paganetto, 13–40. Basingstoke: Macmillan Press.

Siu, D. Y. K. 1999. *The Development of Housing Policy in Hong Kong: An*

Analysis of its Implications for Social Control. Unpublished M.A. thesis, School of Professional and Continuing Education, University of Hong Kong.

Smart, A. 1989. Forgotten Obstacles, Neglected Forces: Explaining the Origins of Hong Kong Public Housing. *Environment and Planning D: Society and Space*, 7.2: 179–196.

Smart, Alan. 1992. *Making Room: Squatter Clearance in Hong Kong.* Hong Kong: Centre of Asian Studies, University of Hong Kong Press.

Smart, A. 1985. *The Squatter Property Market in Hong Kong: Informal Regulation and the State.* Hong Kong: Centre of Urban Studies.

Smith, J. W. 1971. Justice and Democracy. *Monist,* 55.1: 121–133.

Spring, Joel. 2001. *Globalization and Educational Rights: An Intercivilization Analysis.* New Jersey: Lawrence Erlbaum Associates.

Stafford, D. C. 1979. Housing Policy: Efficiency and Equity. *Social Policy & Administration*, 13.1, 37–52.

Steiner, H. 1981. Justice and Entitlement. In *Reading Nozick*, ed. J. Paul, 380–382. Oxford: Basil Blackwell.

Sum, Ngai Ling. 1989. *Housing: Government and Public Affairs.* Hong Kong: Ling Kee.

Sunstein, Cass R. 1997. *Free Markets and Social Justice* New York: Oxford University Press.

Tang, Connie P. Y. 2000. *More Than Housing Providers: How Hong Kong Property Developers Grew Big?* Hong Kong: Chinese University Press.

Taylar, Steven J. and Bogdon, Robert. 1984. *Introduction to Qualitative Research Methods: The Search for Meanings.* New York: John Wiley & Sons.

The Commission on Social Justice. 1998. What is Social Justice? In *Social Policy and Social Justice*, ed. Jane Franklin, 37–49. Cambridge: Polity Press.

Thomas, June Manning and Hwang, Hee-Yun. 2003. Social Equity in Redevelopment and Housing: United States and Korea. *Journal of Planning Education and Research*, 23.1: 8–23.

Titmuss, Richard M. 1973. *Commitment to Welfare.* London: Allen and Unwin.

Tonkiss, Fran. 2000. Social Justice and the City: Equity, Cohesion and the Politics of Space. In *A Companion to the City*, ed. Gary Bridge and Sophie Watson, 591–98. Oxford: Blackwell.

Tse, R. Y. C., and Raftery, J. 1999. Income Elasticity of Housing Consumption in Hong Kong: a Cointegration Approach. *Journal of Property Research*, 16.2: 123–138.

Tse, R. Y. C., and Ganesan, S. 1999. Hong Kong. In *Cities in the Pacific Rim*, ed. J. Berry and S. McGreal, 67–88. London: E & F N Spon.

Tse, R. Y. C., and Ganesan, S. 1999. Matching Housing Supply and Demand: An Empirical Study of Hong Kong's Market. *Construction Management and Economics*, 17.5: 625–633.

Turner, Bengt. 1996. Sweden. *In Housing Policy in Europe*, ed. Paul Balchin, 99–112. London: Routledge.

Ungerson, Clare. 1994. Housing: Need, Equity, Ownership and the Economy. In *Social Policy Towards 2000*, ed. Vic George and Stewart Miller, 190–214. London: Routledge.

Van Parijs, Philippe. 1992. Competing Justifications of Basic Income. In *Arguing for Basic Income*, ed. Philippe Van Parijs, 3–43. London: Verso.

Van Parijs, Philippe. 1995. *Real Freedom for All.* New York: Oxford University Press.

Veit-Wilson, John. 1999. Poverty and the Adequacy of Social Security. In *Introduction to Social Security*, ed. John Ditch, 78–109. London: Routledge.

Wade, M. L. 1992. Hume's Theory of Justice and the Role of Public Policy. In *The Moral Dimensions of Public Policy Choice*, ed. J. M. Gillroy and M. Wade, 429–442. Pittsburgh: University of Pittburgh Press.

Walker, Alan. 1984. The Political Economy of Privatization. In *Privatization and the Welfare State,* ed. Julian Le Grand and Ray Robinson, 19–44. London: George Allen & Unwin.

Wallis, Joe and Dollery, Brian. 1999. *Market Failure, Government Failure, Leadership and Public Policy*. Basingstoke: Macmillan.

Walsh, Adrian J. 1997. *A Neo-Aristotelian Theory Of Social Justice*. Aldershot: Ashgate.

Walsh, Kieron. 1995. *Public Services and Market Mechanisms*. Hampshire: Macmillan.

Walzer, Michael (1983) *Spheres of Justice* U.S.A.: Basic Books

Weale Albert. 1978. *Equality and Social Policy*. London: Routledge.

Wen, Simon Chu-Hsung. 1988. *A Cross-national Study on Housing Development in Asian Transitional Countries: Hong Kong, Korea (South), Singapore and Taiwan (The Republic of China)*. Michigan: UMI Press.

Whitfield, Dexter. 1992. *The Welfare State: Privatization, Deregulation, Commercialization of Public Services: Alternative Strategies for the 1990s*. London: Pluto Press.

Wilding, Paul. 1990. Privatization: an Introduction and a Critique. In *Privatization*, ed. Richard Parry, 18–31. London: Jessica Kingsley.

Wilding, Paul. 1996. *Social Policy and Social Development in Hong Kong*. Hong Kong: Department of Public and Social Administration, City University of Hong Kong.

Wilkinson, Margaret. 1997. *Equity, Efficiency and Market Failure*. Oxford: Heinemann.

Will, B. F. 1978. Housing Design and Construction Methods. In *Housing in Hong Kong*, ed. Luke S. K. Wong, 91–127. Hong Kong: Heinemann.

Williams, Bernard. 1973. *Problems of Self*. London: Cambridge University Press.

Williams, M. S. 1995. Justice Towards Groups: Political Not Juridical. *Political Theory*, 23.1: 67–91.

Wilson, Dorothy J. and Wilson, Thomas. 1995. Social Justice and the Reform of Social Security. *Social Policy and Administration*, 29.4: 335–344.

Wilson, Thomas and Dorothy. 1991. Issues and Objectives. In *The State and Social Welfare*, ed. Thomas and Dorothy Wilson, 3–34. New York: Longman.

Wolff, J. 1991. *Robert Nozick: Property, Justice and Minimal State*. Oxford: Blackwell.

Wolff, R. P. 1977. *Understanding Rawls*. Princeton: Princeton University Press.

Wong, Francis; Yeung, Stanley; and Howes Rodney. 1995. *A Comparative Study of Affordable Housing Development in the United Kingdom, Hong Kong and the People's Republic of China*. Hong Kong: Department of Building & Real Estate, Hong Kong Polytechnic University.

Wong, John. 1991. *Promoting Confucianism for Socioeconomic Development: The Singapore Experience*. Cambridge: American Academy Arts and Sciences.

Wong, L. S. K. 1989. Housing and the Residential Environment. In *The Other Hong Kong Report*, ed. Tsim, T. L. and Luk, B. H. K., 229–43. Hong Kong: Chinese University Press.

Wong, L. S. K. 1990. Housing and the Residential Environment. In *The Other Hong Kong Report 1990*, ed. R. Y. C. Wong and J. Y. S. Cheng, 445–458. Hong Kong: Chinese University Press.

Wong, Luke S. K. 1978. An Overview of Housing Provision and Housing Needs in Hong Kong. *Housing in Hong Kong*, ed. in Luke S. K. Wong, 23–54. Hong Kong: Heinemann.

Wong, Luke S. K. 1978. Socio-economic Characteristics of Public Housing Provision. In *Housing in Hong Kong*, ed. Luke S. K. Wong, 128–157. Hong Kong: Heinemann.

Wong, Luke S. K. 1978. The Squatter Problem. In *Housing in Hong Kong*, ed. Luke S. K. Wong, 204–32. Hong Kong: Heinemann.

Wong, R. Y. C. and Staley, S. 1992. Housing and Land. In *The Other Hong Kong Report 1992*, ed. J. Y. S. Cheng and P. C. K. Kwong, 309–350. Hong Kong: Chinese University Press.

Wong, Y. C. and Liu, P. W. 1986. *The Distribution of Benefits among Public Housing Tenants in Hong Kong Related Policy Issues*, ed. Hong Kong: Economics Department, Chinese University Press.

Wong, Y. C. Richard. 1988. *On Privatizing Public Housing*. Hong Kong: City University of Hong Kong Press.

Wong, Y. C. and Liu, P. W. 1998. The Distribution of Benefits among Public Housing Tenants in Hong Kong and Related Policy Issues. *Journal of Urban Economics* 23.1, 1–20.

Wong, Y. C.; Richard, Chau K. W.; and Lai, Lawrence W. C. 1996. *Prices and Competition in Property Markets: Analysis and Policy Issues*. Hong Kong: Hong Kong Centre for Economic Research.

Wu, Teh Yao. 1987. *The Confucian Way*. Singapore: Institute of East Asian Philosophies.

www.cityu.edu.hk/hkhousing/

Yang Xiao. 1997. Trying to Do Justice to the Concept of Justice in Confucian Ethics. *Journal of Chinese Philosophy*, 24.4: 521–551.

Yeh, A. G. O. 1989. *Unfair Housing Subsidy: the Hong Kong Experience*. Hong Kong: Centre of Urban Studies and Urban Planning, Hong Kong University Press.

Yeh, A. G. O. 1990. Unfair Housing Subsidy and Public Housing in Hong Kong. *Environment and Planning C: Government and Policy,* 8: 439–454.

Yeh, A. G. O. and Fong, P. K. W. 1984. Public Housing and Urban Development in Hong Kong. *Third World Planning Review*, 6.1: 79–94.

Yeung, Y. M. 1987. *The Next Fifteen Years: Public Housing at the Crossroads in Hong Kong*. Hong Kong: Department of Geography, Chinese University Press.

Yeung, Yue-man. 1989. *Fifty Years of Public Housing in Hong Kong: Retrospect and Prospect*. Hong Kong: Hong Kong University Press.

Yip, N. M. and Lau, K. Y. 1997. Housing. In *Social Policy in Hong Kong*, ed. P. Wilding, A. S. Huque and L. P. W. J. Tao, 39–53. Cheltenham: Edward Elgar.

Young, Iris Marion. 1990. *Justice and the Politics of Difference*. Princeton: Princeton University Press

Young, Iris Marion. 2000. *Inclusion and Democracy*. Oxford: Oxford University Press.

Young, Stephen B. 1981. The Concept of Justice in Pre-Imperial China. In *Moral Behaviour in Chinese Society*, ed. R. W. Wilson, S. L. Greenblat and A. A. Wilson, 38–71. New York: Praeger.

Yu, F. L. and Li, S. M. 1985. The Welfare Cost of Hong Kong's Public Housing Programme. *Urban Studies*, 22.1: 133–140.

Yu, S. W. K. 1997. The Hong Kong Government's Strategy for Promoting Home Ownership: An Approach to Reducing the Decommodifying Effects of Public Housing Services. *International Journal of Urban and Regional Research*, 21.4: 537–553.

Yu, S. W. K. 1997. The Sale of Public Rental Housing: British and Hong Kong Experiences. *International Social Work*, 40.2, 209–224.

Sources in Chinese

Chan, K. W. 1999. Housing Policy: the Root of Hong Kong Housing Problems. In *New Social Policy*, ed. K. C. Lee *et al.*, 173–194. Hong Kong: Chinese University Press.

Kam, P. K. *et al.*, ed. 1996. *The Evaluation of Hong Kong Housing Policy*. Hong Kong: Joint Publishing.

Lee, K. C. 2000. *Hong Kong Housing Policy after the Asian Economic Turmoil*. Hong Kong: Department of Public and Social Administration, City University of Hong Kong.

Yeung, Y. M. 1998. *Peaceful Living and Happy Work for Tomorrow: Increased Cooperation for Public and Private Housing*. Hong Kong: Chinese University Press.

Yeung, Y. M. and Wong, K. Y. 2001. *The Evaluation of SAR Government Housing Policy: The Viewpoints of Hong Kong Citizens*. Hong Kong: Institute of Asia-Pacific Studies, Chinese University Press.

Index